FIRST WORDS

by Alice Waters

I have known Nancy for over a decade now, and through the years I have been so inspired by her commitment to the rich food culture of Japan. Nancy has a historian's passion for preserving traditions, and she has dedicated her life to finding and revealing the local flavors and ingredients that have been cornerstones of Japanese cooking for centuries. She has immense respect for all the sustainable artisans of Japan – the organic dairy farmers, the konbu harvesters, the 6th-generation teakettle ironworkers, the potters who are masters of their craft – and shows us the profound depth of experience they bring to their work.

The dishes Nancy has gathered here – from talented chefs she has met all over Japan – have a common, unifying aesthetic and deep respect for their ingredients. These are recipes intimately tied to place and season and provenance, thoughtfully crafted by chefs who live and breathe the sustainable ethos of Slow Food. In today's world the livelihood of these artisans is threatened, so it is increasingly rare to find people who are committed to holding onto these traditional values. Nancy has found them, honored them, and lifted them up. I can think of nothing more important.

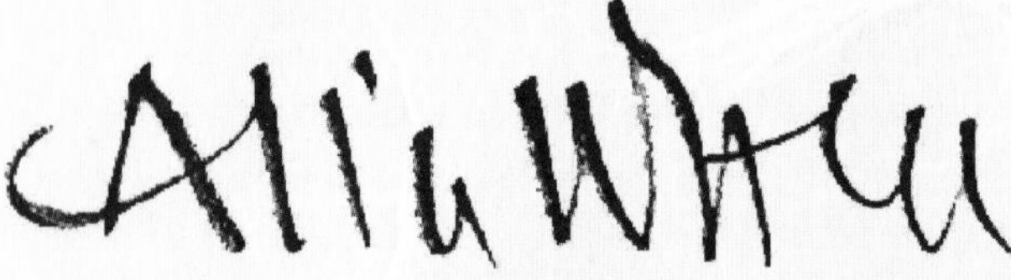

FOOD ARTISANS OF JAPAN

Recipes and stories

日本の食・職人

FOOD ARTISANS OF JAPAN

Recipes and stories

日本の食・職人

Nancy Singleton Hachisu

Photography by
Kenta Izumi and Kenji Miura

Hardie Grant
BOOKS

This book is dedicated to the chefs and artisans who generously gave their time to make the stories and the food come alive.

CONTENTS

TAKING SHAPE

Every project starts with a kernel of an idea, which grows and takes shape as the material is gathered, processed and absorbed. Initially, the plan we make and the direction we think the project will take is only conjecture, a best-guess scenario. As an author and cook, my projects involve books and meal ideas, both of which tend to take detours from their original concepts. But once the framework of a book or menu has taken shape, there is a great feeling of relief – almost euphoria – and with that comes the confidence that the book or menu will come to life almost effortlessly, and will make sense and be wonderful in some way.

This book is the result of a deviation in the path while writing *Japan: The Cookbook*. We hit a snag in the execution of my plan for the book, and it became terrifyingly clear that I had two books on the table. Terrifying in that the two years of travel and thousands of photos would not be used in the book. Yet, I also knew that that body of material deserved its own book, and the *Japan* book would benefit from the separation. Thankfully, Hardie Grant agreed that the artisan concept was exciting, evocative and worth putting together into a book. This book.

I see the compendium of books I write as a never-ending story. The first one was extremely personal, the second timely, the third encyclopedic, while *Food Artisans of Japan* is profoundly close to my heart yet about other people. The recipes come from chefs with whom I have a deep connection, and the myriad stories peppered through the book celebrate a critical community of artisans who make up the landscape of food in this country. Each of the books I write is a whole, and each one follows the next in a logical narrative progression. And I always am looking towards the next books.

In the writing of my second book, *Preserving the Japanese Way*, I began traveling around Japan to explore various traditional Japanese products – especially those made by people following ancient ways without compromising sources of materials. This coincided with a liaison with Fuji TV's *Shinhodo 2001* documentary news show, and later allowed me the chance to bring other Japanese and non-Japanese film crews to visit and record my favorite artisans and local chefs. It was those chefs and artisans who became my focal point for dividing up Japan when tackling the *Japan* book project.

My entree to each area was to be chefs and artisans, and through them I hoped to connect with local grandmas who might still be cooking the traditional foods of the area. Unfortunately, fewer and fewer people are cooking local foods, especially grandmas, because convenience food is so prevalent and ingredients from all over Japan (and the world) are easily accessed. I shifted the plan and turned towards two of the most remarkable home-style cooks I knew: Harumi Kawaguchi and Teiko Watanabe, both cooking teachers of long standing. Kawaguchi-san is now a Zen nun, and Teiko-san is well into her eighties. Each had her own style, but both cataloged a style of gorgeous 'town food' of the 1970s and '80s that is deliciously light and feminine, and exceptionally appealing to me. Ultimately, the *Japan* book was filled out with other food from that era and, voilà, it coalesced perfectly as a whole.

Once I had separated Japan into areas, I approached the chefs and artisans with my plan and set up a schedule of visits, which spanned the course of almost two years. In Japan, relationships are built over time. Introductions are not made lightly. If I introduce someone to an artisan or if I bring a film crew to visit an artisan, I am risking my whole relationship on that introduction. Should something not go well, it will reflect poorly on me, not on the person or group visiting. The intricacy of this particular Japanese attitude cannot be explained with words; it is something felt.

Each chef speaks to me differently, but each one creates food for which I will travel long distances to enjoy.

Lack of understanding of the entrenched obligation and implied responsibility has been the cause of no little consternation in the past when introducing foreign visitors. So when I began my forays into rural areas to reconnect with my chef and artisan contacts in order to access local foods, I knew I was asking big things in terms of their time, commitment and support. Chefs are busy, which made this an even bigger ask. To this day, I remain extremely grateful for their cooperation and willingness to vouch for me personally.

But what came out of those visits was a deepening relationship with each chef and artisan, rather than the local grandmas. So in the end, it was the chefs who inspired me to write this book and to showcase their food. Each chef speaks to me differently, but each one creates food for which I will travel long distances to enjoy. Their commonality is in their love of ingredients and dedication to sourcing, and absolute passion for what they are making and serving. This passion is more rare than one might think.

Also, the chefs profiled in this book infuse their food with their hearts, but not with their egos. Their food is soft on the spirit and has a sense of clarity; a window into the soul of the chef. When you eat their food, you will know them.

SA-SHI-SU-SE-SO: THE FIVE ESSENTIAL ELEMENTS IN JAPANESE CUISINE

The fundamental Japanese flavorings can be reduced to an acronym taken from the Japanese syllabary: *sa* = *sato* (sugar), *shi* = *shio* (salt), *su* = *su* (vinegar), *se* = *seiyu*/*shoyu* (soy sauce), and *so* = miso.

Clear yet complex Japanese dishes are built up from a subtle base using a light hand. Added sparingly and thoughtfully, deeply flavored artisanal raw materials (shoyu, miso, mirin, rice vinegar) will yield the most consistently satisfying results, so don't skimp on these crucial ingredients. That said, if you cannot source well-made versions of each, it is best to select all your ingredients at the same level, for example, mid-range across the board. Using a nuanced, well-made shoyu with ersatz mirin will give your food a jarring note and create a feeling of unbalance in the finished dish. Selecting at the same level means the ingredients will enhance each other equally, without one overpowering another.

Getting to the heart of how these key Japanese ingredients are made is essential to understanding how to successfully incorporate them into your own cooking, because they are not random. They have history.

Shoyu

***Koikuchi shoyu* is the mother of all sauces in Japan.** Typically shortened to shoyu, best known as soy sauce, Kikkoman has made it a household item in most western kitchens and, along with some of the other large Japanese soy sauce makers, sells a wide range of soy sauces. The majority of homes and restaurants probably use the least expensive varieties, but properly fermented soy sauce is very different from the mass-produced version we've become accustomed to. (Truth be told, even the Japanese have only a vague idea of how soy sauce is made or how mainstream soy sauce differs from small artisanal versions.)

Cheaper soy sauces are brewed from non-Japanese defatted soybean grits (a by-product of pressing soybeans for oil), with wheat, table salt and water. Typically, these soy sauce mashes are held for 6 months in a simulated summer environment – heated to speed up the fermentation process. (Many industrial soy sauces skip fermentation altogether and are instead made by chemical hydrolysis.) Large-scale factory–produced soy sauce has the requisite punch of salt, yet lacks the base flavor of fermented soybeans and wheat to offset it. It does the job, but better quality exists.

The finest artisanal Japanese soy sauces are becoming known abroad as shoyu. The best of the best is made from organic Japanese whole soybeans, roasted cracked wheat, Japanese sea salt, and deep well or spring water. The mash ferments naturally, usually going through two summers and at least another year of autumn, winter and spring. This kind of slow-fermented, carefully made shoyu has a round, well-balanced feel in the mouth. It is salty, yet heady with complex fermentation notes.

HOW TO USE SHOYU

Fact: shoyu made from organic Japanese soybeans only constitutes 0.005% of the market in Japan. '*Murasaki*' ('purple') is an old nickname for premium shoyu. The name speaks to the deep, almost purple color of excellent shoyu (and purple is the regal color associated with the emperor). This inherent preciousness is why shoyu should be used sparingly, not as an afterthought or a knee-jerk marinade ingredient like mass-produced versions have encouraged us to do. With artisanal shoyu, a dash goes a long way to introducing that little hint of umami that everyone seems to be chasing.

Used in quiet moderation, shoyu adds a note of flavor depth to western dishes such as stews, gratins, pastas, bechamel-related sauces, vinaigrettes and soups. Just about everything could benefit from a splash of top-shelf shoyu. For dipping sashimi: pour a small pool in the center of the soy sauce dish rather than filling the whole surface of the dish. You can always add more.

Soy sauce has become almost generic, and cost seems to be the prevailing factor in selecting this daily condiment. I prefer to think of it as an extraordinary ingredient that can elevate and enhance any dish.

HOW TO BUY SHOYU

Because the world has become used to soy sauce produced in large factories, soy sauce use has changed in Japan as well as in other countries. Soy sauce has become almost generic, and cost seems to be the prevailing factor in selecting this daily condiment. I prefer to think of it as an extraordinary ingredient that can elevate and enhance any dish.

Defatted soybean grits (*dashi kako daizu*) are dirt cheap and have little redeeming taste value, so soy sauces made from this material are best avoided.

Japanese organic companies bottle and sell shoyu under various proprietary labels, but almost all is produced with Chinese organic beans because they are so cost effective. And more troubling, the Japanese artisanal shoyu houses that sell to these large organic companies (who in turn sell to the large organic companies outside of Japan) must use the Chinese beans as part of their agreement. And at least one large Japanese organic company buys the Chinese beans and sells them directly to the shoyu makers, thus taking profit at both ends.

Just because a product is organic does not mean it is better. Chinese organic beans are cheaper than Japanese conventional beans. Japanese organic beans (both certified and uncertified) are hard to come by and expensive, but responsible soy sauce makers have their own farmers, whom they have supported for generations. I buy from these companies because they are doing something responsible and honest. And such companies also use Japanese sea salt and spring water or deep well water. Companies using Chinese beans are not all as scrupulous about other ingredients, and some use Mexican or other non-Japanese salt. It's a slippery slope.

Our local organic shoyu made by Yamaki Jozo and a few others is slowly becoming available abroad. (The white paper–wrapped Kishibori Shoyu found abroad is made from North American conventional soybeans, but is being sold as a super-premium shoyu.) And several companies outside of Japan are repackaging and selling shoyu: Gold Mine Natural Food Co. (Yamaki Shoyu, under the Ohsawa Nama Shoyu label), Eden Foods and Mitoku (US); Clearspring (UK); and Spiral Foods (Australia).

A WORD ABOUT TAMARI

Nowadays, tamari is thought of as shoyu made from only soybeans, or soybeans with just a small amount of wheat. But '*tamari*' means 'pooled up' and originally referred to the naturally occurring syrup on the surface of miso that results from excess weight on the miso mash: a precious commodity probably best stirred into the mash.

Tamari as a commercial product, however, has a longer history than shoyu. In Japan, tamari is made (and used) in Aichi prefecture. Tamari production is minute compared to shoyu (1.8% versus 84.2%). Due to the lack of wheat to balance out the rich soybeans, well-made tamari is inky in color, pungent, and has a slightly funky taste when compared to shoyu. Cheaper tamari tends to have an unpleasant nose.

Tamari works well for pickling mild vegetables such as eggplant (aubergine) or daikon skin. Although tamari often does contain a small amount of wheat, wheat-free versions are useful for gluten-free dishes. However, tamari should not be used as a blanket substitute for shoyu since just not that much is produced.

A FEW OTHER TYPES OF SHOYU

In the Kansai area (the greater Kyoto and Osaka region), ***usukuchi shoyu*** ('light' soy sauce, not to be confused with 'lite' soy sauce) is commonly, though not exclusively, used, and constitutes 12.4% of the total shoyu market in Japan. *Usukuchi shoyu* has a higher percentage of salt than *koikuchi shoyu* and a different fermentation method (hence the lighter color). Excellent *usukuchi shoyu* is deep amber, salty, yet bright, and spreads throughout your mouth, finally reaching the throat. Until a few years ago, I had never tasted or used *usukuchi shoyu*, but am now a huge fan of this beautiful product. It is commonly used in flavoring *chawan mushi* (steamed savory egg custard) and elegant soups. Unfortunately, artisanal *usukuchi shoyu* is, as yet, a challenge to source outside of Japan, but hope springs eternal ... Fino Foods in Australia and The Japanese Pantry in San Francisco are now selling Suehiro *usukuchi shoyu* from Himeji on my recommendation (the Suehiro Shoyu story will be in my next book).

Pale amber ***shiro shoyu*** (also called white tamari) is an even lighter colored shoyu, because it uses only wheat and a small amount of soybeans. The market share for *shiro shoyu* is only 0.7%, yet it is easily available outside of Japan – perhaps thanks to a great marketing campaign by the *shiro shoyu* makers. *Shiro shoyu* is quite salty and fairly sweet from the addition of shochu (fermented, distilled alcohol). Its flavor is more insistent than *usukuchi shoyu* so should be used cautiously.

Saishikomi shoyu ('refermented shoyu') has another tiny portion of the market at 0.9%. This shoyu is twice-fermented using several different methods. Yamaroku (page 243) uses already fermented shoyu instead of salt water in the shoyu mash (*moromi*). Tsurubishio from Yamaroku is a wild, umami-rich version of the product and is available online. There are two other methods to produce a less dense version of *saishikomi shoyu*, while also controlling the nitrogen. Method one: a thin shoyu is first produced through regular fermentation. Method two: shoyu is produced through regular fermentation, then salt water is added to thin it. At this point in either method, another batch of shoyu koji and salt are added and the mash goes through a second fermentation for an additional 6 months or more (at least one summer).

Thanks to demand from foreign chefs abroad, **smoked shoyu** seems to be having a moment. Suehiro Shoyu is one of the only companies actually smoking the shoyu with wood and fire, and the taste is far superior to other products on the market.

An extremely local yet nonetheless compelling shoyu is a syrupy **abalone liver shoyu** called 'abalone essence' (*awabi no sei*), akin to the best balsamic vinegars in consistency and flavor density – found at Japan Rakuten and Umami Paris (page 274) and used in one recipe in this book (page 41). Avoid the cheap imitation abalone soy sauce (*awabi no shoyu*) that is made by Asamurasaki (containing a long list of ingredients, including corn syrup and MSG) and found on Amazon.

SHOYU-BASED SAUCES

Soy sauce makers also produce various shoyu-based sauces, some of which are difficult to reproduce in the professional or non-professional kitchen. **Ponzu** pairs citrus and shoyu with dashi elements, while **dashi shoyu** is a mixture of just the dashi elements and shoyu. These two would be the first choice of sauces to stock if you can find excellent versions. At our house, we make a simple ponzu with sour orange (*daidai*) juice and shoyu, but it does not keep well. Our local shoyu company in Saitama (Yamaki Jozo) makes a katsuobushi-infused ponzu with a blend of Japanese citrus and vinegar that is stable for 9 months in the fridge. Yamaki's dashi shoyu is similarly infused with katsuobushi and other dashi components, to the extent that it cannot be duplicated, even in the restaurant kitchen.

Whisk a little miso into homemade mayonnaise (shoyu is also delicious). Miso-based vinaigrettes (oil, miso and rice vinegar in a ratio of 2:1:1) are an excellent foil for julienned root vegetables or peppery mizuna leaves.

Miso

Use miso for an earthy umami flavor. Japan is a country that adheres deeply to the concept of '*mottainai*' ('no waste'), and miso embodies that philosophy perfectly. When producing shoyu or tamari, the mash is pressed for the rich salty liquid, and the solids are left behind. Not so with miso: the base ingredient (always soybeans in Japan), koji spore–inoculated grain or pulse (rice, barley or soybeans), salt, and perhaps a small amount of seed miso (miso thinned with water), all come together to make the final product. As a paste, miso is not quite as easy to dash into non-Japanese cooking because of its viscosity and pronounced earthy quality. But if you start with a well-made miso, a little bit can add a deep, round salt note to many foods.

What constitutes a well-made miso? Most important: it should taste good. The salt and fermented beer-like notes should be well balanced with no sourness.

HOW TO USE MISO

Dip carrots, celery, radishes, turnips, green peppers (capsicums) or cucumbers in miso in the summertime for a before-dinner snack.

Whisk a little miso into homemade mayonnaise (shoyu is also delicious). Miso-based vinaigrettes (oil, miso and rice vinegar in a ratio of 2:1:1) are an excellent foil for julienned root vegetables or peppery mizuna leaves. Salt some fish, poultry or pork lightly, then lay a double piece of muslin (cheesecloth) over the top before slathering on a paste made of miso thinned with sake and/or mirin, and leave it to marinate in the fridge for up to several days. Miso also makes a brilliant pickling medium and can be used as is, loosened with sake and/or mirin, or with the addition of aromatics such as *shichimi togarashi* (seven-spice powder), dried red chili or slivered ginger.

A wide range of miso-based sauces is used in vegetable dishes: vinegar miso, mustard miso and dengaku miso (used as a glaze) are classic treatments. *Aemono* ('dressed things') such as *shira-ae* (smashed tofu), *goma-ae* (vegetables in sesame-miso dressing), and *kurumi-ae* (vegetables in walnut sauce) often include miso as a key component and can be incorporated into most non-Japanese meals. The flavor profile and sweet-to-acid balance of these dishes will vary with the cook.

HOW TO BUY MISO

In general, first check the label when buying miso. Authentic and aesthetically pleasing front labels will first catch your eye. Next, pick up the package and read the back label for ingredients. Avoid products with sweeteners, MSG, preservatives, vitamin B2 (for preserving and color enhancement) and alcohol (to stabilize and preserve).

Nothing compares to the highest quality Japanese misos such as our local Yamaki Jozo miso (which is starting to be available abroad). However, there are local miso makers popping up all over the world. Some are better than others. Companies that have been around since the 1970s are arguably doing the best job at making authentic misos, although some I have sampled have been oxidized, and are thus darker and denser than I think they should be. This is not a deal breaker, just something to keep in mind. More concerning is the newer miso companies cropping up that are marketing barely fermented, or poorly fermented, miso, with the iconic miso flavor missing. Worse yet are the miso companies attempting to capture their own wild koji spores for fermentation – without success. The unfortunate result is decidedly NOT miso.

TYPES OF MISO

Kome* (White Rice) Miso:** From quick-fermented **white (*shiro*) miso** and ***Kaga miso to 6-month- or 1-year-fermented **country-style (*inaka*) miso**, *kome miso* represents a fairly wide range of flavors. Quick-fermented varieties are made with an appreciably larger percentage of koji than other misos, and have a sweet and only slightly salty profile. These varieties are good for adding a gentle miso flavor to vegetable dishes or fish marinades. *Inaka miso* is an excellent choice as a starter miso since it is mild, yet still has heady fermentation notes for savory dishes.

***Genmai* (Brown Rice) Miso:** Fermented for 6 months to 1 year (one summer) from soybeans, brown rice koji and salt. Bright and rich, *genmai miso* is probably the most immediately accessible of the darker varieties of miso, and is versatile as a seasoning for most dishes because of its lustrous flavor profile.

***Mugi* (Barley) Miso:** Soybeans, barley koji and salt, traditionally fermented for 6 months to 1 year (one summer). Soft, luscious and fragrant from the barley, *mugi miso* is particularly good in simmered dishes, but absolutely delicious in just about anything. Highly favored in Western Europe – perhaps because *mugi miso* goes well with olive oil.

Mame* (Soybean) Miso:** Long-fermented for 2 to 3 years from soybeans, soybean koji and salt. Dark and deeply flavored with lovely beery notes, *mame miso* makes rich winter broths, and is a good candidate for mixing with lighter miso varieties (*awase miso*) to add overall complexity. ***Hatcho miso is a type of *mame miso* produced in Aichi prefecture in central-eastern Japan and is weighted with massive rocks for 2½ years.

Salt

Japanese sea salt is some of the best in the world and plays an important role in background flavoring, even when using shoyu, miso or *gyosho* (fish sauce).

Japanese artisanal salt production all but died out in the last century, due both to a government salt monopoly that spanned almost one hundred years, and the abolishment of all remaining salt fields in 1971 (page 230).

In recent years, the industry has revived and flourished thanks to a crop of passionate artisanal salt producers. One of my favorite salt makers, Hajime Nakamichi of the Wajima no Kaien company, began making salt because he realized the inefficacy of table salt in creating superior air-dried fish (at the time, his metier). Another salt maker, Toshiki Kaba (page 230), relocated to Shodoshima and, seeing no native salt production, taught himself how to make a bright, flavorful salt and can now barely keep up with demand. Artisanal salt is raked off slowly and gently after purifying and condensing deep seawater, using various methods of evaporation (sun, fire from below, heat from above, etc.).

The resulting salt is well suited for all manners of food preservation and preparation. Harsh, industrially produced salts interfere with the symbiosis of salt, air and sun, which is part of the salt-preservation process. Natural sea salts don't overpower the base ingredient being preserved, and allow the inherent strength of ingredients to interact productively.

Always ask questions regarding the ingredients that go into any given food product.

Gyosho

Closer to salt than shoyu, *gyosho* (fish sauce) takes salt and fish to a whole other dimension. Traditionally fermented from the guts of plentiful fish, the current rendition uses the whole fish for a pleasantly salty, yet not smelly, fish sauce. What was once strictly an ultra-local seasoning that took the place of shoyu in isolated areas where fish was the main source of food, *gyosho* is now being used by chefs all over Japan as a 'hidden taste'.

Japan has only two main fish sauce–producing regions. Akita prefecture in the north primarily uses sandfish and calls their fish sauce ***shottsuru***. In Ishikawa prefecture on the Sea of Japan, northwest of Tokyo, fish sauce is typically made of sardine, mackerel or squid and is called ***ishiri*** or ***ishiru***. Production of sand lance (*ikanago*) fish sauce in the Seto Inland Sea all but died out, however recently the industry is slowly revitalizing.

HOW TO USE GYOSHO

Gyosho should be used as a light, one-time brush before grilling, or a delicate hint in pickles, *nabe* (one pot) dishes, fried rice, gratins, stews ... whatever. It should not be overused. The point is to give the food a feel of the sea rather than an insistent taste of salty fermented fish.

While recent research seems to indicate that consumption of MSG should not have health implications, I still have a problem with its use in food preparations. MSG is ubiquitous in Japanese processed foods, and signals the use of inferior materials in the making of food products. One objection to MSG is that it is used to hide the fact that a food is essentially lacking in flavor. Another objection is its one-sided punch as opposed to the true umami flavors that shoyu, miso or *gyosho* can lend to any given dish.

HOW TO BUY GYOSHO

Moroi Jozo (page 26) is arguably one of the top producers of fish sauce in Japan, and, besides their regular *shottsuru*, they also make a milder one steeped with konbu. The exceptional 10-year-old version, which comes in an elegantly slim 300 ml (10 fl oz) bottle, is mellow and subtle.

Hajime Nakamichi of Wajima no Kaien salt also happens to be vice-president of the Wajima town morning market. When I need fish sauce I contact him, and he sends me his current favorite *ishiru/ishiri*. He might be convinced to do the same for you if you order salt.

Artisanal fish sauce production is not large, and each barrel takes 2 to 3 years to ferment, so the available quantity is finite. When tasting fish sauces side by side, you are looking for a pronounced yet not stinky saltiness. The fermented fish flavor should infuse your mouth with a taste of the sea. Do not be put off by saltiness, however. If a fish sauce is too salty, yet has an intrinsically good flavor, put the bottle in the freezer until the salt crystals solidify. Decant and use.

Rice Vinegar

Artisanal rice vinegar will change your life. Throw out those bottles of low-grade Marukan or Mizkan vinegar made from ethyl alcohol and only a smidge of rice. Do yourself a favor and, at the very least, buy **brown rice vinegar** (called 'black vinegar' in Japan because of the black pots in which it is fermented). All the responsible organic companies around the world are selling excellent versions of these 'black' vinegars, but look out for the beautiful vinegar ranges offered by Iio Jozo, Sennari (Oochi) and Ohyama. Harder to come by outside of Japan is a pure and elegant **white-rice vinegar (*junmai su*)** made from in-house-brewed sake (possibly made from local organic rice). The best of this stuff might have you reaching for rice vinegar over wine vinegar for most of your vinegar needs.

HOW TO USE RICE VINEGAR

Rice vinegar works well with many other sauces. The classic combinations are: *amasu* (sweet vinegar), *nihai sanbaizu* (vinegar, soy sauce and dashi), *nihaizu* (vinegar and soy sauce) and *warisu* (vinegar and dashi). Use them as is, or as a base for other treatments. *Amasu* and *sanbaizu* are useful for quick-pickling vegetables. Add a light or fruity oil to *nihaizu* in a ratio of 1:1 for a Japanese vinaigrette. And *warisu* is beautiful drizzled on blanched, refreshed green vegetables.

HOW TO BUY RICE VINEGAR

Choosing a mass-produced rice vinegar for salads or vegetable preparations is akin to using distilled vinegar (who would?). The harsh vinegar necessitates adding extra sugar to soften the puckery, one-sided dimension of low-quality rice vinegars. An artisanal rice vinegar is aromatic and well balanced. Sadly, artisanal white-rice vinegars are not yet widely available abroad, but that situation is rapidly changing, and, by the printing of this book, perhaps you will already have a bottle of top-shelf *junmai su* in your kitchen.

Sugar

Add some sweetness for balance: sugar, mirin and sake. In our house, we do not have the custom of using sugar in most Japanese vegetable treatments, because my husband grows our vegetables and they are naturally sweet. That said, as I explore other people's food and other areas' flavoring techniques, my mindset tends to shift and become more open. If I use sugar, it is a light tan, organic Brazilian sugar, which resembles granulated sugar in texture, but has a lovely floral profile. Granulated sugar is common in Japan, but there is also an array of Japanese sugars from which to select, and their use depends on personal taste and how much color or flavor the sugar will bring to the finished dish.

TYPES OF SUGAR

***Guranyuto* (Granulated Sugar):** A refined sugar made mainly from sucrose, sometimes translated as caster sugar.

***Johakuto* (Fine White Sugar):** Moist in texture with 1% water content. Made from sucrose and invert sugar (glucose and fructose), the addition of which hastens the caramelization process, so perhaps not appropriate for baked goods.

***Sanonto* (Refined Light Brown Sugar):** 'Three temperature sugar' produced by heating *johakuto* and granulated sugars together several times to lend a caramel color to what is essentially white sugar.

***Kibizato* (Light Brown Cane Sugar):** Made from boiling down the refined cane sugar solution directly, thus preserving the flavor and minerals of the cane itself.

***Zarame* (Coarse Light Brown Sugar):** A shiny, coarse, tan sugar of high purity. Good for simmered dishes and pickling.

***Kurosato/Kokuto* (Black Sugar):** A fine-grained, dark-brown to blackish native Okinawan sugar, which is mineral-rich and made by boiling down the juices pressed from the sugar cane. Different from western dark brown sugar.

***Wasanbon* (Artisanal Japanese Sugar):** A powdery, caramel-colored native Japanese sugar produced in the southern islands, particularly Shikoku. Used for high-level Japanese confectionery.

***Tensaito* (Sugar Beet Sugar):** Produced from sugar beets grown in Hokkaido, said to aid in digestion.

MIRIN AND SAKE

Through visits to small mirin producers around Japan, I have developed a deep appreciation for and understanding of mirin, a naturally sweet cooking 'sake' that is lower in alcohol and often mislabeled as 'sweet rice wine'. The best mirins (such as Mikawa mirin) are fermented from koji-inoculated glutinous rice and in-house-distilled shochu. A top mirin rolls around on your tongue and is beautifully drinkable. The alcohol balance and naturally occurring sweetness from the koji add a depth of flavor that sugar cannot match. Look for *hon mirin* (本みりん). You will not be disappointed.

I use sake in lieu of or in conjunction with mirin to introduce a soft background sweetness to dishes. Sometimes you just want a hint of gentle, clear sweetness; in that case, use sake alone. Some Japanese sake breweries such as Kitsukura Shuzo and Hakusen Shuzo are producing excellent sake specifically well-matched for cooking, but this style of high-quality cooking sake is difficult to obtain, even in Japan. Best select a sake from what is available to you locally. And, much as you would not select the absolute cheapest wine for cooking, choose a mid-range sake – but avoid the cloudy sakes such as *nama-zake* or *nigori-zake* for cooking. Once opened, keep the sake in the fridge.

BEYOND THE BASICS

It is not enough to grab a bunch of Japanese ingredients and throw them into a dish willy-nilly. The combinations and tastes should make sense. And without understanding how these ingredients interact with each other, it will be impossible to use them thoughtfully or to good result. Examples would be pairing *ume* with wasabi, because they will war with each other, or shiso with *sake kasu* (sake lees), because they originate in opposite seasons (summer and winter). Taste first, internalize, then use these Japanese flavors sparingly to complement and enhance rather than overpower a dish.

Dried Fish

KATSUOBUSHI

Given that Japan is a mountainous archipelago with the 6th-longest coastline in the world, creatures and plants found in the sea are integral to Japanese food culture. Katsuobushi is skipjack tuna that in its most artisanal form is smoked then fermented and sun-dried (several times) over the course of 5 to 6 months, and is pure heaven. Award-winning Sakai Shoten in Yamagawa-machi, Kagoshima-ken, is where I head for all katsuobushi needs, though smoked, fermented, sun-dried katsuobushi is still a challenge to source outside of Japan. However, you will easily find bags of pre-shaved smoked katsuobushi (*hanakatsuo*) – just look for the widest and most pinky tan shavings (sold as 'bonito flakes'). The most common use of katsuobushi is as a base for dashi (soup broth), but katsuobushi can be strewn on boiled vegetables, pickles, salads, rice, pasta or pizza (!) by the handful. When I call out, 'Who wants katsuobushi?' at my little preschool in Japan, a dozen grimy hands shoot out.

IRIKO

Sun-dried fishes (*iriko*) are a popular snack, though are classically used for making a gentle dashi reminiscent of the sea (just soak the *iriko* in cold water overnight, and the dashi is ready to use). For western applications, throw a few in a soup or stew to add a subtly imperceptible depth to the dish. *Iriko* are produced in southern coastal areas of Japan where sun and wind are naturally present. These fishes range from the eensy-weensy *eso* of Kyushu to the almost grotesque dried *aji* (horse mackerel) of Amami Oshima. And *yaki ago* – charcoal-grilled, sun-dried juvenile flying fish – is prized for making ramen soup. ***Niboshi*** is the most common *iriko* found outside of Japan.

SURUME IKA

The best *surume ika* (dried squid) is sun-dried and can be identified by the hole at the top of the head; good as a chewy snack after being wafted over low-ember coals, or as a textural component of Hokkaido pickles (*matsumae-zuke*). Shredded *surume ika* is packaged as a drinking snack, but has been processed with MSG and preservatives, so is to be avoided for culinary applications.

SAKURA EBI

Small sun-dried shrimp. Used in stir-fries and deep-fried fritters such as the Dried Shrimp and Green Nori Fritters (page 103). Japanese-sourced shrimp are preferred, but expensive.

KOEBI, ISADA

Very tiny sun-dried shrimp. Used in similar applications as *sakura ebi*, also useful for adding just a hint of the sea to dishes such as Ganmodoki (page 207).

Konbu

Both wild and farmed konbu (kelp) are harvested in Japan over six short weeks from the end of July to the end of August. Konbu can be the base for making dashi, either alone or with dried shiitake, katsuobushi or *iriko*; a wrap for simmered foods; or a vehicle to wick off moisture from raw fish. After a life-changing visit to Rausu at the tip of a narrow peninsula off northeast Hokkaido (page 22), I revere konbu, and toss it into simmering pots of potatoes or stews to infuse them ever so slightly with the taste of the sea. Avoid 'snack' konbu since it is unpleasantly seasoned with MSG and other ingredients.

Sea Greens

There are many other sea greens (page 36) that are harvested and dried in the Japanese spring, though only wakame, arame and hijiki are readily available outside of Japan. These dried sea greens take up little space in the cupboard, have a shelf life of 1 year (or more), and are quickly reconstituted in cold water. They are handy to have on hand, and each has different applications. **Wakame** adds a briny, slippery texture to salads, **hijiki** is often used in steamed or deep-fried tofu dishes, and **arame** can be slipped into simmered or raw dishes.

Last is **nori** (laver), the best of which is *ichibanzumi nori* (first nori), gathered by aqua-farmers in mid-January from the Ariake Sea of Kyushu in southern Japan. Nori is wrapped around rice for sushi or *onigiri* (rice balls), but also makes a striking garnish when snipped into jet-black slivers and scattered over food of contrasting colors.

Nuts and Seeds

ONIGURUMI

Moving inland from the sea, the mountainous areas of Japan produce small walnuts called *onigurumi* ('devil walnuts') due to the hardness of their shells and difficulty in cracking. Oily and fragrant, these walnuts are paired with soba or other mountain-based foods, as well as smashed and used to dress vegetables in lieu of sesame.

SESAME

Sadly, Japanese sesame production is close to nil, so Wadaman (page 212), the top sesame company in Japan, sources each of its shockingly flavorful seed varieties (black, white and gold) from a different country. A 130-year-old company, Wadaman roasts the seeds in a proprietary method that had my jaw dropping in amazement when I visited. They offer a range of organic and conventionally grown sesame-based products, such as whole roasted sesame, ground sesame, sesame oils and sesame pastes. Naturally, these products are more expensive than other sesame products on the market, but their quality is far, far superior and defies comparison. White sesame seeds are a natural pair to delicate spring vegetables, gold sesame is well matched with miso, and black sesame contrasts beautifully with green- and white-hued salads or stir-fries.

GINKGO NUTS

Not really a main ingredient, nonetheless ginkgo nuts deserve a mention. Only available fresh in the autumn, these rubbery, indescribably musky nuts have a short-lived season during the fall and are highly perishable. Shelled and pan-roasted in oil and salt, they are deliciously compelling, though slightly toxic if not consumed in moderation.

Dried and Preserved Fruit

UMEBOSHI

High-quality umeboshi (salt-pickled, sun-dried sour 'plums') are difficult to source even in Japan. However, Yamaki Jozo contracts one of the two commercial farmers in Japan (page 72) who offer organic *ume*-related products, such as red shiso–infused and natural *ume* paste. Currently, the *ume* paste is only available directly from Yamaki Jozo or through Fino Foods in Australia, though negotiations are underway with Nishikidori in France and The Wasabi Company in the UK. *Ume* paste imbues dishes with a puckery yet brightly fruity element, and goes particularly well with white foods such as cod, turnips or cream, and is well worth the effort required to source it.

HOSHIGAKI

Air-dried persimmons (*hoshigaki*) are entirely seasonal. Tannic persimmons must be picked when ripe but not soft, then peeled and hung outdoors to dry. At home, persimmons are usually hung under the rafters that jut out from the roofs of Japanese farmhouses. Artisanal commercial operations need a more practical system, so they hang their persimmons on tiered poles to dry in direct sun. Depending on the weather and the drying method, the dried persimmons are brought in after about a month, when they have sufficiently withered, yet the inside flesh retains a firm, gelatinous consistency. *Hoshigaki* can be munched as an afternoon pick-me-up or sliced up and tossed into salads and smashed tofu treatments (*shira-ae*) to introduce natural sweetness and texture.

YUZU KOSHO

Yuzu peel and green chilies are salted separately in the summer and fermented, before mashing into an unforgettable paste called yuzu kosho (page 270). Besides green yuzu kosho, Kushino Nouen also makes a warm red yuzu kosho from red chilies in the late autumn. A little goes a long way. Mix into vinegar for a spicy mignonette, white sesame oil as a drizzle, or dab into clear broths.

Aromatics

CITRUS

Yuzu is being grown in pockets around the world, so use Google and search it out. Slivered yuzu peel is an essential flavoring note in many Japanese dishes, and is commonly strewn into vegetable treatments, salads, salt pickles, noodles, soups and savory egg dishes.

Beyond yuzu, there are many other interesting, fragrant Japanese citrus, such as ***sudachi*** (slightly more subtle than yuzu), ***kabosu*** (green and brightly acidic but with unusual aromatic zest), and ***daidai*** (a bitter orange used for making ponzu). These citrus varieties are worth clamoring for.

SPICY ROOTS AND RHIZOMES

Freshly grated **daikon**, **ginger** and **wasabi** provide an element of hotness to balance dishes. While chopped or slivered ginger is commonly tossed into stir-fries or simmered meat treatments, garlic is not, and is mostly only used in pickling or Chinese-style dishes. And *myoga*, a beautiful flame-shaped pinky tan rhizome related to (though totally unlike) ginger is lovely in cold soups, salads, pickled, or as a garnish for sashimi.

LEAVES AND HERBS

After the cold winter, vibrant bitter greens spring up all over the mountains and near the streams running icy water.

Cultivated ***seri* (Japanese parsley)** grows upright on stalks similar to conventional parsley, but the wild variety grows in a tangled mass that makes it an excellent candidate for tempura, though a bit of a pain to clean. The pinky stems turn brown overnight so it is important to pick through each strand. *Seri* needs a quick douse of boiling water to tame its raw bitterness, before refreshing, blotting dry, cutting crosswise into 5 centimeter (2 inch) pieces, and adding to salads and soups.

***Mitsuba* (trefoil)**, the haunting green leaves you find floating in soup at Japanese restaurants, is available year-round from hot-house cultivation, but a pungent wide-leafed variety is foraged in the spring from our local mountains, and can be grown in your garden. Mountain *mitsuba* complements egg dishes naturally, smooths out the briny quality of clams and contrasts brilliantly with the earthy tones of miso soup.

Shiso (perilla) reseeds in the summer and is incorporated into dishes containing cucumber, eggplant (aubergine) and green pepper (capsicum) until it goes to seed in the fall. Shiso is not as ubiquitous to Japanese food as it seems to be abroad, so best pause on the blanket use of the leaf and look towards some of the more interesting bitter leaves and alliums.

Another harbinger of spring, ***sansho*** leaves are tiny green leaves from the Japanese prickly ash tree. *De rigueur* for dishes with bamboo shoots (the ultimate spring delicacy in Japan), they are also good torn over miso-simmered foods or vegetables smeared with sweet miso (dengaku).

Like the vast array of Japanese citrus yet unknown to the world, Japanese alliums are myriad and varied in nuance, so worth a closer look.

ALLIUMS

Known as the Japanese 'leek' or 'long onion', ***negi*** is present in many Japanese dishes and is almost irreplaceable. Farmers around the world are starting to grow *negi*, so don't lose heart. In the meantime, substitute fat scallions (spring onions) or French *échalotes vertes*.

In the spring we have a wide range of multiplying onions which happily, and prolifically, reseed: ***rakkyo*** (hot, garlicky, good for pickling), ***asatsuki*** (a shallot eaten raw, not dried), ***nobiru*** (a wild green onion with tiny bulbs, which begs to be eaten raw with miso), and the cultivated ***wakegi*** (very thin, chive-like young *negi* occasionally served as sushi). All of these alliums can easily be grown by farmers outside of Japan, and should be.

Powders

And not to be ignored, there is a small range of spices and powders that are used in Japanese cuisine – some traditional, some not.

Recently, American recipes are starting to call for '*togarashi*'. It is not clear if they are referring to *ichimi togarashi* (powdered Japanese red chili) or *shichimi togarashi* (seven-spice mixture). And it seems that sometimes the writers may not even know. Let's avoid this misnomer.

Togarashi means red chili, and is most often used whole in the dried form. As for the powder, ***ichimi togarashi*** is mildly spicy yet well balanced, and even my kindergarten students request a little sprinkle on the lunch I serve them. Both *ichimi* and ***shichimi togarashi*** (containing a combination of usually seven spices, such as *ichimi togarashi*, hemp seeds, yuzu peel, black sesame, white sesame, *sansho* and green nori) are sprinkled into soupy things, but not without thought. For instance, you would never add either of these to a sweet shoyu-based dipping sauce for udon or soba, though you would for a brothy one. Good sense is the key to using these ingredients.

An extremely spare sprinkling of **green *sansho* powder** can enhance miso-based simmers and earthy treatments, or be rubbed on meat before grilling. Also exciting and equally exceptional is **red shiso powder**. Yamaki Jozo's *ume* farmer (page 72) dips red shiso leaves in the *ume*-pickling brine and sun-dries them three times before pulverizing. The resulting powder is at once vibrant, salty and sour. Sprinkle shiso powder on mayonnaise-based salads, daikon or turnip pickles, rice, beurre blanc, or sake-steamed white fish.

Lastly, top-shelf **dashi powder** produced from Japanese-sourced ingredients (extremely rare, even in Japan) can act as an unexpected alternative to salt and is especially good on red meat or green vegetables.

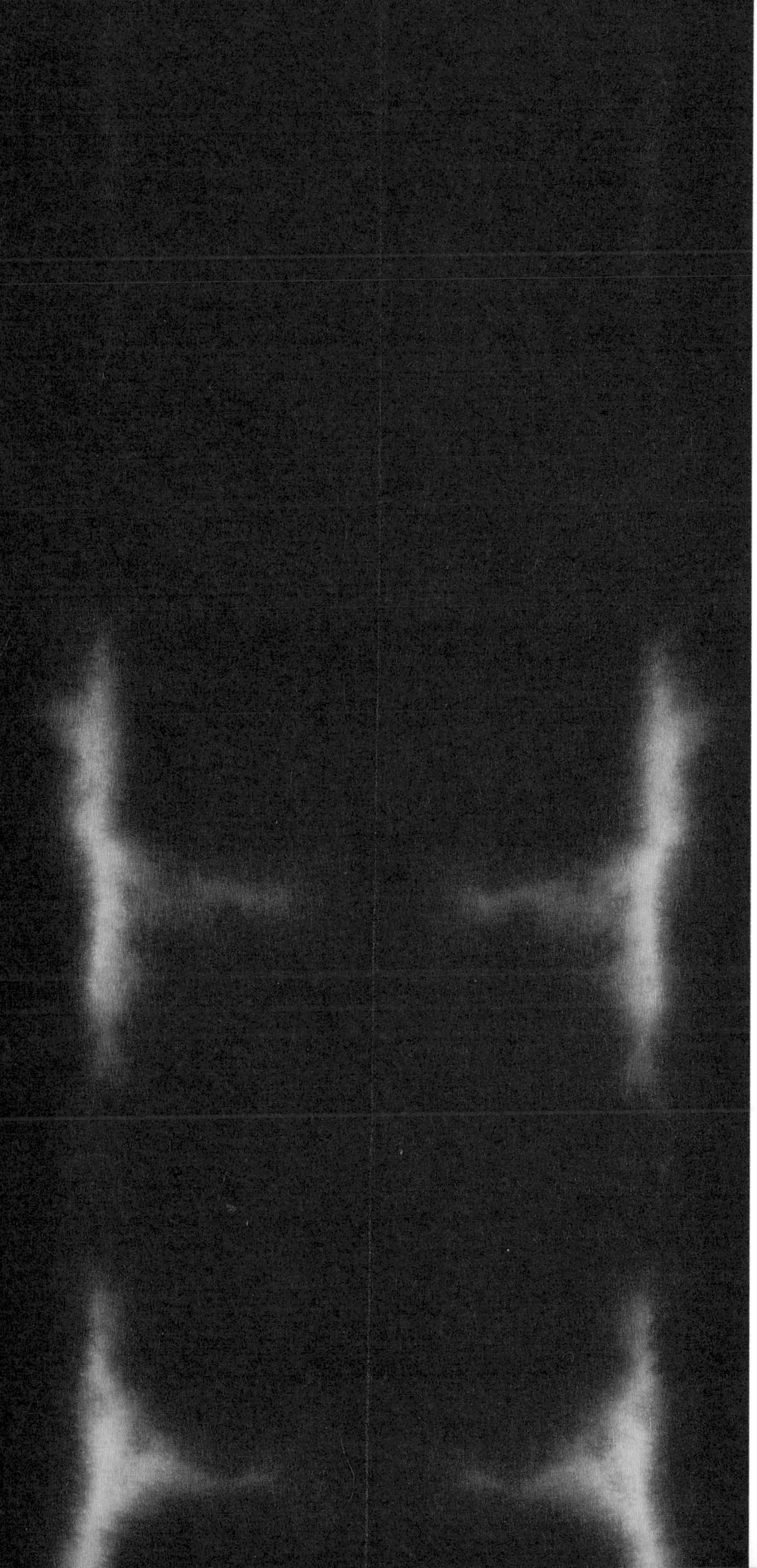

北海道

RAUSU KONBU

After flying in from Tokyo the night before, it took a 2-hour drive snaking through Shiretoko National Park to reach the town of Rausu, situated on the eastern side of the Shiretoko Peninsula, off the eastern tip of Hokkaido. We met up with Katsuhiko Amano at the Rausu Konbu Association office and followed his zippy white van as he drove up the coast to where local fishermen were gathering konbu. Scrambling down the bank to the rocky beach put us smack in the middle of several families processing their harvest. I set out down the beach and was immediately drawn to the wide smile stretching across the round face of Katsuyo Shimakura.

Katsuyo is the wife of Kazumi Shimakura and she runs the beach crew (consisting of friends and family), while her husband is out on the boat gathering wild Rausu konbu.

The season starts around July 19 or 20 each year and ends on August 31. At the outset of the season, the boats are allowed out for a short couple of hours for three days each week. And as the season progresses, so do the allowable hours and days.

We were there in early August, already the height of the season. Kazumi Shimakura motored out every morning at 6 am, heading back in to drop off a load of konbu around 9 am, then returning with a second load at 11 am: the absolute time limit for harvesting konbu. He had been and gone by the time we stumbled upon their operation and found a glistening pile of konbu heaped on the beach, next to a roller-equipped washing apparatus. Katsuyo and her fireman son, Kazuaki, pitching in on his day off, fed the konbu through the rollers into Sachio Kawabata's open arms. Crouched in a wading pool with circulating water gushing out from the apparatus, Kawabata grappled with the slippery kelp to rinse off the seawater before tossing each piece onto the rocks. After washing, the 6-person crew spread the kelp out across the rocky beach to dry in the sun, dispatching the lot swiftly and efficiently.

The Shimakuras are perhaps the only family in Rausu who rely on the sun rather than a kerosene-fueled drying room. While they do possess a drying chamber next to the beach where they work, it is reserved for lesser grade kelp, or as a backup when the weather does not cooperate.

After the first load of konbu had been laid out for half a day of drying, the beach team took a tea-and-smoke break, while Yoshimi Tanaka continued her task of rolling the previous day's konbu. After softening the half-day-dried konbu in the misty evening or early dawn air, the strands are then rolled using a foot-operated spindle to flatten the natural ruffles of the kelp. These rolls are then unfurled and arranged in 20- or 30-layer stacks between rush mats. A thick board weighted by hefty rocks is placed on top of the last stack. This weighting process is a crucial step in 'aging' the kelp, to develop the highly desirable amino acids contained in the best konbu. After aging for at least five days, the konbu is again laid out on the rocky beach for an (almost) final drying process called *hi-ire* ('putting in the sun') – a step done under the sun by all producers. The konbu is brought in, stacked in a zippered silver bag the size of a small room, and held in that non-humid environment until the end of the season. In September, the konbu tips, bottom ends and ruffled edges are snipped off. The konbu is dried one last time before grading and packaging, and the whole year's harvest is warehoused at the Rausu Konbu Association.

We ended up spending most of three days with the Shimakura family and their team, and left with an armload of konbu and a renewed appreciation and love for the seaweed. Truly magical stuff – a square popped into any Japanese or western soup or sauce adds a subtle briny clarity. My Rausu konbu from the Shimakura family is draped across the wooden banister upstairs at my little English-immersion preschool. A fair amount of crystals have formed. The crystals are a combination of salt and

mannitol, and contribute to the umami-rich properties of konbu. Best not brush them off, unless you are chewing the dried konbu as a snack. At the preschool I cut a piece from the strand, and before using it in the day's lunch, offer snipped pieces to the children. Not one kid declines, and most ask for seconds (or thirds).

While wild-harvested Rishiri, Hidaka and Ma konbu all have their own compelling characteristics, I have a penchant for the sun-dried Rausu konbu produced by Kazumi Shimakura, perfectly content with the cast-off strands I shlepped home to Saitama.

Hokkaido produces 90% of Japan's konbu, and the harvesters sell almost all of their product to their local konbu association, which in turn takes it to the Hokkaido Federation of Fisheries Cooperative Association, where it is sold at auction. The konbu is graded by color (red, black, white) and by rank (first, second, third, forth and crude – *zatsu*); separated by wild or farmed; but never differentiated for being sun-dried, so families such as the Shimakuras who put time and effort into sun-drying their konbu are not compensated extra. Their sole reward is the pride they take in producing a superior konbu.

東北

TOHOKU

Akita Prefecture
Iwate Prefecture

Oga-shi, Akita Prefecture

MOROI JOZO

A whopping four and a half hours on the Komachi bullet train from Tokyo to Akita, and another hour on the local train to Oga-shi, brought us to Moroi Jozo, the soy sauce maker who single-handedly revived *shottsuru* production.

Oga-shi is located on a small peninsula jutting out from northwestern Akita prefecture. *Shottsuru* is the fish sauce/condiment made traditionally in Akita prefecture from sandfish (*hata hata*). And although fish sauce was historically made in numerous locales along Japan's almost 30,000-kilometer coastline, nowadays the only significant sauce-producing area besides Akita is Ishikawa prefecture, where the sauce is called *ishiri* or *ishiru*. (*Ishiru* and *shottsuru* are clearly cognate words.) The Seto Inland Sea area has maintained a minute production of sand lance fish sauce (*ikanago shoyu*), and Hokkaido is putting effort into developing salmon fish sauce due to its extensive salmon catch, but fish sauce has historically been a hyper-local ingredient in Japan.

The popularity of Southeast Asian foods in the 1980s brought renewed attention to the condiment, but Japan has yet to reach the same heights of the worldwide craze for the flavor. And conversely, the world has yet to discover that Japan is the best source to satisfy the appetite for well-made versions of the condiment. Japanese fish sauce is generally milder than Southeast Asian varieties, and the gentle flavor is easily incorporated into many foods, both Japanese and western alike, as a hidden taste.

Sandfish are bountiful from December 1 to 20, which is the only period when this traditional *shottsuru* is put up.

Hideki Moroi, 3rd-generation soy sauce, miso and pickle maker, speaks about his relatively recently acquired fish sauce–making craft with a quiet dedication, yet an almost pent-up passion underlies his words. He is also thinking forward towards realizing his mission to introduce *shottsuru* to the world, and is already selling in Australia, Hong Kong and Thailand.

Thirty to forty years ago, about thirty companies were still making *shottsuru* in Akita prefecture. Around 1992–93, the number of *shottsuru* companies took a drastic dive due to aging makers and lack of demand, leaving only eight or nine places still making the condiment.

Moroi, noticing that the viability of commercial *shottsuru* was imminently threatened, and despite being told he was 'stupid', set about entering the market himself. He began experimenting with the process of making *shottsuru* in 1983, and finally, by 2000, he had a product he was proud to sell. In 2004 he attended the inaugural gathering of Slow Fish, organized by Slow Food in Genoa, and it was his involvement with Slow Food that enabled Moroi to initially find routes for selling his fish sauce in Tokyo. Since then, Moroi Jozo's *shottsuru* has become the poster child of the best Japanese fish sauce, and is being used in several of Joël Robuchon's restaurants in Paris.

Sandfish are bountiful from December 1 to 20, which is the only period when this traditional *shottsuru* is put up. It represents 89% of Moroi Jozo's fish sauce. The remaining 11% are other fish sauces that Moroi Jozo began making 3 years ago: oyster, tuna, sea bream, shrimp and squid. The bottles are strikingly designed, and each product has a deliciously distinct profile. Although some of the newer varieties of fish sauce are fermented for a shorter time, Moroi ferments most of his sauce for about 3 years in wooden barrels or enamel tanks, and uses 10–23% sun-dried Japanese sea salt, depending on the fish or shellfish. He also has an impressive 10-year *shottsuru* that is arguably the most elegant and nuanced fish sauce in the world. Pricy, but not overpriced, the sauce comes in a slender, hand-numbered bottle and makes a wonderful gift.

My first contact with Moroi Jozo was about ten or more years ago when looking for Japanese fish sauce to bring as gifts to chef friends in the United States. Down to the last minute, I madly dashed off an email in English asking if Moroi Jozo could dispatch an order swiftly. Not daunted by the English, Moroi responded affirmatively and the package arrived one day later, the bottles carefully bubble-wrapped, with a gold gift bag for each one. This attention to detail and great kindness made Moroi my friend for life, and I have often bought his *shottsuru* as gifts over the years.

When writing my second book, *Preserving the Japanese Way*, I called Moroi Jozo in the hopes of arranging a trip there with my photographer to capture the sandfish catch and making of *shottsuru* in December. Particularly drawn to absorbing the knowledge and heart of older Japanese countrywomen, an extended telephone conversation with Moroi's mother further instilled in me an intense desire to visit. Alas time was not on my side, and that visit was not to be, but I finally made it to Moroi Jozo in July 2018. Walking through the facility and taking in the fermenting vats full of sweetly fragrant fish sauce mash first hand, all of my imagined perceptions of the man and the company were confirmed. Moroi is serious about his craft, and this quietly and naturally complex fermented condiment is poised for the world market.

Although I love many of the new types of *shottsuru* that Moroi is making, I am a creature of habit. And when recently in the United States doing food events, I brought little spray bottles of the original Moroi Jozo *shottsuru* I had first bought ten years before. I sprayed the *shottsuru* on ripe garden tomatoes and drizzled them with a little of my brother-in-law's Frantoio Grove olive oil: so simple, but a standout favorite at the events.

At first glance *shottsuru* might seem foreign or unapproachable, but it can easily be used as a replacement for salt. Think of it as a salt-plus, with a depth of flavor not found in salt. Think of *shottsuru* as umami in a bottle, with all of the good points of MSG but none of the bad.

L'Auréole Tanohata
Tanohata-mura, Iwate Prefecture

KATSUYASU ITO

Katsuyasu Ito ran a successful restaurant in Oshu, a large city in Iwate prefecture, and was winner of the famed Iron Chef competition.

On March 11, 2011, the Tohoku Earthquake triggered a massive tsunami that reached heights of 40.5 meters (133 feet) and traveled up to 10 kilometers (6 miles) inland, killing over 10,000 people. Tanohata-mura, a 3500-person village on the northeast coast of Iwate, was hit by a wave 10 meters (33 feet) high that killed 39 residents, destroyed 200 buildings, and decimated the 565-boat fishing fleet, leaving only 43 afloat.

After working tirelessly in the region to help rebuild from the devastation, including gathering chefs around Japan to participate in an outreach called 'Soul of Tohoku' to bring food to evacuated survivors, chef Ito relocated to this remote locale and opened L'auréole Tanohata in May 2016. Recognizing the potential of the village's natural resources, Ito undertook the mission to introduce chef friends in Tokyo to the bountiful raw materials he found in Tanohata-mura. He also revitalized the school lunch to be local, seasonal and delicious. Tanohata-mura, due to its unique location along a pristine stretch of the Sea of Japan, has a plethora of fish and sea greens, verdant forests with mushrooms of all kinds, as well as walnuts, chestnuts and acorns, flat land with local rice and vegetables, and a grass-fed dairy farm in the foothills (page 52).

Ito uses cast-iron Oigen cookware (page 48) exclusively and, with minimal intervention, takes deeply flavored seasonal ingredients and puts them together beautifully on the plate. Even today, sourcing well-made bread in Japan is a challenge, yet, inexplicably, this tiny town boasts at least two outstanding bakeries, and chef Ito serves bread from both shops. His food is gentle, sensitive, and you do not tire of it, even if you eat it several days in a row (as I do). Counter seats give diners a chance to watch every mesmerizing step of the cooking process, in which Ito uses three key techniques: parboiling vegetables in an iron pot; searing fish and meats while spooning pan juices over them; and covering the sauté pans and leaving them off heat to finish cooking meats and fish from the heat of the pan.

The first time I ate Ito-san's food I was struck by its duality: simple, yet not simplistic. It is elegantly composed with clear flavors. At that first sitting, I instinctually knew him and immediately liked him as a person through experiencing his food.

Upon meeting and observing him further in the kitchen, Ito-san was indeed casual yet flawlessly proficient, working with an economy of movement as he demoed a series of dishes to show us how the Oigen ironware defined his cooking methods and style. After a lifetime of cooking, there are not many new yet classic techniques that grab me, but Ito-san's signature use of his iron pans as partners in the cooking process did.

When embarking on my two most recent books involving all of Japan, I reached out to Ito-san first. Despite Ito-san being a native of Chiba prefecture near Tokyo, I knew he was a strong advocate for, and deeply involved with, the food traditions of Iwate prefecture, his wife's home region. And I have spent many hours with Ito-san one-on-one because I had a close connection to Oigen ironworks, and because he was located in such a remote place. At first he was kind, though unused to hanging out with a foreign woman, but now we have an easy and casual friendship.

Ito-san was involved in a food event with Oigen ironworks called 'Food, Food' – one of the first food events I have attended in Japan where every single dish was well made and delicious. And he introduced me to Teiko Watanabe, a legendary octogenarian Iwate cooking teacher who, along with Ito-san, was a main cook at Food, Food, and also eventually became a big influence on my last book, *Japan: The Cookbook*.

I've traveled to Tanohata-mura three times, and would go back more if I could muster up the time. It takes about a half day to get there from my area of Saitama prefecture, and involves multiple train changes. But upon arrival at L'auréole Tanohata, perched above a secluded cove with a breathtakingly beautiful view, I finally sink into a seat at the counter. Wine glass in hand, the distance and hours disappear. Chef Ito moves effortlessly between his iron pot of boiling water and grill pans. Sprigs of herbs and flowers, oils, vinegars and fish sauces are on the counter close at hand. Lulled by the food and action, a quiet calm envelops me, and I am in my good place – far from home but warmly welcomed.

The village of Tanohata moved me, just as it did Ito-san, for the incredible resources that are concentrated there: an astonishing potato flour (page 56), sea greens of all varieties (page 36), seafood and fish, *matsutake* and other local mushrooms, as well as nuts and game in the forests, and garnet-red azuki beans from open farmland. Driving through town, there are signs marking where the tsunami reached, though they aren't necessary. The demarcation is immediately apparent from the old houses visible above a line of new prefab structures built below. The starkness and in-your-faceness of this line shows you how much devastation there was, but also how close so many other dwellings were to being deluged. The inhabitants of Tanohata seem to have moved on, and are both welcoming and generous with their time. But each trip to Tanohata leaves me feeling viscerally affected by the loss.

One day a local mushroom forager took us up a mountain to hunt for mushrooms that chef Ito could use on his menu. Stick in hand, the forager trod sure-footedly through the forest, but turned and casually admonished us to watch out for bears. Bears! Foraging lost some of its luster at that point.

Another early morning, Ito-san and I hopped into his little station wagon and zoomed over to the house of a nearby fisherman who, with his wife and sister, was prying sea urchin (*uni*) out of their shells – ones he had just harvested that morning. It had been a dream of mine to eat fresh *uni* ever since I saw someone eating it from the shell on TV when I was first in Japan. I gobbled down eight, and was offered more. Not wanting to appear gluttonous, I resisted the urge to eat an additional eight, and still regret that decision today.

Ito-san has taken on the stewardship of this small community. He wanted chef friends from Tokyo to travel to Tanohata-mura, visit the producers, meet the fishermen, walk the forests, and then go back with a deeper understanding of the ingredients that they could use in their Tokyo kitchens. Forging a real connection between the producers and the chefs – beyond the order sheet – galvanized this unfathomable move to almost the very edge of the earth.

There are not many places to stay in Tanohata-mura, and other than Hotel Ragaso, there are only small guesthouses (*minshuku*) of doubtful dependability. But Ito-san is assisting Ragaso to revamp their food using local ingredients, so hope is on the horizon. Otherwise, you can negotiate the hotel's no-food rate and eat all meals at L'auréole Tanohata. That is what I do.

Ika to Yugao Sarada Shiso Vineguretto

SQUID AND YUGAO GOURD SALAD WITH SHISO VINAIGRETTE

Japanese squid is line caught to preserve the gut sacs for culinary applications so the squid meat is sweet and delicate. If you have any doubts about the squid you source, it could benefit from a few-seconds' douse of boiling water followed by an immediate plunge into ice water. This will remove any unwanted smells that might have developed between removing from the sea and getting to your kitchen.

Yugao, an ancient vegetable referenced in *The Tale of Genji*, is a pale green, slender, eggplant-shaped gourd. The flesh is typically sliced into long fine strips and sun-dried to make gourd ribbons (*kanpyo*), but here it is cooked as a vegetable. *Yugao* can be substituted with winter melon (*togan*).

For this bright first course you can either make your own red shiso vinegar, or use bottled red shiso *umesu*.

SERVES 4

Red Shiso Vinegar

20 red shiso leaves

200 ml (7 fl oz) white vinegar

Squid Broth

100 g (3½ oz) dried squid (*surume ika*, page 16)

1 fresh whole squid (*yari ika*), weighing about 300 g (10½ oz)

2 large handfuls of *tengusa* dried seaweed

200 g (7 oz) *yugao* gourd or winter melon, peeled

1 tablespoon shiso buds or seed clusters (*hojiso*)

2 tablespoons red shiso vinegar or red shiso *umesu* (page 72)

60 ml (2 fl oz/¼ cup) extra-virgin olive oil

¼ teaspoon flaky sea salt (omit if using *umesu*)

Make the red shiso vinegar at least 1 day in advance by adding the shiso leaves to the vinegar and leaving them to steep.

To make the squid broth, drop the dried squid into a medium saucepan and add 750 ml (25½ fl oz/3 cups) cold water. Bring to an almost boil over medium–high heat, adjust to a simmer and cook for 30 minutes. Strain the broth and discard the solids. You should have about 300 ml (10 fl oz) broth.

To prepare the fresh squid, gently dislodge the gut sac from the body by running your fingers around the sac. Pull on the tentacles to remove the sac in one piece. Slice off the tentacle portion and reserve for a different dish. Discard the gut sac. Remove the gladius (the plastic-like stick that runs the length of the inner body) and discard. Cut the body to open it out flat, and peel off the skin. Rinse the meat under cold running water, pat dry and freeze for 10 minutes. Cut on a diagonal (*sogigiri*, page 276) into 5 mm (¼ in) slices, then cut these about 2 cm (¾ in) long. Chill until ready to use.

Place the *tengusa* in a medium saucepan and fill three-quarters of the way up with water. Bring to a boil over high heat, adjust to a simmer and cook for 30 minutes. Strain through muslin (cheesecloth), and twist up the cloth to press together the gelatinous solids into a rough rectangle. (Alternatively press into a rectangular mold.) Cool and cut into 1 cm (½ in) thick slices. Cut these into 3 cm (1¼ in) batonnets.

Cut the *yugao* into the same size batonnets as the *tengusa*. Place in a sieve and douse for 10 seconds with boiling water. Shake off excess water and set aside to cool briefly.

Bring the squid broth to a simmer over medium heat and drop in the *yugao*. Simmer for 3 minutes to soften and absorb flavor. Scoop out with a wire-mesh strainer and cool to room temperature.

Toss the *tengusa* and *yugao* in a medium mixing bowl. Add the raw squid – you should have roughly equal parts of each ingredient. Mound attractively on 4 chilled salad plates, strew with a few shiso buds and drizzle with the shiso vinegar or *umesu*, followed by the olive oil. Sprinkle with the salt if using and serve immediately.

Shokko to Kyuri Sarada Kuroninniku, Gyosho-ae

YOUNG YELLOWTAIL AND CUCUMBER SALAD WITH BLACK GARLIC AND FISH SAUCE

The range of strong-tasting flavors comes together in extraordinary harmony in this deceptively simple dish. In Japan, the many stages in the life of a fish have different names. This young yellowtail is known as *shokko* in Iwate prefecture.

SERVES 4

200 g (7 oz) skinless sashimi-grade fillet of young yellowtail (*shokko*)

flaky sea salt

1 small Japanese cucumber, weighing about 100 g (3½ oz)

4 small umeboshi (page 17), finely chopped

½ tablespoon capers, roughly chopped if large

½ tablespoon finely chopped black garlic

1 teaspoon Japanese fish sauce (page 27)

2 tablespoons extra-virgin olive oil

4 small sprigs of fennel, for garnishing

Cut the yellowtail into diagonal slices 7 mm (⅜ in) thick and sprinkle with a pinch of salt.

Cut the cucumber into thin rounds and toss with a small pinch of salt in a small bowl. In a separate small bowl, stir the umeboshi, capers, black garlic, fish sauce and olive oil together to make a dressing.

On 4 chilled plates, make a domino-like line of yellowtail, then cucumber, yellowtail, cucumber, yellowtail, cucumber. Sprinkle a pinch of salt over the fish and cucumber on each plate. Drizzle 1 tablespoon of dressing over each line of fish and cucumber. Garnish with a sprig of fennel and serve as a raw course before dinner.

Kunsei Sanma, Myoga, Shungiku, Kiku

SMOKED PACIFIC SAURY WITH PICKLED MYOGA AND CHRYSANTHEMUM

SERVES 4

Smoked Pacific Saury

4 Pacific saury (*sanma*) weighing about 175 g (6 oz) each, filleted with the skin on

2 teaspoons flaky sea salt

½ small onion, finely diced

½ small carrot, finely diced

¼ celery stalk, finely diced

2 bay leaves

2 small handfuls (about 1 cup) cherry (*sakura*) wood chips, soaked in water for 30 minutes

Pickled *Myoga*

8 *myoga* (page 18)

60 ml (2 fl oz/¼ cup) mild rice vinegar

2 teaspoons granulated sugar

2 tablespoons extra-virgin olive oil, plus extra for oiling the grate

4 small edible chrysanthemum flowers (*kiku*)

1 stalk of edible chrysanthemum greens (*shungiku*, page 278)

pinch of flaky sea salt

½ small red onion (about 50 g/1¾ oz), thinly sliced

¼ medium Japanese cucumber (about 50 g/1¾ oz), sliced into fine rounds

Since smoking one lone fish makes no sense, this recipe calls for four Pacific saury, smoked over cherry (*sakura*) wood chips. You can substitute any other long, thin, silver-skinned fish. Serve the remaining smoked fish as a bite before dinner with drinks, or as part of another salad. It will keep for at least one week refrigerated.

The recipe also yields more pickled *myoga* than you need, but it can be used in sandwiches, in salads or as a side pickle.

To prepare the Pacific saury, cut the fillets crosswise into thirds and sprinkle both sides with the salt. Toss with the onion, carrot, celery and bay leaves, and marinate overnight in the refrigerator.

Remove from the refrigerator and discard the vegetables. Pat the fillets dry in spongy paper towels and set on a rack to allow the flesh to air dry for about 30 minutes.

Prepare charcoal in a barbecue and once the charcoal embers are red and dusted with white ash, push them to one side of the barbecue. Set a drip pan next to the charcoal and strew the soaked wood chips over the hot coals. Place the cooking grate in the barbecue and rub the area over the drip pan lightly with olive oil. Cover with the lid, open the vent holes half way and allow the barbecue to fill with smoke. Working quickly, open the lid slightly and place the fillets, skin side down, on the oiled portion of the cooking grate. Cover and smoke the fish for 15 minutes, until cooked through but not dry. Cool to room temperature.

To make the pickled *myoga*, place the *myoga* in a sieve and pour boiling water over for 10 seconds. Heat the rice vinegar and sugar in a small saucepan over medium–high heat, until the liquid has come to a boil and the sugar has melted. Place the *myoga* in a small jar and pour the hot liquid over them. Allow to cool to room temperature before refrigerating overnight to pickle.

Remove the petals from the chrysanthemum flowers and drop into a sieve. Bring 500 ml (17 fl oz/2 cups) water to a boil in a medium saucepan and dip the petals in and out of the boiling water. Pat dry in a clean dish towel. Scrape into a small bowl and marinate with 1 tablespoon of juice from the pickled *myoga*.

Pick the leaves from the chrysanthemum stalk and toss them with 1 teaspoon of the olive oil and the salt in a small bowl.

Place 2 pickled *myoga* on a board and halve lengthwise. Turn them cut-side down and slice into fine threads.

Take 4 pieces of smoked Pacific saury that are not tail pieces. Set one on each of 4 plates. Top the fillets with the dressed chrysanthemum leaves, followed with the red onion, marinated chrysanthemum petals, cucumber and sliced *myoga* – building artfully up. Drizzle with the remaining olive oil and serve.

FISHERMEN'S WIVES AND SEA GREENS

The seasonality of fruits, vegetables, nuts and fungi growing in the fields and mountains around Japan is fairly obvious to most Japanese residents, but the seasonality of the sea still eludes even the food-savvy.

Having spent over three decades cooking in Japan, and the most recent one writing Japanese cookbooks, my education regarding the bounty of the sea is yet a work in progress. The fishmongers at my local fish market are my patient yet enthusiastic teachers, and under their tutelage my knowledge has grown exponentially. Once the purview of my Japanese husband, buying fish has become an exciting endeavor to which I look forward with great anticipation. No longer lacking in confidence, I relish the opportunity to cut down a squid and toss it with its corally intestines (*shiokara*), or gut a fish before hanging it outside for drying (*himono*, page 186). But even more than the creatures of the sea, the greens enthrall me for their myriad shapes, flavors and textures.

Spring is the season for fresh sea greens, and local Japanese fish markets will have a wide variety of fascinating types for sale. Fluffy, almost spongy semi-dried fresh nori (*aosa-nori*) can be tossed in flour and deep-fried for a tasty snack. Viscous konbu buds (*mekabu*), julienned and chartreuse green from a lashing of boiling water, are wonderfully slurpable and delightful as a simple cold salad. Jagged small fern-like strands (*matsumo*) and burnished red seaweed (*akamoku*) need only a quick dip in and out of boiling water before eating with ponzu. Red tangled tendrils (*funori*) are lovely in udon or soba soups, and tiny jet-black pieces of hijiki are often folded into smashed tofu dishes to enhance the mild flavor of the bean curd. But wakame (page 17), the humblest of all sea greens, is arguably the most versatile and most appealing.

Wakame adds color and texture to vinegar treatments (*sunomono*) and miso soups. Gently reminiscent of the sea, this mahogany brown seaweed is shocked into a jade green and becomes meltingly soft when swished through boiling water. In seaside areas, strands of freshly harvested wakame can be seen draped over bamboo poles, drying under the mild spring sun. And semi-dried wakame is often tossed in salt and packed in plastic bags to preserve.

In years past, an insistent countrywoman hailing from some remote village on the Sea of Japan came door-to-door to hawk her wares in our neighborhood. I bought a 1-kilogram bag of wakame from her whenever she turned up, whether I needed it or not. But now she comes no more, and once the season passes for fresh sea greens at our local fish market, I rely on the dried wakame and other sea greens processed by the fishermen's wives of Tanohata-mura in Iwate prefecture.

Tanohata-mura, on the northeast corner of Iwate, is a plucky village of 3500 inhabitants. Washed over by the devastating tsunami following the Tohoku Earthquake in 2011, the line of devastation is immediately discernible by the hastily slapped together small structures that dot the town several meters above sea level. Although tiny, the town is resourceful, and that quality inspired me to visit multiple times recently – although never in the spring. The fishermen's wives' association dry, pack and dispatch the sea greens they gather, working out of an inauspicious post-earthquake building near the docks. And, unusually for such a local product, the packaging is adorned with an extremely cool label designed by Takahashi Design in Morioka city.

I travel to the United States periodically to do collaboration dinners at like-minded restaurants on both coasts, and always bring the crucial artisanal Japanese ingredients needed. Shoyu, mirin, rice vinegar and miso weigh a ton, but dried sea greens such as wakame are light as a feather. Reconstituted wakame swells up an impressive five to six times its dried volume, so two 20-gram packs are enough for a 90-person dinner. And given the attractive packaging, the fishermen's wives' dried sea greens make a light and affordable gift from Japan.

Sea greens, commonly called seaweed, are perhaps the most overlooked treasure of Japanese food culture. When dried, they literally keep forever, and they take up little space in the larder. Full of nutrients, fiber and flavor, sea greens can be added at the last minute to dishes – western or Japanese – almost as a garnish.

When traveling in far-flung areas of Japan, I recommend visiting the local JA (Japan Agriculture) or JFA (Japan Fisheries Association) stands, because these spots are where the locals shop. You won't find much fresh fish at a JFA stand, but there will be all sorts of dried sea-related products, including sea greens. Bring your discoveries home and experiment. The one sure thing is that there is nothing offensive about sea greens, unless you object to their slightly rubbery texture or natural slipperiness. Sea greens are immensely friendly to any country's cuisine, and add a note of gorgeousness to a hastily thrown together meal. What is there not to like about that?

Soi no Itame, Zukki-ni, Papurika So-su

PAN-SEARED BLACK ROCKFISH AND ZUCCHINI WITH ROASTED PEPPER SAUCE

Zucchini (courgette) is grown all over Japan these days, and western peppers (*papurika*) are popular for sauce in many restaurants. Here the pan does the work of cooking the fish to perfection, and as a light first course this has a particularly lovely balance of flavors. The recipe for squid ink salt makes more than needed for the dish – store it in the refrigerator to use in seasoning other seafood dishes or meat stews.

SERVES 4

Squid Ink Salt

1½ tablespoons squid ink

3 tablespoons flaky sea salt, plus more if needed

1 large thick-fleshed yellow pepper (capsicum)

1 large thick-fleshed red pepper (capsicum)

90 ml (3 fl oz) extra-virgin olive oil

¾ teaspoon flaky sea salt

1 medium zucchini (courgette)

8 edamame pods

4 small fillets of black rockfish (*soi*), skin on, weighing about 60 g (2 oz) each

2 teaspoons *egoma* mustard, or substitute 1 teaspoon *moutarde a l'ancienne* (French mustard with seeds)

Make the squid ink salt by slowly stirring the ink into the salt in a small bowl, mixing until the salt grains are black but still distinct. You will want to sprinkle the salt to finish the dish, so if the ink has not been completely absorbed by the grains, add a bit more salt.

Roast the peppers in an oven or over a low flame until lightly charred. Peel and pulse the yellow pepper with 2 tablespoons of the olive oil and ¼ teaspoon of the salt. Repeat with the red pepper.

Trim the ends from the zucchini, cut it lengthwise into 12 mm (½ in) slices and sear for 30 seconds on each side in a ridged cast-iron grill pan over medium–high heat, until crisp-tender. Cook the edamame pods in the same pan for about 3 minutes, turning occasionally, until charred in spots. When cool enough to handle, remove the beans from the pods and reserve in a small bowl.

Spoon a few teaspoons each of the yellow pepper and red pepper sauces side by side in a random fashion on each of 4 small salad plates. Set 2 pieces of zucchini a short distance apart in the middle of each plate.

Sprinkle the fish fillets on both sides with the remaining ¼ teaspoon salt. Heat the remaining 2 tablespoons olive oil in a medium cast-iron frying pan over medium heat and grill the fillets, skin side down, for 2 minutes. Flip the fish, cover the pan, and let sit for 1 minute off the heat.

Lay a piece of grilled fish across the zucchini on each plate. Strew with edamame and spoon a few small dollops of mustard here and there. Sprinkle each plate with a few pinches of squid ink salt and serve immediately.

Awabi, Shimeji, Uni no Shiozuke

ABALONE AND SHIMEJI MUSHROOMS WITH SALTED SEA URCHIN

Raw or smoked abalone freezes well, so savvy chefs buy abalone when the price drops to keep on hand in the off-season. Chef Ito chose to serve this dish on an iron plate made by Oigen (page 48), which has little divots in the surface where the sauce can pool up. The nasturtium leaves simulate umbrellas over these 'puddles' of sauce.

Salt-preserved sea urchin (*uni no shiozuke*) is a delicacy of Iwate prefecture and Hokkaido and might be difficult to source, but is easy to reproduce approximately at home, though you will need to start early in the day as it requires at least three hours to cure. You will end up with more salt-pickled sea urchin than needed, but leftovers can be served as a condiment for a bowl of white rice.

SERVES 4

Salt-pickled Sea Urchin

1 tablespoon flaky sea salt

150 g (5½ oz) sea urchin scooped from the shell

1 large handful (about 75 g/ 2¾ oz) *sakura shimeji* (page 279) or other shimeji mushrooms

1 small abalone, about 9 cm (3½ in) diameter

4 tablespoons unsalted butter

flaky sea salt

2 tablespoons brandy

125 ml (4 fl oz/½ cup) Fond de Veau (page 42), or use chicken stock reduced by 75%

½ teaspoon abalone liver soy sauce (*awabi no kimo shoyu*, page 10), puréed abalone liver, or shoyu

4 nasturtium leaves, for garnishing

To make the salt-pickled sea urchin, line a small rectangular pan with a bamboo sushi-rolling mat (*makisu*, page 275), topped with a piece of muslin (cheesecloth). Sprinkle a thin layer of the salt onto the cloth and place the sea urchin side by side on the salt in 1 layer. Lay another small piece of muslin on top of the sea urchin and pat it down carefully around the sea urchin to enclose. Sprinkle the rest of the salt on top of the flat mounds of sea urchin and leave at room temperature for 3 hours to cure. Pat dry and store in the refrigerator, but use within a few days.

Brush the shimeji clean and trim their bases. Quarter the abalone, and cut about 4 lengthwise slits around each quarter, which will create a sort of oblong star effect when cooked.

Heat 3 tablespoons of the butter in a medium cast-iron frying pan over medium–low heat and sear the abalone and shimeji gently on all sides, sprinkling in a pinch of salt while cooking. Swirl in the brandy, adjust to high heat, and tilt the pan to flambé.

Add the fond de veau or chicken stock, and the abalone soy sauce, puréed liver or shoyu, and simmer for 1 minute before stirring in the remaining 1 tablespoon of butter and another pinch of salt.

Spoon 1 piece of abalone and a few mushrooms onto each of 4 small plates. Dot a few small pieces of salted sea urchin around each plate and drizzle over the sauce. Garnish with a nasturtium leaf and serve immediately.

FOND DE VEAU

Simmer the combined stock down 'until it is delicious', according to Ito-san. Or until the aromas of your kitchen seep into your soul, according to me. This is a classic French building-block stock, which chef Ito has personalized. Freeze in small portions and add to daubes (French meat and wine stews) to enhance complexity, or as a sauce base with butter to nap meat dishes.

MAKES 750 ML (25½ FL OZ/3 CUPS)

4 tablespoons unsalted butter, at room temperature

1 kg (2 lb 3 oz) veal bones

2 kg (4 lb 6 oz) veal 'muscle meat', cut into 3 cm (1¼ in) pieces

2 medium onions, halved and sliced 1 cm (½ in) thick

2 medium carrots, scrubbed and sliced into 1 cm (½ in) rounds

1 medium celery stalk, sliced 1 cm (½ in) thick

2 bay leaves

400 g (14 oz) tomatoes (fresh or canned), roughly chopped

1 teaspoon freshly ground black pepper

250 ml (8½ fl oz/1 cup) red wine

250 ml (8½ fl oz/1 cup) white wine

Preheat the oven to 190°C (375°F). Melt the butter over low heat in a large, wide stockpot. Stir in the bones, meat, onion, carrot, celery and bay leaves. Place the pot in the oven and roast for 30–40 minutes, stirring occasionally, until the bones, meat and vegetables are brown and fragrant. (If your pot does not fit in the oven, do this step on the stove over medium heat, but stir a little more frequently to distribute the heat well.)

Remove the pot from the oven and place on the stove over medium–high heat. Stir in the tomatoes and pepper, and add the wine to deglaze, scraping the bottom to free any adhered bits. Once most of the liquid has evaporated, add 5 liters (169 fl oz) water and transfer to a medium, tall stockpot. Bring to an almost boil, then adjust to a bare simmer and cook for 6 hours.

Strain out the 'first stock' and reserve. Dump the strained solids back into the stockpot, then add 5 liters (169 fl oz) water again. Bring to an almost boil, adjust to a bare simmer, and cook for 5 hours this time around. Strain out the 'second stock', discard the solids, then mix the first and second stocks together in a clean medium saucepan. The first stock has the flavor, while the second stock has the gelatin; mixed together they form a whole. Simmer the stock down on very low heat for about 2 hours.

Hotate, Matsutake

SEARED SCALLOPS AND BRAISED MATSUTAKE

Matsutake are highly prized mushrooms in Japan and, much like French or Italian truffles, fetch exorbitant prices when they appear in the autumn. Chinese or Korean imports are less expensive but lack depth of flavor.

SERVES 4

- 4 large sea scallops, in their shells
- 1 medium *matsutake* (page 279), brushed clean, base trimmed
- ⅛ teaspoon flaky sea salt
- 1 tablespoon extra-virgin olive oil

Pry open the scallops and dislodge the contents of the shells into a bowl, taking care not to lose the precious juices. Separate the white scallop meat and set aside. Slide the other parts of the scallop and the juices into a medium saucepan. Add cold water to cover, and bring to a simmer over medium heat. Adjust to a low simmer and cook for 30 minutes to concentrate flavor. Strain the scallop broth and discard the solids.

Quarter the *matsutake* lengthwise, and place directly on a wire rack set over a gas flame. Grill about 1 minute on each side, until the juices sizzle. Drop the *matsutake* into a small saucepan with 250 ml (8½ fl oz/1 cup) of the scallop broth. Bring to an almost simmer over low heat, gently infusing the broth with the aroma of *matsutake*. Keep warm but do not simmer or overcook.

Sprinkle the scallops on both sides with the salt. Heat the olive oil in a medium cast-iron frying pan over medium heat and sear the scallops for 1 minute on each side. Remove from the heat and allow to rest briefly in the pan.

Place a scallop in each of 4 bowls (or individual lidded pots) and divide the *matsutake* between them. Ladle about 60 ml (2 fl oz/¼ cup) scallop broth into each and serve warm.

Hirame, Mizu Nasu

SEARED FLOUNDER AND EGGPLANT WITH EGGPLANT PURÉE

Eggplant three ways gives this dish texture and nuance. Make it in the height of summer when eggplant (aubergine) is at its best. Ito-san uses *mizu nasu* here, a small plump eggplant that has a slightly juicy character, which also lends itself to pickling. Since these might be hard to find, you can substitute any Japanese eggplants.

SERVES 4

4 small fillets of flounder (*hirame*), weighing about 60 g (2 oz) each, plus the center bone and head from 1 small flounder

3 small *mizu nasu* eggplants (aubergines), weighing about 225 g (8 oz) in total (if unavailable, use any Japanese eggplants)

extra-virgin olive oil

flaky sea salt

1 small western eggplant (aubergine) – *bei nasu* – weighing about 75 g (2¾ oz)

12 wild arugula (rocket) leaves, for garnishing

Make a broth from the flounder bones and head by first rinsing the bones and splitting the head in half. Cut down further if necessary to fit into a medium saucepan, and fill with cold water. Bring to an almost boil over medium–high heat and adjust to a gentle simmer. Cook for 30 minutes. Strain into a small saucepan and discard the solids. Keep warm.

Grill the Japanese eggplants on a rack set over a flame until soft and blackened all over. When cool enough to handle, trim the ends and peel the eggplants. Tear the flesh in half lengthwise. Reserve 4 fat strips for serving, and purée the rest in a blender or mini food processor with 2 tablespoons olive oil and ¼ teaspoon salt.

Lightly brush a ridged cast-iron grill pan with a little olive oil and heat over medium–high. Quarter the western eggplant lengthwise, and grill the pieces for 2 minutes on each side, or until soft.

Sprinkle the flounder fillets on both sides with ¼ teaspoon salt. Heat a medium cast-iron frying pan with 1 tablespoon olive oil over medium–high heat and sear the fillets, skin side down, for 30 seconds. Flip, swirl in 250 ml (8½ fl oz/1 cup) of the flounder broth, cover, and remove from the heat. Let sit for 1 minute cooking in the heat of the pan before uncovering.

Spoon a quarter of the eggplant purée just left of center on each of 4 salad plates. Set the grilled eggplant quarters over part of the purée, and lay the peeled strips of eggplant alongside, creating a three-way eggplant framework. Rest the flounder fillets across the eggplant and garnish with the arugula, adding some flaky salt and a drizzle of olive oil. Serve hot as a first course.

Shake, Mu-rugai, Tomato, Ingen

SALMON WITH MUSSELS, TOMATOES AND GREEN BEANS

The salmon broth coupled with the savory juices exuded from the mussels and scattering of flavorful summer vegetables help keep the salmon moist and aromatic. The intent of this recipe is to start with a whole fish, using the head for the broth, so you will need to find a use for the remaining salmon and broth.

SERVES 4

1 small salmon weighing about 2.5 kg (5½ lb), scaled and cleaned, reserving the head, liver and – if a male – the milt (*shirako*)

12 small mussels, scrubbed and debearded

8 green beans, trimmed and cut into 3 cm (1¼ in) lengths

½ teaspoon flaky sea salt

2 tablespoons extra-virgin olive oil

12 small cherry tomatoes

1 tablespoon tiny dried shrimp (*isada*, page 16), or substitute chopped small dried shrimp (*koebi*, page 16)

Cut through the salmon to make 4 steaks weighing about 140 g (5 oz) each, and set aside. Whack the head of the salmon in half to create 2 identical pieces, then cut these in half crosswise. Rinse the head pieces and drop them into a large saucepan. Cover generously with cold water and bring to an almost boil over medium–high heat. Adjust to a simmer and cook for 30 minutes.

While the broth is cooking, soak the mussels in several changes of cold salty water to purge them of any lingering sand. Blanch the green beans in boiling water for 1 minute.

Strain the salmon broth into a medium saucepan. Before discarding the solids, pull the grey-edged, clear gelatinous cartilage (*hizu*) from the boneless pocket at the top of the head area behind the eyes, and tear by hand into small pieces. Reserve half the *hizu* for this dish, and toss the remaining portion with sweetened vinegar for a savory bite with beer.

Cut the liver and milt, if using, crosswise into 2.5 cm (1 in) pieces. Sprinkle the salmon steaks with the salt. Thread 2 short bamboo skewers through the thin protruding belly sections of each steak to prevent them from breaking off during cooking.

Reheat the salmon broth. Heat the oil in a large cast-iron frying pan over medium–low heat and sear the salmon steaks and liver and milt pieces for about 2 minutes on each side. The salmon should have cooked through by about 80% at this point. Strew in the green beans and tomatoes and spoon up any juices over the ingredients in the pan as they cook for about 2 minutes more. Add the purged mussels and 250 ml (8½ fl oz/ 1 cup) of the hot salmon broth and cook over high heat, covered, for a few minutes until the mussels open. Scatter in the reserved half of the *hizu* and the dried shrimp, and cover again for 1 minute, off heat, to warm.

Remove the skewers from the salmon steaks and serve one per person in a shallow soup bowl. Divide the other ingredients between them along with a drizzling of the pan juices.

OIGEN IRONWORKS

The cavernous building was filled with a symphonic *gung, gung, zzz, pish, pish* from the gargantuan machines that released fire and steam at regular intervals. A film of black blanketed the surfaces in the Oigen iron foundry, and a worker constantly swept the floors. Another worker muscled wheelbarrows of coal and scrap iron through the maze of machinery at a breakneck pace. We jumped aside to avoid his path.

That day the cupola, a monstrous cylindrical coke-fueled furnace, was in use. Although the cupola creates a finer mix of iron, it is only fired up once a week due to the work involved in tending it, and the resulting atmospheric emissions. The faces of the workers tending the cupola were eerily lit by the fire below, and periodic blasts of air made me flinch. The great gusts of air aid in the combustion of the iron mix, which contains 50–70% recycled iron. I was mesmerized by the energy captured in the cupola and its deadly bucket of 1550°C (2820°F) liquid iron. The men were awe-inspiring in their sure handling of the beast-like molten iron. It resembled a living thing in its fluidity and vitality.

Kuniko Oikawa, 6th-generation president of the Oigen ironworks, in the Nambu region of Iwate prefecture, holds herself gently yet solidly, and her face lights up when speaking of the process, the history, the artisans and the wares. While a female president is certainly an anomaly in what clearly is a male-dominated industry, Kuniko-san's daughter is already designated to be the 7th-generation president of the ironworks. Kuniko-san has nothing to prove in this man's world. She walks the floor as if she owns it. Which she does.

Kuniko-san doesn't just run the day-to-day operations of the company. Like her father, Hideharu Oikawa (now retired), she looks towards the future of Nambu ironware (*Nambu tekki*). Hideharu Oikawa began exporting Oigen ironware in 1966, and soon after had the perspicacity to respond to the Europeans' desire for color on small teapots (*kyusu*). Thus started the trend in today's bright-hued brewing pots. In a move to further elevate the brand, Hideharu Oikawa began commissioning designers in the 1960s to create original cookware lines for Oigen. These designers have included Komin Yamada and Jasper Morrison as well as chef Katsuyasu Ito (page 28).

Despite the aim of maintaining the spirit of tradition while modernizing production techniques, Kuniko-san has taken one huge step backwards. Recognizing the decline in artisans creating handcrafted teakettles (*tetsubin*) used for heating water for tea, Kuniko-san took on the commitment of reviving that lost art in her own family foundry.

In 1970 there were eighty companies producing *Nambu tekki* ironware in the three cities designated as official producers: Morioka, Mizusawa and Oshu. Now there are fourteen. Of those fourteen, only two companies have a family member designated to take over. These bleak numbers are sobering.

Although Oigen ironworks had not produced artisanally made *tetsubin* since before World War II, Kuniko-san now has one worker learning the craft (there were two, but one quit). Tatsuya Ono was born into a tree-trimming family, but felt the call to create handcrafted cast-iron kettles and teapots, and joined as an apprentice at Oigen several years ago at the age of 22.

All of our eyes are drawn to Ono's long, gentle fingers as he makes small indentations in the wall of a *tetsubin* mold, which has taken him ten days to create from sand and clay from the local riverbed and mountainside. Although the mold can be reused, it will lose integrity each time.

The craftsman first creates a metal plate from a design originally drawn on paper. The plate is a half section of the pot's intended shape, and is rotated like a compass to create the sand and clay mold that forms the inside shape of the finished kettle.

Ono mixes six types of sand (from coarse to fine) with clay as a binder, each in a separate bucket. He packs the sand into the mold in distinct layers, allowing each layer to dry before applying the next one. This takes two days. The last layer will be the outside of the *tetsubin,* and the outer design of the *tetsubin* is drawn by hand while the sand is still pliable.

Dots are fashioned by pressing a thin iron rod into the surface of the sand. The dots should be evenly spaced from each other and appear as concentric circles on the finished pot. The top row of dots contains the same amount as the bottom. This typical design, known as *arare moyo* ('hail pattern'), is applied freehand.

The level of difficulty of the *tetsubin* design raises the rarity of the piece and consequently the price, since few artisans have the skill to produce the more intricate drawings of flowers, horses, birds and landscapes, or the powerfully majestic large dots known as *oni arare* ('devil hail'), delicately etched *kushime maru gata* ('round fine-combed pattern') or the deceptive *hata* ('skin') pattern, which looks like it was created naturally, though is actually drawn by an artist.

We follow Ono into the bowels of the ironworks where he sets up three molds on top of an iron frame over a bed of glowing charcoal embers. As one worker dips a bucket into the hot iron of the cupola, sparks are flying madly as if from friction on steroids. Another worker guides the bucket along a wire pulley system towards the molds. Ono dons thickly padded, elbow-length gloves and ever so carefully carries the bucket towards the molds. He pours the surface fire out of the bucket, and waves a wadded torch into the combusting air to fuel the coal fire underneath. We are engulfed by the smoldering smell of molten iron. With a fluidity of motion, Ono picks up the bucket once again, fills each mold, and sets the bucket back down. He immediately removes the collars, and tips out the extra molten liquid from the top.

Back at the workstation, the anticipation is palpable as Ono unveils the casting. He digs the sand out of the spout area and wraps his arms around the mold to pull the upper portion away from the lower. The silvery bottom of the *tetsubin* is now visible. He replaces the upper portion of the mold, turns the mold upside down, and pries the mold away from the *tetsubin* by splitting it in half vertically. He dislodges the sand from the emerging pot and sets it aside to free a second one. Once he has two *tetsubin* to display, he holds them up shyly but proudly, his eyes tearing as we exclaim compliments on his handiwork. Ono is a natural at this work and exceptionally talented after only a few years of practice. He is a serious young man who studies his craft at night when he goes home. Kuniko-san has invested several years of his salary with no immediate return, and will continue that investment for several more years hence, before Ono's work becomes worthy of selling as artisanally produced *Nambu tekki.*

A master craftsman comes to work with Ono once a month; otherwise, he practices his solitary craft in an airy, well-lit space of the factory. Tools of the trade donated by retired local artisans are strewn about on tables and workbenches. Molds etched with past designs are stacked on the floor and in grey metal shelving, alongside *tetsubin* Ono has made over the last few years. When asked how much Ono's *tetsubin* will fetch, Kuniko-san laughs, 'Zero! He must make many, many more before we can ever sell them. It's not about the money. Ono will teach future generations. I am investing in the future of Japan.'

Kamo, Negi

PAN-SEARED DUCK BREAST WITH BRAISED NEGI

One large duck breast can stretch to serve four if you are not counting on this dish to be a main course. The philosophy of 'less is more' is representative of Japan's overall cultural approach to food. There is a saying: '*Hara hachi bu me ni isha irazu*,' meaning if you always only fill your stomach 80%, then you will never need a doctor.

SERVES 4

1 large boneless duck breast, skin on, weighing about 400 g (14 oz)

1 tablespoon extra-virgin olive oil

1 medium *negi* or fat scallion (spring onion), cut into 3 cm (1¼ in) lengths

1 small bunch Malabar spinach (page 278) or regular spinach, cut into 3 cm (1¼ in) lengths

½ teaspoon flaky sea salt

Duck Broth

bones from 2 small ducks, weighing about 600 g (1 lb 5 oz)

1 large *negi* or 3 fat scallions, weighing 150 g (5½ oz), trimmed but left whole

1 large onion, weighing 150 g (5½ oz), halved and sliced 1 cm (½ in) thick

1 large carrot, weighing 150 g (5½ oz), scrubbed and sliced into 1 cm (½ in) rounds

1 medium stalk celery, weighing 75 g (2¾ oz), sliced 1 cm (½ in) thick

pinch of flaky sea salt

pinch of freshly ground black pepper

1 bay leaf

Make the duck broth early in the day. Rinse the duck bones and drop into a medium stock pot. Add 4 liters (135 fl oz/16 cups/4 quarts) of water and bring to an almost boil over medium–high heat. Skim off scum. Roast the *negi* or scallions on a grate set over a medium flame, for 1–2 minutes, turning with tongs until fragrant. Drop into the pot of duck bones and add the onion, carrot, celery, salt, pepper and bay leaf. Simmer gently for 4 hours, periodically skimming off scum. Strain and discard the solids. You will have about 1 liter (34 fl oz/4 cups/1 quart) of stock.

Score the duck skin in a crosshatch pattern, taking care not to cut down to the meat. Heat the oil in a medium cast-iron pot over low heat and sear the duck, skin side down, for about 10 minutes until golden brown. Spoon up the melting fat over the breast as it cooks, to give heat to the exposed side. (Note: duck breast should always be served red inside.) Remove the duck from the pot and let it rest. Do not wash the pot.

Bring a medium pot of water to a boil. Meanwhile, pour off all the accumulated fat in the duck pot except about 1 teaspoon. Sear the *negi* or scallion pieces over medium heat in the remaining duck fat. Add the duck broth and bring to a simmer.

Using a sieve, dip the spinach in and out of the pot of boiling water, then stir it into the duck broth and boil over high heat for about 1 minute, to soften the greens and reduce the liquid. There should only be a small amount of broth remaining in the pot.

Slice the duck crosswise at an angle 12 mm (½ in) thick, and lay the slices carefully back in the pot with the *negi* and spinach. Sprinkle with the salt. Set on a trivet at the table.

Horakuyaki Horo Horo to Jagaimo

PINE NEEDLE–ROASTED GUINEA FOWL AND POTATOES

The technique of roasting fish on pine needles and large pebbles is called *horakuyaki*, and delivers a moist, aromatic result – traditionally the pot was cooked over hot embers, so the stones helped conduct the heat. A riff off that classic technique, here guinea fowl is flame-roasted in a cast-iron pot, thus creating an oven-like environment.

SERVES 4

top portion of a guinea fowl weighing about 1 kg/2 lb 3 oz (back portion and thighs removed), plus its liver, heart and gizzard

2 teaspoons flaky sea salt, plus extra for finishing

60 ml (2 fl oz/¼ cup) extra-virgin olive oil

3 medium potatoes (about 300 g/10½ oz), cut in half

2 small pine branches, cut to fit inside the pot

2 tablespoons unsalted butter

Pat the guinea fowl's skin and body cavity dry, then season inside and out with the salt. Rinse and pat dry the liver. Remove any bloody spots or fat from the heart. Rinse and pat dry. Slice the gizzard open and rinse out the food and small gravel particles. Halve lengthwise, and pare off the hard inside cartilage covering and the thin outside silvery muscle tissue.

Heat the oil in a medium cast-iron pot over medium heat. Once the oil is shimmering but not smoking, sear the fowl and potatoes quickly on all sides, spooning the oil over the bird. The skin should begin to crackle and crisp up, 8–10 minutes.

Throw in the liver, heart and gizzard pieces and cook for 4–5 minutes, spooning the oil and juices over the contents of the pot to encourage even browning, and to cook the liver, heart and gizzard. Remove the potatoes and fowl to a plate, and the liver, heart and gizzard to a small bowl.

Preheat the oven to 160°C (320°F). Do not wash the pot, but line the bottom with the pine branches and return the fowl and potatoes to the pot. Place in the middle of the oven without a lid and roast for about 25 minutes, until the fowl is cooked through. (Poke a skewer into the place where the breast and small wings meet – the juices should not be red. If they are, cover the pot with a lid and let sit for about 5 minutes.)

Spoon the butter into the pot along with the liver, heart and gizzard and tip the pot to melt the butter and distribute. Sprinkle with a few pinches of salt and let rest uncovered for 5 minutes before cutting and serving.

DAIRY IN JAPAN

Significant milk production did not come to Japan until the beginning of the 20th century, during the Meiji period (1868–1912). By 1975, there was already one dairy cow to every sixty-two people in Japan, and milk had been a standard component of school lunches for at least two decades. Dairy farming has the benefit of all-year income compared to seasonal crops such as rice, soybeans and wheat. On the other hand, having dairy cows requires daily early morning and evening feeding and milking, so precludes leaving the farm. Needless to say, there are few sons or daughters who are taking over small-enterprise dairy farms.

No stranger to milk scares (the famous one being in 2000, when 13,000 people became ill from Snow Brand contaminated milk), Japan lags behind other countries in pasture-based dairies. In the West, grass-fed cow milk has become mainstream, while in Japan it is scarce in supermarket refrigerator cases. One reason for this phenomenon could be traced back to the local nature of pasture-based dairies, thus placing them outside supermarket distribution channels. Also, due to the lateness of the dairy boom, arable land suitable for grass-feeding cows was perhaps no longer available, except in the northern areas of Japan.

There are not many, yet forward-thinking dairies do exist in Japan. These dairies are pasturing their cows and directly marketing their grass-fed milk to the public. Near us in Ota township of Gunma prefecture, Tomorakuno Dairy pastures their cows by the Arakawa River and has a delivery system that reaches into Tokyo. Our family has been buying their milk for over twenty years, but I have never visited the farm. Nonetheless, I have had the chance to visit two other pasturing dairy farms in Japan: one in Hokkaido and one in Iwate prefecture.

Hiroaki Shinmura is a 4th-generation dairy farmer in the Tokachi area of southeast Hokkaido. Quietly self-confident, Shinmura convinced his father to convert Tokachi Shinmura Ranch, their family farm, to be wholly pasture-based in 1994. Recognizing that the health of the soil was paramount to the quality of the grass and thus the overall wellbeing of the cows and the taste of the milk, Shinmura began the several-year process of restoring the natural power of his pasture soil. Having been subjected to years of chemical fertilizers, the soil had become weak, and earthworms and microorganisms could not survive. But as the microorganisms and insects increased, the ecosystem began to function in a healthy cycle where decomposing cow dung was broken down efficiently and the grass began to flourish.

Shinmura believes that grazing dairy cows fosters the future of the earth. If the grass is delicious, then the cows will eat it, and when the cows eat the grass, there will be no need for imported feed. No reliance on imported feed leads to energy savings in terms of the fossil fuels required for the transport of feed. Thus a grass-fed dairy contributes to global environmental preservation.

But beyond that, the milk tastes better. The cows thrive in a stress-free environment. They wander where they want, and even in the winter are out in the field most days. At milking time, a fence is opened and the cows amble contentedly back to the barn. The raw milk is remarkably clear and refreshing on the palate with a sweet aftertaste.

When Kimio Yoshizuka first stepped on his plot of mountainous land in the northeastern tip of Iwate prefecture, he felt a deep tug of emotion and a sense of belonging. A transplant from Chiba prefecture near Tokyo, Yoshizuka believed that Iwate was more suitable for creating pastureland. His home prefecture was overrun with golf courses, while Hokkaido, the obvious choice as a producer of 52% of Japan's milk, nonetheless does not have a rainy season, and rain is essential for growing grass.

Inspired by Kyoji Naohara, a pioneer advocate of grass-fed dairy farming practices in Japan, Yoshizuka and his wife, Toshiko, converted their land into pasture over the course of a couple of decades, starting by planting and propagating *shiba*, Japan's native wild grass. Yoshizuka and Toshiko raised seven children, without electricity for the first ten years, living at subsistence levels as they painstakingly encouraged the *shiba* to spread across the mountainsides, while also, little by little, increasing their head of cows. Today the hills of their Tanohata Yamachi Rakuno dairy farm are carpeted with lush green grass, and the two older sons are working in the dairy with their parents.

When in the area, I stop by for a chat in the hope that some of their perseverance and mettle might rub off. Toshiko is engaging, generous and kind, while Yoshizuka is passionate about his metier, and an enthusiastic teacher. He hauls out charts and photo albums, to which I am riveted each time with renewed awe at the herculean project they have accomplished: converting hectares of mountainous land to grassy pastures. They pour me a glass of milk, and I drain it willingly before asking for more. The milk is truly addictive.

These pasture-based dairies give hope for the future of Japanese dairy farming. The decline rate is certainly rising for small farms; however, slowly but surely, conscientious farmers are increasing, and they are taking responsibility for their stewardship of the land.

As for milk, it makes all the sense in the world to buy direct from the source, from people who have raised the cows and processed the milk in-house. These people are not only doing crucial work for the planet, but they are also invested in keeping the milk untainted and pure.

Imo Dansu, Azuki So-su, Miruku Aisu

POTATO DUMPLINGS IN RED BEAN SAUCE WITH MILK ICE CREAM

The most common term for ball-like confections is '*dango*', but that changes with locale and size. Here they are called '*dansu*' because they are small. This dish originated in Tanohata-mura, the village where chef Ito has relocated his restaurant, L'auréole. There is a producer of excellent potato flour in the village (page 56), and the mountain dairy nearby produces beautifully sweet and grassy milk (page 52), elevating this ice cream to unforgettable heights. Ito-san infuses the milk with a piece of *kuromoji* branch, a woody deciduous shrub (*Lindera umbellata*), which he also uses to flavor the water he serves to guests at the restaurant.

SERVES 4

Milk Ice Cream

1 liter (34 fl oz/4 cups) whole (full-cream) grass-fed cow's milk

150 g (5½ oz) granulated sugar

150 g (5½ oz) fine white Japanese sugar (*johakuto*, page 14)

10 cm (4 in) branch of *kuromoji*, optional

Red Bean Sauce

100 g (3½ oz/½ cup) azuki beans

100 g (3½ oz) granulated sugar

⅛ teaspoon fine sea salt

Potato Dumplings

215 g (7½ oz/1⅔ cups) potato flour (*imo no kona*, page 56)

To make the milk ice cream, heat the milk with the sugars and *kuromoji* branch (if using) over medium heat, stirring until the sugars have completely melted but the milk has not come to a boil. Remove from the heat and cool to room temperature, then chill. Once cold, remove the branch and freeze in an ice cream maker following the manufacturer's directions.

To make the red bean sauce, place the azuki beans in a large, heavy saucepan with the sugar, salt and 1.5 liters (51 fl oz/6 cups) water. Bring to an almost boil over high heat, adjust to a gentle simmer and cook for about 1½ hours, until the beans are completely soft and easily squished between two fingers, and the soup is thick and dark red.

Make the potato dumplings while the bean sauce is still cooking. Bring a medium pot three-quarters full of water to a boil. Adjust to a brisk simmer. Slowly mix about 300 ml (10 fl oz) warm water (50°C/120°F) into the potato flour in a medium mixing bowl, until you have a resilient dough that feels like an earlobe to the touch. Knead the dough in the bowl until smooth. Roll the dough out into a long log 3 cm (1¼ in) in diameter. Cut crosswise into 2 mm (⅛ in) discs.

Poach the discs in batches in the briskly simmering water until they bob up to the surface, about 7 minutes. Scoop out with a wire-mesh strainer, shake off, and slip into the red bean sauce. Once all the *dansu* are cooked, simmer them gently in the sauce for 8 minutes, or until they have absorbed azuki flavor all the way through.

Spoon a few *dansu* and some warm sauce into each of 4 shallow bowls. Top with a scoop of the milk ice cream and serve immediately.

IWATE POTATO FLOUR

Said to be the last person producing potato flour (*imo no kona*) commercially in Japan, Hidemitsu Kikuchi, assisted by his mother, Fuchi, should be heartily applauded for his steadfast work each year to create this local food of Tanohata-mura in Iwate prefecture. The process defies imagination, and the possibilities for this naturally silky flour are endless.

In the area around Tanohata-mura, a tiny village on the Sanriku Coast in northeastern Iwate, little 'dumplings' (*dango*) or steamed buns (*manju*) were traditionally made from the flour. Chef Ito of L'auréole Tanohata (page 28) has revitalized this homely flour into a genius bechamel put together with local grass-fed milk and a dab of butter, which he uses as a base for a white stew of seafood and leafy greens.

According to Stuart Brioza at State Bird Provisions in San Francisco, Peruvians living near the Andes (where potatoes originate) make a similar flour but use it in a chicken and vegetable stew.

With interest generated among Tokyo chefs and food-savvy cooks in Japan, perhaps local young people will see the potential in producing this versatile flour, currently made only by Kikuchi and his mother. Potato flour also has the virtue of being gluten-free.

Although a few additional varieties of potatoes are slowly appearing in Japan, the majority of potatoes grown here are may queen or danshaku. May queen are slightly creamy, thin-skinned, and oval. Danshaku are round, a bit starchy, and eventually develop a thick skin. Potatoes are cropped in June and stored for use throughout the year.

In January, after New Year, Kikuchi hauls his may queen potatoes out of storage (the optimal storage temperature is 20°C/70°F) and lays them out in the cold Iwate winter air to freeze for two to three days. Once frozen, he and his mother bring the potatoes inside to peel, rubbing and scraping the peels off using their bare fingernails as the potatoes thaw. Now soft enough to stab through the center with a long, heavy needle, they thread them onto thick twine, making long ropes of potatoes butted up against each other. These fat strands are tied together in groups of five or six and anchored onto a rope dangling into an icy stream. The potatoes soak in the snowy water over the course of two weeks to take off bitterness, and tiny cavities in the porous potatoes fill with water, to facilitate quick freezing when removed from the stream. At this point 'the potatoes are still weak,' Kikuchi says, so they need to be hung out in the bitter winter air for two or three days to freeze once again. And there they will stay for at least a month to dry naturally, hanging in the winter sun. By the end of February, the potatoes have completely dried and resemble balsa wood. These light, off-white, slightly misshapen ovoids are packed into feed bags and kept in a cool, dry place until being milled as needed into flour. The potatoes will keep whole until the rainy season in June, at which time they risk developing mold, and should be milled and stored carefully.

The process of drying these potatoes, and the image of the strands submerged in the icy stream, captured me in a way I have not often experienced. And the fact that there is nothing exactly like this unassuming yet incredibly versatile ingredient fills me with terror that it will disappear.

Recently I have been introducing interesting Japanese ingredients to my good pal, ex–Chez Panisse chef Jérôme Waag, co-owner of the Blind Donkey in Tokyo. I tried to describe the flour to Jérôme but could not get past the inevitable preconception of the flour creating something akin to a potato slurry. This is a truly revolutionary flour that looks and acts like wheat flour in many of its good ways, but does not gum up or have gluten, and also has a lovely flavor. Thus far, I have guarded the existence of this flour lest the limited supply be gobbled up by the chefs in Tokyo, but with this book, I am finally ready to share this secret with the world.

Tanohata-mura was half-destroyed by the tsunami that followed the Tohoku Earthquake of 2011. The town has vast native resources, but is remote, so would benefit from more Japan-wide recognition to hasten the progress towards revitalization. There is local woodwork such as cutting boards and *surikogi* (Japanese grinding pestles) sold at the farmstands along with the potato flour and seaweed dried and packaged by the fishermen's wives (page 36). The surrounding mountains are full of game, mushrooms, nuts and wild plants, and the lush hills above town are home to an inspirational grass-fed dairy, planted by hand with Japanese native grasses (page 52). What's more, chef Ito's outstanding eatery, L'auréole, uses only local ingredients.

Getting to Tanohata-mura is no small feat from most places in Japan, but the last leg of the journey involves a clickety-clack train ride along the Sanriku Coast on a picturesque vintage train fitted with wooden tables for eating your bento. For the food-obsessed, Tanohata-mura is certainly a destination worth exploring, and potato flour an ingredient worth trying.

Potato Bechamel and Fish Stew: Make a bechamel with 1 liter (34 fl oz/4 cups) milk and 3 tablespoons Iwate potato flour – no need to make a roux, just simmer the potato flour and milk gently for about 20 minutes. If needed, stir in a bit more milk if the bechamel becomes too thick, as it should be silky smooth, not gloopy. Finish with 2 tablespoons butter and 2 teaspoons sea salt. Add 500 g (1 lb 2 oz) white fish seared in olive oil, a couple of handfuls of shimeji mushrooms, and a small quartered and blanched head of bok choy. Garnish with chopped delicate herbs such as chives and chervil.

関東

KANTO

Saitama Prefecture
Tokyo
Chiba Prefecture

Soba Ro and Soba Ra
Honjo-shi, Saitama Prefecture

KANJI NAKATANI

Kanji Nakatani does not run his two restaurants with the bottom line in mind. He approaches his work and the ingredients in a visceral, extremely personal way. Since I share this approach to food and life, I find myself time and time again drawn to his restaurants, as well as to his presence. Affectionately known as 'Kanchan' by his customers and friends, he suffers no fools and is an exacting taskmaster in the kitchen. Although he has a fine-honed aesthetic sense, he is impatient with shallowness, and his credo is: 'If you love what you do, money will follow.'

Kanchan opened Soba Ro, a gorgeous Japanese structure set on the edge of some rice fields, in 1994. Located in Kodama-machi, the town adjacent to ours, it quickly became almost the only place in the area where we ate. Ro is made up of a collection of Japanese rooms aimed at secluded yet convivial dining, and is surrounded by Japanese gardens, which create a feeling of tranquility.

As the years passed by, Kanchan also built a second restaurant, Soba Ra, again of traditional architecture, but this time a building with high, beamed ceilings reminiscent of Japanese inns or gathering spots. Antique British library–style chairs, and tables made from local wood, are punctuated by kilim rugs to create distinct spaces. Soba Ra also has three 'Japanese-style' rooms separated by washi-papered sliding doors that can be removed to create a spacious room for a larger group. At both establishments, the art and cloth hangings make an impression: eclectic, interesting, provocative.

But the heart and excellence of the food is where Soba Ro and Soba Ra succeed in capturing their loyal following. Visiting Soba Ra for a solitary Sunday lunch at the counter is sometimes the only way I can restore my energy to meet the next week head on. Food people seem to be heading to Japan in droves, and I know quite a few of them, so get my share of emails regarding 'coming to visit the farm'. Depending on the person, schedule permitting, I acquiesce to a visit, and the first stop on the 'tour' is lunch at Soba Ra, conveniently located a few minutes drive from our local bullet train stop, on the edge of bamboo woods.

Kanchan is jovial yet deeply serious about his metier, and he expects much from himself as well as from his staff.

I have known Kanchan since 1995 (the year my second son, Andrew, was born), and he has been, and remains, an important mentor to all three of my sons. A man's man, Kanchan was originally my husband Tadaaki's friend, with me as a sidekick anomaly. But now, since publishing cookbooks (that have always included some of his recipes), and especially through working on this book, Kanchan and I are firmly friends on our own terms.

Kanchan is jovial yet deeply serious about his metier, and he expects much from himself as well as from his staff. His dishes have intent – there is a reason why each one evolves. Kanchan's style is precisely classic, yet uniquely his own. His food is well thought out, and he enhances the intrinsic flavors of ingredients using impeccable technique. Like most Japanese chefs, Kanchan is a highly skilled master with fish, and his sashimi plates (page 78) are probably some of the most diversely gorgeous in Japan. The colors and range of aromatics that Kanchan uses to create these stunning plates are certainly inspired by his visits to Bob Cannard's various farms in Sonoma County, California, and the four dinners Kanchan has staged at Chez Panisse.

Of course soba is the star attraction at any soba restaurant, but hands down my favorite dishes from Kanchan are his gelée-based seafood salads. Salad and sashimi are the two foods I love best in the world, and Kanchan combines them into eye-popping, zingy-tasting creations at my behest, such as the Fish Gelée Salad with Fig and Nashi (page 97), or the Vinegared Persimmon and Chayote with Salmon Roe (page 99). And each and every time the salad is unique. Often starting with a base of cabbage and komatsuna gelée, it always includes raw or cured fish, blanched vegetables, seasonal fruit, and perhaps katsuobushi mixed with shoyu (*okaka*). The always surprising combination of ingredients on these salads showcases Kanchan's imagination and originality, and are way more interesting than the soba dishes (though to admit this is heresy).

Japanese chefs tend not to travel, and there is some unspoken attitude that they need to get it right in Japan before they go abroad. The genesis for Kanchan's soba dinners at Chez Panisse was an over-exuberant going-away party for Sylvan Mishima Brackett (now chef-owner of Izakaya Rintaro in San Francisco), after a stint Sylvan did at Soba Ro a decade or so ago. In the cold light of day Kanchan tried to wriggle out of the plan, because he was breaking ground on his new restaurant, Soba Ra. But I told him that 'Alice is waiting', and being her huge fan, he could not say no.

Kanchan has now traveled to Russia and the Philippines consulting on soba restaurants, and the world has opened up for him despite his imperfect English. But what he lacks in vocabulary, he makes up for in confidence, hutzpah and knowledge of the kitchen, so somehow words become less important. It is all about the heart of the chef and the soul of the food.

Shiromi-zakana no Tsutsu-mushi

STEAMED WHITE FISH ROLL

Steaming white fish scraps in a log is an excellent way to use up the bits and pieces that did not make it onto the sashimi plate, but which cannot be thrown away. The *zensai* plate is where a chef often repurposes odds and ends from the dishes he is cooking and creates delicious little savory bites as a starter to accompany a cold beer or glass of sake.

SERVES 4

300 g (10½ oz) boneless, skinless, lean white fish such as snapper or bream

½ teaspoon fine sea salt

3 tablespoons finely chopped *negi* or scallion (spring onion)

Cut the fish into small cubes, sprinkle with the salt, and finely chop by hand with a thin-bladed, sharp knife. Sprinkle with the *negi* or scallion and fold in with the knife blade.

Set a large piece of heavy, food-grade plastic wrap across your work surface. Form a 3 cm (1¼ in) wide log of fish along the middle of the wrap. Fold the bottom edge of the wrap up over the log, smoothing down the surface of the log to encase it tightly. Fold in the side edges and roll up to seal.

Steam for 15–20 minutes in a bamboo steamer set inside a large wok over rapidly boiling water. The cooked log should have firmed up with little resistance.

Remove from the steamer and cool to room temperature. Chill overnight, or for at least half a day, before unwrapping, slicing and serving. This keeps for about a week if well wrapped and refrigerated.

See image on page 64

Fukuden Maki

TOFU POUCH VEGETABLE ROLL

Good-quality tofu pouches (*usuage*, also known as *abura-age*, page 280) can be hard to find abroad, although some local tofu companies around the world are producing fairly decent versions. At Japanese grocers outside of Japan, look in the freezer section for the pouches made by House, one of the largest food manufacturers in Japan, so of adequate (though not great) quality. Avoid the canned pre-seasoned ones called '*inarizushi no moto*', which contain preservatives and MSG.

SERVES 4

2 tofu pouches (*usuage*, page 280)

375 ml (12½ fl oz/1½ cups) Happo Dashi (page 126)

½ small carrot, scrubbed

¼ small thin burdock (*gobo*, page 277), scrubbed

2 komatsuna leaves or 4 large spinach leaves with stems

1 large shiitake, stem removed

½ tablespoon granulated sugar

Lay the *usuage* out side by side, vertically, on a large board. Roll over the *usuage* with a wooden rolling pin from the bottom edges to the top, to assist in the eventual prying open of each pouch. Put the *usuage* in a sieve and douse with boiling water for 10 seconds. Shake off and drop into a medium saucepan with 125 ml (4 fl oz/½ cup) of the happo dashi. Lay a drop lid (*otoshibuta*, page 275) or piece of parchment (baking) paper on top of the *usuage* and bring to a low boil over medium heat. Adjust to a slow simmer and cook for 5 minutes. Drain and discard the simmering liquid.

Return the *usuage* to the board. Halve crosswise and slide a very sharp, thin knife into the opening of each half pouch. Slice open the sides while leaving the bottom edge intact. Open up like a book and lay each opened-up pouch next to each other, vertically, on the board. Set aside.

Cut the carrot and burdock lengthwise into 5 mm (¼ in) thin batonnets, about 4 cm (1½ in) long. Bring a medium saucepan full of water to a boil over high heat. Drop in the carrot and cook for 1 minute. Scoop out with a wire-mesh strainer. Cook the burdock for 2 minutes in the same water, then scoop out and add to the carrots. Poke the komatsuna or spinach leaves into the boiling water for 30 seconds. Drop into a bowl of cold running water to refresh, squeeze out excess liquid and chop roughly.

Place the carrot, burdock and shiitake in a small saucepan with the remaining happo dashi and the sugar. Set a drop lid or piece of parchment (baking) paper across the surface and bring to a simmer over medium heat. Adjust to low and cook gently for about 5 minutes, until soft. Drain and discard the simmering liquid. Cut the shiitake into a 5 mm (¼ in) dice.

Place a thin line of carrot, shiitake, komatsuna or spinach, and burdock next to each other about a quarter of the way up on each open piece of *usuage*. Roll tightly and allow to set for about 10 minutes. Slice each roll into 3 thick rounds. Serve as an appetizer, or as part of a *zensai* plate.

See image on page 64

Tataki Gobo
Dengaku Miso

BRAISED BURDOCK WITH DENGAKU MISO

Burdock (*gobo*), a long, thin, earthy-flavored root, is a common ingredient in Japanese stir-fries and soups. This versatile method of preparing burdock breaks down the fibers a bit, so the kaketsuyu simmering liquid can seep into the very core of the burdock. Substitute ground roasted sesame seeds for the sweet miso as a variation.

SERVES 4

300 g (10½ oz) burdock (*gobo*, page 277), scrubbed

300 ml (10 fl oz) Kaketsuyu (page 127)

2 tablespoons Dengaku Miso (page 127)

Lay the burdock horizontally on your workspace and use a Japanese grinding pestle (*surikogi*, page 275) or small rolling pin to gently rap the burdock to just barely break down the fibers. Halve or quarter the burdock lengthwise depending on the thickness, and cut crosswise into 4 cm (1½ in) lengths. Put in a medium saucepan and add water to cover. Bring to a boil over high heat, then drain and return to the saucepan.

Add the kaketsuyu and bring to an almost boil over medium heat. Adjust to a simmer and cook for 10–15 minutes, until the burdock is soft but not mushy. Drain and discard the simmering liquid.

Make a small mound of burdock on 4 small plates and spoon the dengaku miso on top. Serve as a bite before dinner, with beer if you like.

Shake to Hakusai,
Kobu no Hasami Suzuke

LAYERED NAPA CABBAGE WITH SALMON

This stunning preparation can be a little tricky to eat with chopsticks, so I recommend cutting the loaf into smaller pieces for ease of handling at the table.

MAKES 6–8 SMALL SQUARES

2 tablespoons rice vinegar

60 ml (2 fl oz/¼ cup) Shiro Dashi (page 126)

200 g (7 oz) sashimi-grade salmon fillet

¼ teaspoon fine sea salt

5 large napa (Chinese) cabbage leaves

2 × 10 cm (4 in) squares of konbu leftover from making dashi

Line a 10 × 20 cm (4 × 8 in) loaf pan with a layer of plastic wrap so that it drapes over all sides with enough to wrap back over the top.

Heat the vinegar in a small saucepan over medium heat until the sharp vinegar aroma wafts up to you. Measure 1 tablespoon of the hot vinegar into a small bowl with the shiro dashi. Pour the remaining vinegar into another small bowl. Cool both to room temperature.

Cut the salmon at a diagonal with a fine, razor-sharp knife into 5 mm (¼ in) sashimi-like slices. Sprinkle both sides of the fish with the salt from 30 cm (1 ft) above (*tateshio*), and toss with the small bowl of cooled vinegar that was not mixed with dashi.

Bring a large pot three-quarters full of water to a boil over high heat. Drop the cabbage leaves in and blanch for 1 minute. Scoop out with a wire-mesh strainer and shake off excess water. Lay the leaves side by side on a clean dish towel (or two if needed) and roll to blot dry.

Snip the konbu into 6 mm (¼ in) strips, then crosswise into 2 cm (¾ in) lengths.

Cut the cabbage leaves in half. Line the bottom of the pan with half of the stem pieces, followed by half of the soft, light green leaves. Lay two-thirds of the salmon over that layer, followed by the darker green portions of the leaves and about half of the remaining light green leaves. Next, lay the konbu strips crosswise across the surface. Top this layer with the remaining salmon and the last light green leaves. Lay the remaining stem pieces lengthwise across the surface to form a thick top.

Place another 10 × 20 cm (4 × 8 in) loaf pan on the surface and press down firmly on the cabbage to exude excess liquid. Drain that out and discard, while still holding the pan against the surface of the cabbage. Pour the vinegar and dashi mixture over the surface, and fold the plastic wrap over the top to tightly encase. Chill in the refrigerator overnight. Cut into small squares and serve. Keeps for about 1 week.

See image on page 64

Surimi no
Kenchin Mushi

STEAMED CHICKEN AND VEGETABLE ROLL

Steaming in plastic wrap is a convenient method for making little log-shaped terrines that can be sliced up as a bite before dinner, as part of a *zensai* plate, or to accompany a simple green salad. This keeps for about a week if well wrapped and refrigerated. Here, '*kenchin*' refers to the trio of carrot, burdock and shiitake, often used in temple food.

SERVES 4

150 ml (5 fl oz) Happo Dashi (page 126)

½ small carrot, scrubbed

¼ small, thin burdock (*gobo*, page 277), scrubbed

1 large shiitake, stem discarded

1 large komatsuna leaf or 2 large spinach leaves with stems

300 g (10½ oz) chicken breast, diced

½ teaspoon flaky sea salt

1 egg at room temperature

Reserve 1 tablespoon of the happo dashi for seasoning the chicken. Pour the remaining happo dashi into a small saucepan.

Cut the carrot, burdock and shiitake into a 5 mm (¼ in) dice. Slide into the saucepan with the dashi. Lay a drop lid (*otoshibuta*, page 275) or piece of parchment (baking) paper across the surface and bring to a simmer over medium heat. Adjust to low and cook for 2 minutes to flavor the vegetables. Drain, discard the simmering liquid, and cool the vegetables to room temperature.

Blanch the komatsuna or spinach leaves for 1 minute. Drain and refresh under cold running water. Squeeze out excess water and chop finely.

Pulse the chicken in a food processor with the salt, egg and reserved tablespoon of happo dashi until a smooth paste has formed. Scrape into a medium mixing bowl and fold in the greens and simmered vegetables.

Set a large piece of heavy, food-grade plastic wrap across your work surface. Shape the chicken mixture into a 3 cm (1¼ in) thick log in the center of the wrap. Fold over the bottom and side edges before rolling up tightly.

Steam for 15–20 minutes in a bamboo steamer set inside a large wok over rapidly boiling water on high heat until completely set and no resistance is felt when the surface is pressed.

Remove from the steamer and cool to room temperature, then chill overnight before unwrapping, cutting and serving.

See image on page 64

RED BEAN SQUARES

Kuzu-kintoki

MAKES 8–12 SMALL SQUARES

100 g (3½ oz) medium-sized Japanese red beans (*kintoki mame*), soaked overnight or for at least 2 hours

750 ml (25½ fl oz/3 cups) Shiro Dashi (page 126)

3 tablespoons mirin

1 teaspoon fine sea salt

50 g (1¾ oz) kudzu powder (*kuzuko*, page 280), well crushed

See image on page 70

Most often served as sweet squares for a tea break or at the end of a traditional Japanese restaurant meal, here the red bean squares are savory, yet still naturally sweet, so add balance to a *zensai* plate.

Place the drained beans in a medium saucepan and fill with plenty of cold water to cover by at least 5 cm (2 in). Bring to an almost boil over medium heat, adjust to a simmer and cook gently for 30 minutes. Drain the beans and return to the pan, fill again with cold water, and simmer for 30 more minutes, until the beans have softened. Drain. Rinse the pan quickly and return the beans to it with the shiro dashi, mirin and salt. Place a drop lid (*otoshibuta*, page 275) or piece of parchment (baking) paper on the surface, and bring to a simmer over medium heat. Cook gently for 30 minutes, until the beans are soft and deeply flavored.

Put the kudzu in a small bowl and add a small spoon or two of the simmering liquid. Stir to dissolve, and scrape back into the pan of beans. Stir over low heat for about 5 minutes, until thickened and sticky.

Scrape into a 10 × 20 cm (4 × 8 in) loaf pan and cool to room temperature. Chill for 2 hours before cutting into small squares and serving. Keeps in the refrigerator for 3 or 4 days.

SAVORY SOBA DOFU

MAKES 8–12 SMALL SQUARES

50 g (1¾ oz) Japanese buckwheat flour (*sobako*, page 280)

50 g (1¾ oz) kudzu powder (*kuzuko*, page 280), well crushed

500 ml (17 fl oz/2 cups) Shiro Dashi (page 126)

small sprigs of *sansho* leaves (page 19), for garnishing

See image on page 70

Soba dofu is a variation on *goma dofu* (page 71) that appears on *zensai* plates at soba restaurants, but can easily be prepared at home, for serving as a bite with sake before dinner. Both are thickened with kudzu, which renders them almost unctuous in texture. Enjoying the delicate flavor of buckwheat in a different texture from soba noodles gives one a feeling of delight in the unexpected. A small ground cherry (cape gooseberry) with its dried husk artfully arranged also makes a lovely garnish instead of *sansho* leaves.

Whisk the buckwheat flour and kudzu together in a small heavy saucepan until well mixed. Slowly whisk in the dashi until a smooth paste has formed. Set over low heat and cook, stirring continuously with a flat wooden spoon, until the mixture starts to thicken. Start stirring vigorously, scraping the bottom of the pan to avoid scorching, until the mixture has a glue-like consistency. It should take about 15 minutes in total.

Scrape into a 10 × 20 cm (4 × 8 in) loaf pan and allow to cool to room temperature. Chill for at least 2 hours. Cut into small squares and serve garnished with a sprig of *sansho* leaves. Keeps for about 3 or 4 days, if refrigerated.

TAMAGO DOFU

SERVES 6–8

5 medium eggs at room temperature

125 ml (4 fl oz/½ cup) Kaketsuyu (page 127)

125 g (4½ oz) enoki mushrooms

150 g (5½ oz) spinach leaves

100 g (3½ oz) fresh picked crabmeat

a few sprigs of buckwheat flowers, for garnishing (optional)

One of our most favorite dishes at Soba Ro and Ra, *tamago dofu* is a juicy, dashi-steeped savory egg square that is fairly easy to make, as long as you take care to steam it slowly. Also avoid adding extra ingredients, since packing the egg mixture too full will hinder the cooking process and cause the need to overcook in order to get the custard to firm up. Making this recipe in larger quantities in an oversized pan will also create issues regarding even cooking.

Whisk the eggs with the kaketsuyu until well emulsified. Strain through a fine sieve into a pitcher or jug.

Bring a medium pot three-quarters full of water to a boil over high heat. Place the enoki in a sieve and dip them in then out of the boiling water. Shake off and blot dry on a clean dish towel. Drop the spinach leaves into the water and cook for 30 seconds. Scoop out with a wire-mesh strainer and refresh in a bowl of cold water. Run more cold water until the spinach is completely cool to the touch. Drain and squeeze. Chop roughly.

Bring a large wok filled one-third with water to a boil over high heat. Adjust to a gentle simmer and place a bamboo steamer over the simmering water.

Strew the enoki, spinach and crab evenly across the bottom of a 10 × 20 cm (4 × 8 in) loaf pan. Pour in the egg mixture and set the pan inside the bamboo steamer. Cook over low heat for about 30 minutes, until set. You want to avoid surface bubbling on the custard, as this means the steaming temperature is too high. Check that the egg is cooked by inserting a bamboo skewer into the center. It should come out clean.

Cool to room temperature, then chill for at least 2 hours before cutting into 6 or 8 squares. Lift the squares carefully out of the pan with a small spatula and serve on individual plates with some of the pooled juices from the bottom of the pan. Garnish each piece with a small sprig of buckwheat flowers if you can find some.

See image on page 70

GOMA DOFU

MAKES 8–12 SMALL SQUARES

100 g (3½ oz) Japanese sesame paste (white, black or gold)

25 g (1 oz) sesame seeds the same color as the paste, finely ground (optional)

500 ml (17 fl oz/2 cups) Shiro Dashi (page 126)

50 g (1¾ oz) kudzu powder (*kuzuko*, page 280), well crushed

1 teaspoon freshly grated wasabi, for serving

A cornerstone of temple food, *goma dofu* is deceptively difficult to prepare well. The key to success is a zealous (and long) stirring process that is not for the faint of heart, so the job given to new acolytes at Zen Buddhist temples. Nonetheless, well-made *goma dofu* is sublime; so worth the effort. *Goma dofu* can be served with a tiny drizzle of shoyu if not serving on a *zensai* plate with other preparations.

Put the sesame paste and ground seeds, if using, in a single layer of muslin (cheesecloth) and twist up to make a bundle. Tie well with a piece of kitchen twine.

Heat the dashi in a medium saucepan over low heat and drop in the bundle of sesame paste. Heat slowly to melt out the sesame paste and extract flavor from the ground sesame seeds. Press down on the bundle with a spoon so that all the paste mixes into the dashi and only the seed solids remain. Remove the bundle, squeeze it one last time into the pan, and discard the contents.

Stir a little of the sesame dashi into the kudzu powder in a small bowl, to dissolve the powder and emulsify. Scrape back into the saucepan and stir madly over low heat as the mixture thickens and becomes glossy and extremely sticky. This will take a good 15 minutes of stirring continuously and strenuously. By the end, the mixture will almost have a life of its own as it lifts out of the pan.

Scrape into a 10 × 20 cm (4 × 8 in) loaf pan and cool to room temperature. Chill for 2 hours before cutting into small squares and serving with a dab of wasabi as a small bite before a meal. Keeps for about 3 or 4 days, if refrigerated.

Shira-ae Warabi

FIDDLEHEAD FERNS WITH SMASHED TOFU

SERVES 4

small handful of hardwood ash

2 small bunches fiddlehead ferns (about 250 g/9 oz)

300 g (10½ oz) *momendofu* (page 279) or Japanese-style soft block tofu

⅛ teaspoon fine sea salt

½ tablespoon fine white Japanese sugar (*johakuto*, page 14)

Fiddlehead fern is a delicate mountain vegetable that appears in the spring. Although not all fiddleheads need their natural bitterness (*aku*) removed by soaking in ash, Kanji Nakatani performs this step here. Simply use hardwood ash from a fireplace.

Combine the ash and fiddleheads in a medium saucepan and cover with boiling water. Place a lid on the pan and let cool to room temperature. Leave to soak overnight.

Discard the ash water and rinse the fiddleheads well, removing all traces of ash. Clean the pan and fill with cold water. Drop in the fiddleheads and leave to soak for another 4 hours or more. Drain, pat the fiddleheads dry in a clean dish towel, and chop finely.

Put the tofu in a fine sieve set above a bowl. Place a small saucepan half full of water on top of the tofu and set aside for 20 minutes, allowing the tofu to express excess water.

Drop the drained tofu into a Japanese grinding bowl (*suribachi*, page 275) and smash it to a smooth paste. Stir the salt and sugar into the tofu, and fold in three-quarters of the chopped fiddlehead. Serve in small mounds garnished with the remaining fiddlehead, on a *zensai* plate or as a first course.

SOUR PLUM FARMER

Umeboshi (brined, sun-dried sour 'plums') date back 3000 years to China, and were introduced 1500 years ago into Japan as a medicine. *Ume* contain organic acids, which are good for your stomach and also act as a natural sterilizer in your body. Not just a food, umeboshi are to this day viewed in Japan as essential to good health, much akin to the western idea of 'an apple a day keeps the doctor away'.

Impressive history and health-giving properties notwithstanding, there is a recent trend abroad of attempting to make umeboshi from apricots and other fruit. On the one hand this makes sense, since *ume* might be challenging to source outside Japan. On the other hand, the obsession of taking Japanese traditional foods and remaking them into something they are not is sometimes perplexing.

Ume is related to the apricot, so to some degree unripe apricots may work as a substitute, though the theory is dubious. *Ume* are toxic if consumed raw, only becoming edible when brined and dried, when steeped in alcohol with sugar to make *umeshu*, or when cooked, making the fruit intrinsically different from an apricot.

There are two farmers in Japan growing *ume* commercially and organically to make umeboshi and its brine, which is sold as plum vinegar (*umesu*). One is located in Shimonita (a town famous for natto) nearby us in Gunma prefecture. Masanori Yoshida works with his father in a small operation sun-drying umeboshi from a couple of massive wooden barrels of brined *ume* they put up after harvesting their trees in June. I was confounded to observe those barrels of brining *ume*, because my *ume* would disintegrate if I left them in brine. As a farmwife pickler and preserver, sometimes the science of it all escapes me. I use 8% salt, whereas the Yoshida farm uses a massive 25%, which naturally decreases to 24% when the *ume* release their juices in the weighting process. The salt percentage in the *umesu* brine is adjusted to 20% by blending in hot water.

I hesitate to increase the salt percentage when making my own umeboshi, because to me they seem perfect as they are (though they do need to be closely monitored for mold during the salting and weighting stage). Unfortunately, I was in Australia at the exact time I needed to pick and soak the *ume* to start the umeboshi-making process last summer. My husband picked the *ume* instead, and he followed his own method, so I could not put the increased salt theory to the test. Perhaps next year.

The first time I visited the Yoshida farm, it was summer, and red shiso leaves were drying on long tables in the hot sun, shielded from any rain by greenhouse roofing. A big fan of the red shiso powder made for Yamaki Jozo by Yoshida-san and his father, I was fascinated to learn that they dip their organic red shiso leaves in the *ume* brine and air-dry the leaves three times to bring out the natural red shiso flavors and fully infuse the leaves with the sour, salty, fruity *ume*. Red shiso powder is reminiscent of sumac, but so much more intriguing, and so much more complex. Sprinkle it on mayonnaise-based seafood salads, on rice, or on radish or turnip pickles, or just take it by the spoonful as a pick-me-up.

Over the years, I have visited artisanal food producers of all kinds, both in Japan and abroad, and have come to the realization that the at-home method and the small-scale commercial method are fundamentally different. And as such, farmwives should follow farmwife methods, since they match the rhythm of how we actually live or how we make something. We are not professionals; we do not need to generate a product consistently throughout the year, because we are not selling it. We get one chance at it per year. This is extremely humbling when you put it in the perspective of the finite number of years each person actually has to make one seasonal thing, be it jam, fruit vinegar, or preserved fruit or vegetables.

Green Ume Essence: Wipe clean 4 kg (8 lb 13 oz) green but ripe *ume*. Halve with a sharp paring knife and remove the pits. Pulse in batches in a food processor to break down the *ume* to the smoothest purée possible. Scoop in batches into a large piece of muslin (cheesecloth), twist up into a bundle, and squeeze out as much juice as you can into a bowl. Discard the solids. Simmer the juice in a small heavy saucepan, stirring frequently. Take care not to burn or let the liquid dissipate too quickly. As the liquid simmers, it will turn from pale green to brown. Cook down to a densely dark liquid of about 60 ml (2 fl oz/ ¼ cup). Remove from the heat, pour into a small jar, and store in a cool, dry place. Take a drop or two of the intensely bitter essence when you are feeling peaked, or combine with a spoonful of honey in hot water as a restorative.

Shiro-ni Daikon
Tori Miso

DASHI-SIMMERED DAIKON WITH MISO CHICKEN SAUCE

Daikon becomes juicy and succulent when simmered in dashi. All you need is some sort of miso dressing to complete this refreshing yet deeply flavored morsel.

SERVES 4–8 AS A SMALL BITE

2 slices of daikon about 2 cm (¾ in) thick, cut into quarters

500 ml (17 fl oz/2 cups) Konbu Dashi (page 126)

½ tablespoon unroasted sesame oil

100 g (3½ oz) chicken breast, finely chopped to a paste

150 ml (5 fl oz) Shiro Dashi (page 126)

4 tablespoons Dengaku Miso (page 127)

Drop the daikon into a medium saucepan. Cover with cold water and bring to a boil. Drain immediately.

Return the daikon to the empty pan and add the konbu dashi. Bring to a boil over medium–high heat, adjust to a gentle simmer and cook for about 20 minutes, until the daikon pieces are translucent and soft through to the center. Scoop out and cool to room temperature. Reserve the simmering liquid for storing any leftovers for a day or two.

Heat the oil in a medium saucepan over medium heat. Once hot, add the chicken and fry, stirring continuously with a flat wooden spoon, for about 8 minutes, until pebbly. Add the shiro dashi and simmer down over low heat, stirring occasionally, for about 8 more minutes until the dashi has evaporated. Stir in the dengaku miso and cook over low heat for 3–5 minutes, until glossy.

Place a piece or two of daikon on small plates, setting them down on one of their flat sides so the rounded sides are standing up. Spoon a dollop of the miso chicken sauce on top of the curve of each piece and serve as a bite before dinner. Good with beer.

Shakushina Goma Miso

BOK CHOY WITH SESAME MISO

Shakushina is a variety of bok choy native to the Chichibu mountain region of northwest Saitama prefecture. The stems are a bit smaller than bok choy, the leaves more rounded, and the bunches often curve outwards like a blossoming flower. It is commonly air-dried for a day then salt-pickled. Bok choy is a good substitute.

SERVES 4

200 g (7 oz) *shakushina* (page 278) or bok choy

1 tablespoon Goma Miso (page 128)

Bring a medium pot three-quarters full of water to a boil over high heat. Grasp the *shakushina* or bok choy in a bundle by the leaves and lower the stems into the boiling water for 30 seconds, then drop the bundle into the water, pushing down to submerge. Cook for another 30 seconds. Scoop out with a wire-mesh strainer, and cool with cold running water to refresh. Shake off excess water and squeeze by handfuls.

Align the stem ends horizontally across a chopping board and cut crosswise into 3 cm (1¼ in) lengths. Stack small mounds of the greens on individual dishes or as part of a *zensai* plate. Spoon a small dollop of the goma miso on top of the greens and serve.

Ninjin Kinpira

CARROT KINPIRA

Kinpira is a classic Japanese dish of stir-fried vegetable that is usually seasoned with shoyu, though can have salt instead. A sprinkling of sesame seeds is optional, depending on the mood. Here the flavors are understated to interact well with other dishes on a *zensai* plate.

SERVES 4

200 g (7 oz) carrot, scrubbed

1 teaspoon white sesame seeds

1 tablespoon unroasted sesame oil

3 tablespoons Happo Dashi (page 126)

1 teaspoon fine white Japanese sugar (*johakuto*, page 14)

Cradle the carrot in your non-dominant hand and shave off thin flat strips, cutting away from your body with a sharp knife (*sasagaki*, page 276).

Gently warm the sesame seeds in a small dry frying pan over low heat until fragrant. Scrape the seeds into a small bowl.

Heat the oil in a medium frying pan over medium–high heat. Toss in the carrot and stir-fry for 1–2 minutes, until starting to soften. Stir in the happo dashi and sugar and cook for 1–2 minutes more, to reduce the liquid to a light glaze. Sprinkle in the sesame seeds and serve immediately or at room temperature, as a vegetable side dish or a bite before dinner.

JAPANESE MISO

While most miso is fermented to some degree, there is a wide range of differences in the ratio of koji used, as well as in the fermentation period.

Koji (*Aspergillus oryzae*) – the spore that has been used in Japan for thousands of years – is the mysterious, magical element that enables complex fermentation of traditional foods including shoyu, rice vinegar, mirin and miso.

Miso with a high percentage of koji tends to be barely fermented, or perhaps better put, is matured rather than fermented, and has a mild profile. Barely fermented miso is more like a salty-sweet condiment – much loved in the areas where it is made, and often used for classical preparations in restaurants, such as miso-marinated grilled fish (*saikyo yaki*). Due to the inherent sweetness of this style of miso, typically it is the one added to cookie or cake batters to give a subtle boost of flavor. But I would argue that a fermented miso is the better choice for desserts, because it is more complex, and just a small amount will enrich and enliven a sweet.

In areas where fermented miso is made, local people crave its mellow and savory characteristics that develop naturally over time. The nuanced fermentation notes and heady aromas are highly valued, as well as virtually addictive. This kind of miso should be considered a savory, salt-plus style of condiment.

Miso makers pride themselves on making their own proprietary koji, since it is one of the key factors determining taste. It is said that you can never make the same miso twice, even when using the same ingredients, because koji always develops variations in its flavor profile.

Virtually all (if not all) Japanese miso makers buy their koji spores from one of seven spore laboratories. One hundred grams of koji spores can inoculate 100 kilograms of rice (a ratio of 1:1000). But for some reason, chefs and at least one commercial miso maker abroad are wildly experimenting with fermenting miso from spores they have tried to propagate themselves. The only such misos I have tasted were total failures: sour, not pleasant, with no apparent koji present. There is a reason why artisanal food makers in Japan source their spores from dedicated spore labs. Also, koji-inoculated grains need a protein such as soybeans to ferment properly, but some amateur miso makers are incomprehensibly attempting to make miso from grain only. I am not sure whether to laugh or cry at the arrogance of these New World chefs bastardizing this 1000-year-old Japanese tradition.

Miso types are determined by the koji-inoculated grain/bean they use (i.e. rice, barley or soybean). Making miso, whether automated or artisanal, involves a two-step fermentation process. The grain or bean is soaked overnight, drained, steamed 80%, and cooled to body temperature, then inoculated with the spores and held in a humid and anaerobic environment to propagate for 48 hours. The koji-inoculated rice, barley or soybean is mixed with soybeans that have been soaked overnight and steamed, plus salt and sometimes a little 'seed miso' (*tane miso*) from the previous year's batch. The mash is packed in cedar barrels, enameled steel tanks or fiberglass vats and left to ferment for weeks, months or years, depending on the miso. Good bacteria transform simple sugars into various organic acids, which in turn impart distinctive flavors and prevent spoilage.

Miso may be the most versatile seasoning you can have in your kitchen. Think of it as a richly aromatic, deeply flavorful salt alternative. Used as a hidden taste (*kakushi aji*), miso can literally be put in anything. Fermenting provides the benefit of preservation, while making foods more digestible and nourishing. Fermented foods are central to artisanal and traditional foodways and defy globalization and industrialization of food in the modern world.

Japan is *the* country of fermentation, and the Japanese method of making miso has stood the test of time without variation over a millennium. The beautifully simple method follows the natural rhythm of the seasons and the autumn soybean and rice harvest, deserving all the respect it commands.

一四七

SPRING SASHIMI PLATE

Kawari Zukuri Santen Mori

Less a recipe than a key to open the door to creating your own gorgeous sashimi plates.

Kanji Nakatani first selects the actual plate to be the canvas for his painting. Next, using only the most pristinely fresh seasonal fish at its most optional condition, he 'paints' them into their own corners to anchor the creation. And then, with Jackson Pollack–like brushstrokes, he deftly and surely pinches mounds of chopped fresh and blanched greens and aromatics to enliven and enhance, and grated wasabi and ginger to cleanse. A work of art every time, whether a solitary order for me, or a stunning order for eight. Emulating Kanji Nakatani's sashimi plate is how we become more intuitive and creative in our own rights.

Tsuma are the vegetables and aromatics that grace a sashimi plate and have a dual function as eye-catching splashes of color and as palate cleansers. For this vibrant spring plate, Nakatani used raw carrot fronds, purple mizuna, and boiled, refreshed and squeezed flowering brassica (*nanohana*, page 278).

Typically, Soba Ro and Ra give each person two small dishes of shoyu, not because you are supposed to add the fresh grated wasabi and ginger to each one (because you are not), but because some errant fragments of wasabi or ginger might fall off from where you have pinched them onto the sashimi when you dip a corner of the fish in the sauce. One dish is for dipping fish you are eating with ginger, and the other for fish with wasabi.

Adjust your sashimi plate according to the fish, vegetables and aromatics available in the season. Cut the fish at a diagonal or straight down, thick or thin – as you like – but use a razor sharp knife. And incorporate the following three key techniques.

Kobujime

Lightly sprinkle skinless, boneless, lean white fish fillets (Nakatani used grouper – *hata*) with flaky sea salt (5 g/ 1 teaspoon per 450 g/1 lb fish). Lay each fillet, belly side down, on a piece of konbu the same size as the fish. Stack together without konbu on top and wrap in spongy paper towels, then in plastic wrap, and leave for at least 4 hours in the refrigerator to wick out moisture from the fish. If you like, cut the konbu into small squares to act as a resting place for the sashimi slices, or into a fine julienne to mound alongside the fish.

Yubiki

Fatty fish such as yellowtail (*buri*) benefit from a hot water treatment to firm up the texture. Place the fish fillet in a medium bowl and add boiling water to cover. Drain immediately and plunge into an ice water bath to shock the flesh. Pat dry.

Yakishimo

Char the skin and scales of fish fillets such as sea bream (*kobudai*), bream (*tai*), sea bass (*suzuki*) or rosy sea bass (*nodoguro*) quickly over low-ember coals in a Japanese tabletop brazier (*shichirin*, page 275), or with a butane torch. If charring on a *shichirin*, thread the fillets onto 2 metal skewers. Be careful not to cook the flesh. This fish is sliced with charred skin and scales intact.

How much sashimi you serve per person is totally up to you. Is the sashimi meant as a light starter before a longer meal? Or will you be gorging on all of your special favorites as the unifier of the meal? If the latter, I would follow with miso soup and rice and pickles to complete the meal. If the former, any segue would work, even a light, bright western meal. However, one sage piece of advice I can give is to serve the sashimi with a purely elegant sake – cold, slightly warm or at room temperature – to complement the delicately nuanced raw fish. Sake is the only constant when approaching a sashimi plate.

Anko no Kimo

MONKFISH LIVER WITH MOMIJI OROSHI

Monkfish liver is often compared to foie gras, but I would venture to say it has a much more pleasing texture and flavor. Though perhaps I am biased living in Japan, where the fish is arguably the best in the world, since fishermen have been catching and treating it as if it were to be eaten raw for centuries. Monkfish livers vary greatly in size, so if the one you find is large, halve or quarter it lengthwise before wrapping and steaming.

SERVES 4

1 small monkfish liver weighing about 400 g (14 oz)

1 tablespoon Momiji Oroshi (page 129)

1 tablespoon finely chopped chives or thin scallion (spring onion) tops

2 tablespoons Ponzu (page 128)

Pare the tendons from the liver and peel off the outside skin. Lay a large piece of heavy, food-grade plastic wrap across your work surface. Position the liver in the center and roll up tightly, shaping it to form a 3 cm (1¼ in) log. Twist the ends closed and tie securely with kitchen twine.

Place in a bamboo steamer positioned inside a large wok over boiling water. Steam for about 15 minutes, or until set. There should be a small amount of give when the liver is pressed gently (you want the center to be cooked but still pink). Cool to room temperature, then chill for at least 3 hours.

Unwrap and cut into 5 mm (¼ in) slices. Arrange attractively on 4 small plates with the momiji oroshi and chives or scallions alongside. Serve with a small saucer of ponzu for each person.

Namako no Kyuri-su

SEA CUCUMBER WITH GRATED CUCUMBER IN SWEET VINEGAR

Not for everyone, but I am an aficionado of the chewy, crunchy texture of sea cucumbers. Their gentle briny profile makes them a natural candidate for vinegar treatments, such as *nihaizu*. Cucumber from the land is a natural yet whimsical pairing with these cucumbers from the sea.

SERVES 4

4 very small, very fresh sea cucumbers

1 teaspoon fine sea salt

5 g (¼ oz/½ teaspoon) *bancha* tea leaves

125 ml (4 fl oz/½ cup) Nihaizu (page 128)

1 small Japanese cucumber, weighing about 100 g (3½ oz)

Cut a small slit in the bottom of the sea cucumbers using a sharp knife. Pry out the guts with your finger and discard. Rinse the sea cucumbers inside and out with cold water.

Sprinkle the salt on a large board and vigorously roll the sea cucumbers in it to work out some of their surface slime. Place them in a sieve and rinse under cold running water to remove viscosity.

Pour 750 ml (25½ fl oz/3 cups) water into a medium saucepan and add the *bancha* leaves. Bring to an almost boil over medium heat. Drop in the sea cucumbers and adjust the heat to a 60°C (140°F) simmer. Cook gently, turning with chopsticks, for about 5 minutes, until a skewer can be easily inserted into the center of the sea cucumbers. Drain and chill in a bowl of ice water. Cut the sea cucumbers crosswise into 5 mm (¼ in) slices, keeping the shape of the cucumbers intact. Place each sea cucumber in a small bowl and spoon the *nihaizu* over them.

Trim the ends of the cucumber and grate on a fine-toothed metal grating plate (*oroshigane*, page 275). Scrape into a sieve set over a small bowl to drain for 10 minutes.

Dollop a mound of grated cucumber next to each sea cucumber and serve with a cold glass of sake as an appetizer.

THE JAPANESE POTTER

Prior to a recent discovery of earthenware from 20,000 years ago in the Jiangxi province in southern China, it was thought that Japan and China shared the longest history of pottery, dating back to Japan's prehistoric Jomon period (c. 12,000–400 BCE). Nonetheless, Japan's earthenware tradition of 18,000 years is still stupefying to imagine. While China's recent resurgence of artisanal ceramics focuses on a collective effort, Japanese pottery has a long history of celebrating the individual potter. Japanese ceramic styles have reached far across the globe, influencing potters throughout the world. In 1954, the Japanese government's Cultural Property Preservation Act implemented a system for recognizing the holders/preservers of important Intangible Cultural Properties (ICP), which was quickly nicknamed the more pithy Living National Treasure (LNT) system by the newspapers. Pottery is one of eight ICP categories, and 35 potters had been certified by 2018.

Saitama prefecture is not an area well known for pottery, but we have our share of artisans. Our oldest son, Christopher, a gifted ceramicist who has been making ceramics for eighteen years, has started his own pottery line, and is currently creating prototypes and glaze samples for restaurants. His father and brothers have also done pottery for years. The dishes we use every day are either Japanese pottery made by people we know, or antique ceramics. We have scores of bowls, cups, plates and vases crafted by my husband and sons, as well as a collection bought from Australian potter Richard Ballinger, who apprenticed with LNT Tatsuzo Shimaoka in Mashiko. And we have the odd piece from local potter friends Isao Kimura and Hanayumi Ishizuka, both of whom sell to Soba Ro and Ra (page 61).

A Japanese restaurant is only as good as its food and tableware. The tableware does not have to be pricey, though often is. But it does need to have heart. Early recorded menus of the Edo period (1603–1868) sometimes included the specific plate used for a dish, revealing that tableware is of equal importance as the food in Japan. This cannot be stressed more.

We have a saying in Japan: '*aji ga aru*', meaning 'something has taste'. Not in the meaning of 'good taste' but that it tastes good, like the tangible/intangible thing is so cool you could consume it with your whole being. It elicits a visceral reaction: it has soul. It could be an imperfect piece, perhaps mended (touched with gold lacquer at the mends, called *kintsugi*); intrinsic quality is relevant; expense is not. (LNT Shoji Hamada's response upon being chided at hefty prices for spontaneous, 30-second decorations on pots: 'This has taken 60 years plus 30 seconds.')

Personality in pottery is what draws me in, in the same way that the personality of a chef comes through in the food. My husband and sons studied pottery every week with Hanayumi Ishizuka's father for years, and after each periodic firing of the kiln, they brought home a large box of pottery. Matthew, my ultra-creative youngest, tended toward interesting shapes such as a flower plate with actual petals, or a heavily glazed white plate that appears in one of my full-page book photos and is a personal favorite. Andrew, my second son, has a large heart and that always showed through in his pottery. He tackled big shapes fairly quickly, and was not afraid to use clay. Christopher was always about technique and favored a very thin, fine style of ceramics, always pushing himself to become better in terms of shape and glaze. No surprise that he made about 300 plates as gifts to give guests at his wedding. And Tadaaki, my husband, was always bold in his approach to pottery, stretching the boundaries of what he could make, sometimes creating pieces that we could never use, but were nonetheless interesting and well made for their genre. Tadaaki was a bold user of glazes and even began mixing and experimenting with his own, something that Christopher is doing now as well.

Matthew was five when our boys began visiting the Ishizuka pottery studio and, famously, he walked over to a large standing vase that Ishizuka Sensei had just finished. He poked the vase with his finger and the lip collapsed. Tadaaki gasped in horror, but Sensei walked over and with some deft movements, incorporated the collapse into the piece itself, creating a new feel. 'Pottery is a living, fluid thing,' he said with a shrug.

The potter I have been friends with the longest is Isao Kimura. Kimura lives in the mountains nearby, and we used to drive up to see him when my father and his wife came to visit. They were big pottery aficionados. Kimura has a nonchalant, understated style, and to date does not sign his work. 'No need,' he says with characteristic modesty. He fires two kilns, and the pottery is stacked higgledy-piggledy on every available outside surface. My father and his wife would rummage through the pieces, pick out some gems, and negotiate a price. Always undervalued, Kimura's pottery was a bargain then, and is still quite affordable today.

Over the years I have taken many visitors to Kimura's workshop, finding him sometimes there, sometimes not. (In one hermit stage, visitors were eschewed.) With the encouragement and patronage of Kanji Nakatani from Soba Ro and Ra, Kimura suddenly blossomed and became positively bright. He began wearing pink! Around this time, he started making the *osechi ryori* plates (page 131) for Soba Ro, and was busier and more prolific than ever. In the summer of 2016, I was astounded by his transformation. He invited us into the house for the first time.

Kimura lives in a traditional-style Japanese home on a mountainside. The rooms open up to each other, and the pottery is very visible, stacked in the corners of the rooms. Rather than perched precariously on shelves or exposed to the elements catching rain as before, the pieces are arranged by size and shape and type. And Kimura's style has evolved, becoming more refined, more personal, more compelling. He always had heart, but in a rough-hewn style. Now his pottery is thoughtful if not stunning.

A plate, a bowl, a cup should speak to you in the moment – or perhaps after a sensitive pause. Life is too short not to be honored and nourished by the entire ambience of the table as well as the food.

Shiozuke Daikon no Kakiyose

LAYERED DAIKON, WATERMELON RADISH AND NAPA CABBAGE

Kanji Nakatani is a fan of pressed layered vegetables because they are quick to execute, attractive to serve, and handy to have on hand for adding to a pickle or *zensai* plate. And, of course, also quite tasty.

MAKES 6–8 SMALL SQUARES

150 g (5½ oz) watermelon radish, scrubbed

150 g (5½ oz) daikon, scrubbed

150 g (5½ oz) napa (Chinese) cabbage leaves

¾ teaspoon fine sea salt

See image on page 86

Halve the watermelon radish and daikon lengthwise and cut crosswise into 5 mm (¼ in) slices. Put each into a separate small mixing bowl. Cut the stems out of the cabbage and drop the stems and leaves into another mixing bowl. Sprinkle ¼ teaspoon of salt into each bowl and use your hand to massage in without breaking the vegetables.

Line a 10 × 20 cm (4 × 8 in) loaf pan with a piece of plastic wrap large enough to cover the bottom and sides and drape down the outside of the pan. Layer the watermelon radish evenly across the bottom of the pan. Lay the soft green cabbage leaves over the top, followed by the daikon. Finish by placing the cabbage stems lengthwise across the surface.

Press down firmly on the surface of the layers with another same-sized loaf pan. Pour off the excess liquid while holding the empty pan against the surface. Cover the top with the plastic wrap and chill.

Remove the pressed vegetables from the pan, cut into small squares and serve.

Hakusai Dashi Oshi

DASHI-STEEPED NAPA CABBAGE

Another simple dish that is prepared by steeping cabbage in warm dashi, which makes for a refreshing addition to a pickle plate since it is made without salt or vinegar.

MAKES ABOUT 150 G (5½ OZ)

10 napa (Chinese) cabbage leaves, weighing about 200 g (7 oz)

250 ml (8½ fl oz/1 cup) Shiro Dashi (page 126), warmed

See image on page 86

Drape the cabbage leaves across the bottom of a deep-sided rectangular container and pour the warm dashi over the top. Press another rectangular container of the same size on top of the leaves and press down to firmly compact. Remove the container used for pressing. Allow the cabbage to cool to room temperature, and refrigerate for at least 2 hours.

Remove 1 or 2 leaves at a time for serving. Shake off excess liquid, halve lengthwise and cut crosswise into 3 cm (1¼ in) pieces. Mound onto small individual plates or as part of a pickle plate.

Kabu, Kuro Daikon, Koshin Daikon no Shiomomi

SALT-MASSAGED DAIKON, BLACK DAIKON AND WATERMELON RADISH

More often than not, Japanese pickles are the quick salt-massaged style. There is no fermentation involved and no vinegar, just salt to render the vegetables off-raw or 'pickled'. Here the different radish varieties give a colorful presentation.

MAKES ABOUT 400 G (14 OZ)

150 g (5½ oz) watermelon radish, scrubbed

150 g (5½ oz) white daikon, scrubbed

150 g (5½ oz) black daikon, scrubbed

2 teaspoons flaky sea salt

See image on page 86

Pat the vegetables dry with a clean dish towel. Halve the watermelon radish and white daikon lengthwise, and cut crosswise into 1 cm (½ in) thick half-moons. Drop each variety in a separate small mixing bowl. Cut the black daikon into 5 mm (¼ in) thin rounds and put in a third bowl. Sprinkle the salt evenly between the bowls and massage gently into the slices. Let sit for at least 10 minutes before pressing the vegetables in a clean dish towel to blot off any moisture that has accumulated and salt crystals that have not dissolved.

Slice 1 half-moon of the watermelon radish and white daikon crosswise into 5 mm (¼ in) wide rectangles, but keep the half-moon shapes intact. Lay the half-moons side by side so they make a two-colored circle on an individual plate or as part of a pickle plate. Fan 3 thin rounds of black daikon on top.

Keeps, if refrigerated, for 2 or 3 days, but will leach out liquid so might need another sprinkling of salt for serving.

Mizuna no Shiomomi

SALT-WILTED MIZUNA WITH CHILI

Salt-wilting is an ingenious way to break down the fibers in a bitter green such as turnip tops or a peppery green such as mizuna, to 'pickle' them and render them easier to eat. The chili is essential to add spark.

MAKES ABOUT 200 G (7 OZ)

300 g (10½ oz) mizuna

9 g (¼ oz) flaky sea salt

½ small dried red chili (*chile japones*, page 278), sliced into fine rounds

See image on page 86

Align the mizuna stems, and cut the stems and leaves crosswise into 1 cm (½ in) pieces. Toss into a medium mixing bowl and massage in the salt until the mizuna is completely wilted and dark green. Massage the chili in gently and mound the mizuna into small saucers or as part of a pickle plate. Keeps refrigerated for 3 or 4 days.

Ninjin Yubiki

WILTED CARROT WITH ITS TOPS

Traditional Japanese cuisine seldom includes raw vegetables, unless as a garnish. More often vegetables are salt-massaged, blanched or hot water–wilted.

MAKES ABOUT 150 G (5½ OZ)

1 medium carrot with its fronds, weighing about 200 g (7 oz) in total

½ teaspoon fine sea salt

Cut the fronds off the carrot and remove any brown or yellow parts. Rinse the fronds if needed and blot dry in a clean dish towel. Slice into 3 cm (1¼ in) pieces. Drop into a small mixing bowl and massage in the salt until the fronds are juicy and have completely broken down. Squeeze out excess moisture and reserve in a small bowl.

Scrub the carrot. Cut it into thin rectangular slabs (*tanzaku-giri*, page 276), keeping the stacks together. Set the stacks in a small bowl and pour boiling water over to cover. Press a drop lid (*otoshibuta*, page 275) or sieve onto the surface of the carrots to hold them in place, and dump the boiling water. Cool to room temperature.

Set small stacks of carrot, standing up on their long sides, on small saucers or a pickle plate. Pinch mounds of salt-massaged fronds on top and serve as a palate cleanser or bite before dinner.

Kyarabuki

SOY-SIMMERED BUTTERBUR

Butterbur (*fuki*, page 277) is prized for its haunting bitterness and can grow to an impressive 2 meters (6½ feet) in Akita prefecture in northwestern Japan. A mountain vegetable, *fuki* buds are a harbinger of spring, and are eaten as tempura or as a condiment made by sautéing and folding into sweet miso. *Fuki* benefits from a salt rub (*itazuri*), and larger stems need to be de-stringed before using.

SERVES 4

½ teaspoon fine sea salt

3 thin stalks of butterbur (*fuki*, page 277)

125 ml (4 fl oz/½ cup) Kaketsuyu (page 127)

Sprinkle the salt on a large cutting board and, pressing down firmly, roll the *fuki* to break down the fibers. Quarter crosswise and drop into a medium pot of boiling water. Immediately scoop out with a wire-mesh strainer and rinse under cold running water. Cut the *fuki* lengthwise into long fine slabs, and crosswise into 3 cm (1¼ in) pieces. Slide into a medium frying pan with the kaketsuyu and cook over medium heat, stirring to evenly distribute the kaketsuyu, for about 3 minutes until the liquids have evaporated and the *fuki* has softened.

Mizu Nasu Dashi Hitashi, Myoga, Okura, Furi Goma

EGGPLANT IN DASHI WITH OKRA, MYOGA AND SESAME

Eating raw eggplant (aubergine) seems counter-intuitive, but salt-massaging takes the raw edge off and 'cooks' it ever so imperceptibly. Typically, finely sliced rounds of Japanese eggplant are salt-massaged until wilted, then soaked in ice water with aromatics to perk up and stay vibrant. Here, thin eggplants are quartered, salt-massaged and steeped in dashi. This is a very spare, light dish, which is perfect for a summer evening.

SERVES 4

4 thin Japanese eggplants (aubergines), weighing about 200 g (7 oz) in total

½ teaspoon fine sea salt

250 ml (8½ fl oz/1 cup) Happo Dashi – Variation 2 (page 126)

3 small okra, cut into 5 mm (¼ in) rounds

2 small *myoga* (page 18)

2 teaspoons gold sesame seeds, slightly warmed

Halve the eggplants lengthwise, and cut those halves again to make long quarter pieces. The pieces should not be more than 1 cm (½ in) at their widest, so if need be, cut the pieces lengthwise again and trim off a bit of their spongy centers. Massage gently with the salt in a medium mixing bowl, taking care not to break their shape. Leave for 10 minutes to macerate. Rinse in cold water and pat dry. Stack attractively in deep-sided salad plates or shallow soup bowls. Ladle 125 ml (4 fl oz/½ cup) happo dashi over the eggplant stacks.

Place the okra in a small saucepan with the remaining dashi and bring to a simmer. Remove from the heat and cool to room temperature. Drain and discard the dashi.

Cut the *myoga* in half lengthwise, then place cut side down and slice thinly, lengthwise.

Dollop a small mound each of okra and *myoga* side by side in the middle of each stack of eggplant. Sprinkle with the sesame seeds and serve.

Hotaru Ika Sumiso

FIREFLY SQUID WITH SWEET VINEGAR MISO

Seafood from the Sea of Japan is soft and succulent, and beautifully enhanced by sumiso (sweet vinegar miso). The coastal area of Toyama prefecture, due east of the bottom of the Noto Peninsula, is famous for firefly squid, a small squid that has the ability to light up like a firefly. The aromatic green garnish here is the leaves of barely sprouted soybean plants from the field. These could be hard to source, so any cress or peppery green such as mizuna would make a fine substitute.

SERVES 4

16 small firefly squid

small handful of very young soybean leaves, or cress or mizuna, roughly chopped

2 tablespoons Sumiso (page 128)

Pinch off the outside eyes from the squid and the beak located in the center of the tentacles. Pull out the thin plastic-like gladius from the bodies. Drop the whole squid in a sieve and rinse under cold running water. Shake off and slide into a medium mixing bowl. Pour boiling water over to just cover. Drain immediately and plunge into a bowl of ice water to shock. Once cool to the touch, drain and blot dry in a clean dish towel, and chill for at least 2 hours in the fridge.

Serve in small individual saucers or in 1 or 2 shallow soup bowls for the table. Make an attractive pile of the firefly squid on the left side of the saucer or bowl, tentacles facing towards the edge, and a pile of aromatic leaves alongside, to the right of the squid. Spoon the sumiso next to the squid and serve.

DASHI-MAKI TAMAGO

Do not be deterred by the intimidating reputation this omelette has for taking years of practice to perfect. All true – but with good ingredients, you should still end up with an absolutely delicious result. Traditionally, *dashi-maki tamago* is made in a rectangular tin-lined copper pan (*tamagoyaki nabe*). But do not be too proud to use the non-stick version until you are proficient enough to graduate to a true *tamagoyaki* pan. Being a bit generous with the oil also aids the cooking process when using the copper pan.

SERVES 4

6 fresh eggs, at room temperature

180 ml (6 fl oz) Kaketsuyu (page 127)

2 tablespoons refined light brown Japanese sugar (*sanonto*, page 14)

1 tablespoon unroasted sesame oil

2 tablespoons grated daikon

1 teaspoon shoyu (optional)

Crack the eggs into a small mixing bowl and stir with a pair of cooking chopsticks (*saibashi*, page 276), 'cutting' the eggs using back-and-forth movements as opposed to stirring in a circular fashion.

Stir the kaketsuyu into the sugar in a medium bowl and add the eggs, continuing to use the 'cutting' style to incorporate. Pour into a pitcher or jug for ease of pouring.

Place the oil in a small bowl next to the stove. Fold up 1 sheet of spongy paper towel to make a 3 cm (1¼ in) thick square for dabbing the oil. Heat a rectangular Japanese omelette pan over medium–high. Wipe the pan with the oil. Give the eggs a quick mix, and slurp a thin layer into the pan, tipping the pan so that the egg covers the whole surface. When half set and still a bit wet on top, roll the egg towards you gingerly, nudging it with your chopsticks along the bottom of the pan. (You might need to do this off heat if you are not yet adept at getting this step accomplished swiftly.) Swab the pan with more oil and pour in another thin layer of egg, lifting the roll up so the mixture can seep under to the edge of the pan. When half set, roll the omelette away from you this time. Continue this process 1 or 2 more times, repeating the oil swab, thin layer of egg mixture, slight cook, and roll sequence to use up the egg mixture.

Tip the omelette out onto a cutting board and slice crosswise into 2–3 cm (approximately 1 in) pieces. Serve on small individual saucers or a rectangular ceramic plate for the table. Mound the grated daikon next to the omelette and drizzle it with a little shoyu if desired. Serve hot if possible, but still good at room temperature.

Ama-togarashi Kurogoma-yaki, Shoyu-Katsuo-soe

SWEET PEPPERS GRILLED WITH BLACK SESAME AND MISO

Manganji peppers are an elongated sweet green pepper (capsicum) native to Kyoto, but appear in the markets in our area northwest of Tokyo as well. Substitute Japanese green peppers (*piman*, page 278), but not thick-walled western bell peppers. Mild poblano chilies are the best possible alternative if Japanese green peppers are unavailable, but beware that some might be quite spicy.

SERVES 4

1 teaspoon black sesame seeds, warmed

2 teaspoons Tama Miso (page 127)

4 Kyoto-style green peppers (*manganji*, page 278) or small Japanese green peppers (*piman*, page 278)

2 tablespoons Okaka (page 129)

Preheat the broiler (grill). Mix the sesame seeds into the tama miso and spread on 1 side of each pepper. Arrange on an oven pan with the miso facing up, and place under the broiler 10 cm (4 in) from the heat. Cook until the miso is bubbling and slightly charred.

Set 1 pepper on each of 4 small plates, and pinch a small mound of the okaka next to the peppers. Serve hot if possible, or at room temperature.

Shiro Nasu no
Tai Miso Yaki

WHITE EGGPLANT GRILLED WITH SEA BREAM MISO

Miso treatments complement fried eggplant (aubergine), but are often fairly sweet. Here the miso sauce has a more savory profile, and the addition of sea bream gives it a depth of flavor that goes well with the creamy eggplant. Since Japanese white eggplant might be difficult to find, substitute with any long, thin white or purple Asian eggplant.

SERVES 4

3 tablespoons white (*shiro*) miso

7 tablespoons kome koji miso – or half white (*shiro*) miso and half brown rice (*genmai*) miso or barley (*mugi*) miso

1 teaspoon refined light brown Japanese sugar (*sanonto*, page 14)

250 ml (8½ fl oz/1 cup) Shiro Dashi (page 126)

2 tablespoons mirin

100 g (3½ oz) skinless sea bream fillet, sliced sashimi-style

4 small Japanese white eggplants (aubergines), weighing about 400 g (14 oz) in total

neutral oil such as canola, safflower or peanut, for deep-frying

Stir the misos together in a small saucepan with the sugar. Add the dashi and mirin slowly, stirring to a smooth paste. Bring to an almost boil over medium heat, adjust to a simmer and cook for 30 minutes, stirring occasionally, or until thickened and reduced by 30%.

Place the sea bream in a small mixing bowl and pour boiling water over to cover. Drain immediately and plunge into an ice bath to cool. Drain and slide the fish into the miso mixture. Simmer for 10 more minutes, until the fish has broken apart and become incorporated into the miso sauce.

Trim and peel the eggplants, and slice in alternating diagonal cuts giving rough triangular chunks (*rangiri*, page 276), about 1.5 cm (½ in) thick.

Heat 10 cm (4 in) of oil in a heavy medium saucepan over medium–high heat. Once hot but not smoking, deep-fry the eggplant pieces in batches for about 2–3 minutes, until golden brown. Drain on paper towels.

Preheat the oven to 200°C (400°F). Mound the eggplant on 2 or 4 ovenproof earthenware plates. Spoon the sea bream miso into the middle, so that it drips down and covers about 50% of the eggplant. Bake for 15 minutes in the center of the oven.

Serve burning hot as an appetizer, or with a bowl of rice on the side for a light meal.

Kisetsu no Yasai no Zeri-yose Shiro Doressingu

GELÉE SALAD WITH BROCCOLI AND CAULIFLOWER

No visit to Soba Ra is complete without ordering a signature salad. Each time the salad is a delightful surprise. This version features pieces of vegetable, strawberry and persimmon suspended in a dashi gelée (jelly). Kanji Nakatani made a similar version at Chez Panisse in September 2018 using windfall fruit and field vegetables from Bob Cannard's Sobre Vista farm.

MAKES ONE 20 CM (8 IN) SQUARE GELÉE

50 g (1¾ oz) broccoli florets

50 g (1¾ oz) cauliflower florets

50 g (1¾ oz) watermelon radish, scrubbed

3–4 turnip greens, cut into 3 cm (1¼ in) pieces

50 g (1¾ oz) peeled firm non-astringent (fuyu) persimmon, cut into 1 cm (½ in) pieces

50 g (1¾ oz) strawberries, cut into 1 cm (½ in) pieces

700 ml (23½ fl oz) Happo Dashi (page 126)

1 teaspoon fine sea salt

1½ tablespoons powdered gelatin

Mayonnaise Dressing

1 medium egg yolk, at room temperature

½ teaspoon rice vinegar

200 ml (7 fl oz) canola, safflower or peanut oil

1 tablespoon finely grated onion

1 garlic clove, squeezed through a garlic press

1 tablespoon finely ground gold sesame seeds

1 teaspoon shoyu

Bring a medium pot three-quarters full of water to a boil over high heat. Cook the broccoli for 5 minutes, scoop out with a wire-mesh strainer, and refresh under cold running water. Set aside. Do the same with the cauliflower. Drop the watermelon radish into a strainer and dip in and out of the boiling water.

Dip the turnip greens in and out of the boiling water. Refresh under cold water and squeeze well. Roughly chop the turnip greens and squeeze again.

Cut the cauliflower, broccoli and watermelon radish into 1 cm (½ in) cubes, and squeeze each gently.

Strew the vegetables, persimmon and strawberry pieces attractively across the bottom of a 20 cm (8 in) square pan.

Heat the happo dashi with the salt over medium–low until dissolved. Add a tablespoon of water into the gelatin in a small bowl, and immediately stir the mixture into the warm dashi. Once well mixed, pour over the fruit and vegetables in the pan. Cool to room temperature, then cover with plastic wrap and chill overnight.

To make the mayonnaise dressing, whisk the egg yolk with the vinegar in a medium bowl. Slowly add the oil in a thin stream, whisking constantly, until the mixture starts to emulsify. Keep adding the oil until it has all been incorporated. Stir in the onion, garlic, sesame and shoyu. Chill for at least 2 hours.

Cut the gelée into squares and place on small plates. Nap a corner of each square with the dressing, allowing some to flow onto the plate.

Gyokai no Sarada

FISH GELÉE SALAD WITH FIG AND NASHI

SERVES 4

Kochi Nikogori

400 g (14 oz) collar and center bone from a flathead (*kochi*)

700 ml (23½ fl oz) Konbu Dashi (page 126)

½ teaspoon fine sea salt

2 tablespoons fine white Japanese sugar (*johakuto*, page 14)

½ tablespoon powdered gelatin

4 small okra, halved lengthwise

25 g (1 oz) fish skin

50 g (1¾ oz) squid flesh, scored in a fine crosshatch

50 g (1¾ oz) razorshell clam meat, prepared kobujime style (page 78)

50 g (1¾ oz) sea bass fillet, prepared kobujime style (page 78)

12 delicate inner romaine (cos) lettuce leaves

8 wedges of nashi (Asian) pear cut 1 cm (½ in) thick

1 large fig, peeled, quartered lengthwise and halved crosswise

12 blueberries

2 tablespoons Nihaizu (page 128)

Summer brings richness to the plate, both in the fish, which are acquiring fat for the winter, and in terms of the range of fruit. In this perfect nexus of the seasons, early summer blueberries and nashi (Asian) pear meet the late-summer figs. And the fruit juxtaposes nicely with the natural fish gelée (*nikogori*), here aided by gelatin to encourage setting. *Nikogori* can also be cut into cubes to use as part of a *zensai* plate.

Kobujime is a spectacularly easy yet spectacularly lovely method to firm up fish flesh, involving nothing more than a light sprinkling of flaky salt and wrapping the fish with a layer of konbu for four hours. Feel free to substitute plain sashimi fish for the kobujime, or other fruits and vegetables, following Kanji Nakatani's method as a rough guide for building a gorgeous seafood salad.

To make the *nikogori*, rinse the flathead collar and center bone and drop into a medium pot. Cover with cold water, bring to a boil, and drain. Whack with a heavy fish knife into 5 cm (2 in) pieces and remove all bones, but keep the flesh, skin and any cartilage (rubbery soft tissue). Chop the flesh, skin and cartilage finely, and return to the clean pot.

Stir the konbu dashi, salt and sugar into the chopped fish. Bring to a simmer over medium–high heat, and cook briskly for 3–5 minutes. Remove from the heat. Dissolve the gelatin with a tablespoon of water and stir into the dashi and fish. Pour the contents immediately into a 20 cm (8 in) square pan and cool to room temperature. Chill for at least 3 hours.

Bring a medium saucepan three-quarters full of water to a boil, and blanch the okra halves for 30 seconds. Drain.

Put the fish skin in a small bowl and douse with boiling water. Drain immediately and plunge into ice water. Pat dry in a clean dish towel and cut into fine strips. Do the same with the squid.

Cut the razorshell clam crosswise into fine slices and the sea bass at a diagonal into 6 mm (¼ in) thick slices.

Line 4 chilled ceramic salad plates with 3 lettuce leaves each, positioning the stems in the center and fanning out the leaves attractively. Spoon a heaping tablespoon of *nikogori* onto the stems. Nestle 2 slices each of clam and sea bass next to the *nikogori* in 2 spots. Artfully place the squid strips and fish skin as well. Add 2 slices of nashi to each plate, a few pieces of fig and 3 blueberries. Drizzle with the nibaizu and serve immediately.

Kaki to Hayato Uri no Sunomono

VINEGARED PERSIMMON AND CHAYOTE WITH SALMON ROE

SERVES 4

Cured Salmon Roe Sac (*Sujiko*)

1 salmon roe sac, weighing about 200 g (7 oz)

2 teaspoons fine sea salt

60 ml (2 fl oz/¼ cup) Kaeshi (page 127)

60 ml (2 fl oz/¼ cup) Sanbaizu (page 128)

½ teaspoon fine white Japanese sugar (*johakuto*, page 14)

4 radishes with 1 cm (½ in) stem attached, halved lengthwise

¼ teaspoon fine sea salt

300 ml (10 fl oz) Happo Dashi (page 126)

1 handful of leaves from small brussels sprouts

1 large red mizuna leaf, cut into 2 cm (¾ in) pieces

100 g (3½ oz) fillet of flathead (*kochi*) with skin

200 ml (7 fl oz) Cabbage and Komatsuna Gelée (page 129)

100 g (3½ oz) peeled chayote (choko), finely sliced

100 g (3½ oz) peeled firm non-astringent (fuyu) persimmon, finely sliced

1 tablespoon finely slivered yuzu (or Meyer lemon) zest

Late autumn might be my favorite season: if we are lucky, a few hardy summer vegetables still appear from the field, persimmons finally make their appearance, and chayote (choko) is at its peak. Autumn fish is revered in Japan for being in optimal condition. Female fish yield roe sacs bursting with plump eggs, which are paired here with early winter vegetables crisp from the cold ground or air, and there is a glorious feel to the food.

Make the cured salmon roe 2–3 days in advance. Place the roe sac in a resealable freezer bag with the salt. Leave for 1–2 days in the refrigerator. Pry out a small egg or two and taste: it should be a bit salty. Remove the roe sac from the bag and wrap in spongy paper towels to blot off moisture for 30 minutes. Place in a clean resealable freezer bag with the kaeshi and leave to soak for 1 day in the refrigerator. Before serving, cut the cured roe sac crosswise into 2 cm (¾ in) slices (leftovers can be served in another seafood salad or on a sashimi plate).

Bring the sanbaizu and sugar to a simmer in a small saucepan to dissolve the sugar. Leave to cool to room temperature.

Massage the radishes with the salt. Leave to sit for 10 minutes before blotting off excess salt and liquid.

Bring the happo dashi to a boil over high heat. Drop the brussels sprout leaves into a sieve, dip into the dashi for 30 seconds, then shake off and leave to cool. Drop the red mizuna into the sieve and dip in and out of the dashi. Leave to cool.

Place the flathead in a medium bowl and pour over boiling water to cover. Drain immediately and plunge into ice water. Pat dry and cut diagonally into sashimi slices.

Mound the cabbage and komatsuna gelée into the center of 4 chilled salad plates. Thinking about a balance of color, curl several slices of flathead together and rest against the gelée. Set a piece of cured salmon roe sac in an opposite area on the plate and start adding the other ingredients. Stand some slices of chayote against the roe, and the persimmon against the flathead. Poke in some mizuna, brussels sprout leaves and a couple of radish halves. Drizzle with 1 teaspoon of the sweetened sanbaizu, and lay several yuzu slivers across the top. Serve immediately as a light lunch.

Nasu to Kabocha Tenpura

EGGPLANT AND KABOCHA TEMPURA

Kanji Nakatani uses one egg per kilogram (2 lb 3 oz) of flour for his tempura batter, but recommends skipping the egg for small batches. Excellent tempura relies on good-tasting flour, high-quality oil, seasonal vegetables and timing. Be ready to serve and eat quickly.

SERVES 4

125 g (4½ oz) lightly peeled kabocha (pumpkin)

2 small Japanese eggplants (aubergines), weighing about 100 g (3½ oz) in total

neutral oil such as canola, safflower or peanut, for deep-frying

1 quantity of freshly made Tempura Batter (page 127)

8 medium green shiso leaves

1 teaspoon flaky sea salt, for serving

Cut the kabocha into wedges not wider than 1 cm (½ in) at their thickest part. The pieces should not be longer than 5–6 cm (2–2½ in). Halve the eggplants lengthwise leaving the calyx attached, and place the pieces cut-side down on the cutting board. Cut all the way through the eggplant at 5 mm (¼ in) intervals from right below the calyx to the base so that the eggplant flesh can fan out a bit.

Heat about 10 cm (4 in) of oil in a heavy medium saucepan over medium–high heat. Once hot but not smoking, test the temperature by adding a drop of batter into the oil. If it sinks to the bottom, the oil is not hot enough. If it bounces up to the surface as a tiny ball, the temperature is perfect. If the ball becomes quickly browned, the oil is too hot.

Drop the kabocha pieces in the tempura batter. Pick up one or two at a time with a pair of chopsticks, shake off excess batter and slide into the oil. Continue until all the kabocha is in the oil. Fry for about 2–3 minutes, until golden brown. Drain on paper towels. Fry the eggplant the same way, taking care not to allow batter to seep inside the fanned portion. Dip and fry the shiso leaves for only 20 seconds.

Serve on a communal plate or individual plates with the flaky salt for dipping.

Kaki, Ninjin-ha, Hayato Uri Tenpura

PERSIMMON, CARROT FROND AND CHAYOTE TEMPURA

Chayote (*hayato uri*) is a soft green gourd that becomes juicy when fried or cooked as gratin. The varied textures and flavors of firm persimmon, crunchy carrot frond and juicy chayote make an innovative selection for autumn tempura.

SERVES 4

125 g (4½ oz) peeled chayote (choko) – approximately ½ chayote

1 firm non-astringent persimmon (such as fuyu), peeled

neutral oil such as canola, safflower or peanut, for deep-frying

1 quantity of freshly made Tempura Batter (page 127)

8 sprigs of soft carrot fronds

1 teaspoon flaky sea salt, for serving

Place the chayote, cut-side down, on a chopping board and cut into 5 mm (¼ in) slices. Cut the persimmon into 8 small rounded wedges.

Heat about 10 cm (4 in) of oil in a heavy medium saucepan over medium–high heat, until hot but not smoking. To test the temperature, add a drop of batter into the oil: if it bounces up to the surface as a tiny ball, the temperature is perfect. (If it sinks to the bottom, the oil is not hot enough, and if the ball browns too quickly, the oil is too hot.)

Dip the chayote pieces in the tempura batter, shake off the excess, and fry for about 2–3 minutes until lightly golden. Drain on paper towels. Dip and fry the persimmon pieces for about 1 minute, just until the batter crisps. Dip and fry the carrot fronds for 15 seconds.

Serve on a complementary ceramic plate with a mound of flaky salt.

Sakura Ebi no Kakiage

DRIED SHRIMP AND GREEN NORI FRITTERS

Kakiage is essentially a version of tempura where finely chopped ingredients – seafood such as shrimp (prawns) or scallops; vegetables such as eggplant (aubergine), carrot or potato; and *negi* (page 19) and aromatic greens – are folded into the batter. The trick is to cook the fritters until they are crispy on the outside with only a touch of a soft center. Too much crisp or too much spongy center and the *kakiage* will disappoint. If possible, source *sakura ebi* since they are far and above superior to other (cheaper) ones available.

SERVES 4

neutral oil such as canola, safflower or peanut, for deep-frying

30 g (1 oz) small dried shrimp (*sakura ebi*, page 16)

1 teaspoon green nori powder (*aonori*)

1 quantity of freshly made Tempura Batter (page 127)

¼ teaspoon flaky sea salt, for serving

Heat about 10 cm (4 in) of oil in a heavy medium saucepan over low heat.

Fold the *sakura ebi* and *aonori* into the tempura batter. Adjust the heat beneath the pan to medium–high and once hot but not smoking, drop 4 dollops of the batter at a time into the side of the oil. Fry for 4–5 minutes, until golden brown (keep pushing the *kakiage* down into the oil, and poking them with a pair of cooking chopsticks – *saibashi*, page 276 – to help cook the centers). Drain on paper towels and serve hot with the flaky salt.

Kinmedai no Nitsuke

SHOYU-SIMMERED RED SNAPPER

Whole-fish presentation is stunning, and if using a red snapper (or a red-skinned bream), the vibrant colors shine through the shoyu-flavored juices, so it is exceptionally eye-catching. Kanji Nakatani prepares the fish with elegance and a perfect balance of seasonings. A spoon is essential for capturing the juices when serving.

SERVES 4 GENEROUSLY

1 fresh red snapper weighing about 1 kg (2 lb 3 oz)

600 ml (20½ fl oz) Kaketsuyu (page 127)

60 ml (2 fl oz/¼ cup) sake

1 tablespoon refined light brown Japanese sugar (*sanonto*, page 14)

6 small shiitake

2 cm (¾ in) ginger, finely sliced, plus 1 tablespoon finely slivered ginger for serving

100 g (3½ oz) komatsuna (or spinach) leaves, blanched, refreshed, squeezed and cut crosswise into 2 cm (¾ in) pieces

Set the snapper in the kitchen sink and scrape off the scales using the back of a knife, a fish scaler or a steel scrubby (though not steel wool). Slice open the belly, making a shallow cut (so not to puncture the intestines) from the small opening near the back lower fin up to the gill area. Scoop out the innards and discard. Run cold water inside the cavity and brush out any lingering red tendrils with a toothbrush. Pat dry with spongy paper towels. Score the fish on both sides by cutting a shallow crosshatch pattern about 3 cm (1¼ in) apart with a sharp knife.

Mix the kaketsuyu, sake and sugar together in an oval pan large enough to hold the snapper. Drop in the shiitake and sliced ginger and bring to a boil over high heat. The broth should develop a creamy layer on its surface as it begins to boil. Gently slide the whole fish into the bubbling broth (it should almost come to the top of the fish), and cook uncovered for about 10 minutes, or until the broth has reduced by two-thirds and the flesh of the fish is white.

Carefully lift the whole fish from the pan to a large plate or platter by sliding 2 round skimming implements under each end of the fish. Scoop out the shiitake and arrange artfully on the plate. Spoon over the syrupy broth and serve with a mound each of ginger threads and komatsuna (or spinach).

Tairagai to Tougan no Taki Awase, Furi Yuzu

JAPANESE PEN SHELL WITH SIMMERED WINTER MELON

Silky winter melon is often simmered and served with its juices lightly thickened with potato starch. Here the melon is simmered in dashi so remains naturally juicy, and its texture juxtaposes nicely against the chewy shell meat. *Tairagai* are similar to scallops in appearance, but have a totally different texture and shell. The shell is large, dark and fan-shaped. Only the inner round meat is used – the other connected parts are discarded. Substitute other locally available species of pen shell.

SERVES 4

100 g (3½ oz) peeled and seeded winter melon, cut into 3 cm (1¼ in) cubes

1 Japanese pen shell (*tairagai*), halved crosswise

400 ml (13½ fl oz) Shiro Dashi (page 126)

½ teaspoon fine sea salt

1 teaspoon fine white Japanese sugar (*johakuto*, page 14)

1 small green yuzu (or key lime)

Bring a medium saucepan three-quarters full of water to a boil over high heat. Drop in the winter melon and drain immediately. This step will remove bitterness (*aku nuki*).

Return the winter melon to the empty saucepan with the *tairagai*. Add the dashi, salt and sugar, and bring to a simmer over medium heat. Adjust to a gentle simmer and cook for 2–3 minutes, until the *tairagai* has firmed a bit and is half cooked. Remove the *tairagai*, but continue simmering the winter melon slowly for about 20 minutes more, until meltingly soft. Cool to room temperature in the dashi, before chilling for at least 2 hours. Place the *tairagai* in the refrigerator as well, but slice it into thin cross-sections before serving.

Spoon 3 cubes of winter melon into each of 4 small dishes. Prop 2 slices of *tairagai* next to the winter melon, and grate a small amount of yuzu zest over the top with a microplane. Serve as a bite before dinner with a cold glass of elegantly light sake.

Dashi Tamago

SLOW-COOKED EGGS IN DASHI

Gorgeous in its simplicity, this dish elicits a warm smile whenever it is served.

SERVES 4

4 medium farm eggs, at room temperature

100 ml (3½ fl oz) Kaketsuyu (page 127)

100 ml (3½ fl oz) Shiro Dashi (page 126)

½ teaspoon fine sea salt

1 teaspoon mirin, or to taste

a few pinches of finely slivered yuzu (or Meyer lemon) zest

Bring a medium saucepan of water to a boil over high heat. Adjust to low and gently lower the whole eggs (still in their shells) into the water. Use a candy thermometer to monitor the temperature, and cook the eggs slowly at 60°C (140°F) for 30 minutes. Scoop out and plunge into a medium mixing bowl of ice water. Once completely cooled, break each egg into a small ceramic bowl, taking great care not to break the yolk.

Bring the kaketsuyu, shiro dashi, salt and mirin to a boil over high heat. Pour over the eggs in each bowl, pinch in a few threads of yuzu zest, and serve immediately as an appetizer with a glass of gently warmed delicate sake.

Ebodai Shioyaki
Shira-ae

SALT-GRILLED BUTTERFISH WITH SMASHED TOFU

Salt-grilling could be the most foolproof method to cook fish. Also, the salty, crusty skin is eminently tasty. A dollop of smashed tofu (*shira-ae*) on the side serves to mitigate the salt and give balance to the dish.

SERVES 4

Shira-ae

100 g (3½ oz) *momendofu* (page 279) or Japanese-style soft block tofu

⅛ teaspoon fine sea salt

¼ teaspoon fine white Japanese sugar (*johakuto*, page 14)

2 cm (¾ in) piece of medium carrot, scrubbed and julienned

2 cm (¾ in) piece of burdock (*gobo*, page 277), scrubbed and julienned

200 ml (7 fl oz) Konbu Dashi (page 126)

2 small butterfish, weighing about 125 g (4½ oz) each

1 teaspoon flaky sea salt

2 × 5 mm (¼ in) squares of yuzu zest (or Meyer lemon)

Place the tofu in a fine sieve set over a bowl and weight with a small saucepan for 10 minutes. Drop the drained tofu, salt and sugar into a Japanese grinding bowl (*suribachi*, page 275) and grind with the wooden pestle (*surikogi*, page 275) to form a smooth paste.

Put the carrot and burdock in a small saucepan, add the konbu dashi and bring to a simmer over medium–low heat. Cook gently for 5–7 minutes, until soft. Cool to room temperature in the dashi. Drain and fold into the smashed tofu.

Preheat the broiler (grill). Slice open the belly of the fish and pull out the guts. Cut out the gills, scale the fish lightly, and rinse and pat dry. Make 5 mm (¼ in) deep crosshatch slits through the skin into the flesh on both sides. Rub with the salt.

Grill the fish 10 cm (4 in) from the top of the broiler for 5 minutes on each side, until the inside flesh is snowy white and the skin is crispy golden brown in spots.

Place each fish horizontally on a rustic ceramic plate and add a mound of *shira-ae* below the back third of the fish. Set a piece of yuzu zest on the *shira-ae* and serve as a communal course.

Tonyu Guratan Ni Shu

SOY MILK GRATIN TWO WAYS

These two gratins celebrate autumn with foraged *hon shimeji* mushrooms from the local hills surrounding Soba Ra. Oysters and crab also make appearances in the restaurant's signature gratins, as does eggplant (aubergine), broccoli and cauliflower. And blanched, refreshed, squeezed, chopped spinach or komatsuna would provide a nice balance to the rich soy bechamel.

SERVES 4

50 g (1¾ oz) enoki mushrooms, bottoms cut off

100 g (3½ oz) *hon shimeji* mushrooms (page 279), broken apart at the bottom

3 peeled shrimp (prawns) weighing about 50 g (1¾ oz) in total, cut into 1.5 cm (½ in) pieces

2 large scallops weighing about 50 g (1¾ oz) in total, cut into sixths

90 ml (3 fl oz) unroasted sesame oil

30 g (1 oz) unbleached all-purpose (plain) flour

500 ml (17 fl oz/2 cups) best-quality soy milk

pinch of fine sea salt

50 ml (1¾ fl oz) Mori Tsuyu (page 127)

Halve the enoki and shimeji mushrooms crosswise. Mix them across the bottom of 2 small ceramic gratin dishes measuring about 15 cm (6 in) wide. Scatter the shrimp pieces into one dish, and the scallops into the other.

Preheat the oven to 200°C (400°F). Heat the oil over medium–high heat in a medium frying pan. Add the flour and cook for about 2–3 minutes, stirring constantly, until paste-like and slightly colored. Adjust the temperature to low and slowly stir in the soy milk, stirring vigorously so the mixture doesn't develop lumps. Once all the soy milk has been incorporated and the sauce is smooth, add the salt and mori tsuyu and continue stirring until creamy but still spoonable and not gluey.

Scrape the sauce over the gratin ingredients, and bake in the middle of the oven for 15 minutes, until bubbling and nicely browned.

Matsutake Dobin Mushi-sutairu

MATSUTAKE SOUP

Matsutake have become quite dear over the years, so soup is a lovely way to stretch these elusive mushrooms with their hauntingly musky aroma. If you do not have the little *dobin mushi* pots, you will need to use your ingenuity to rig up a suitable alternative.

SERVES 4

2 small *matsutake*, brushed clean, bases trimmed, quartered lengthwise

50 g (1¾ oz) skinless, boneless snapper or bream fillet, cut into 1 cm (½ in) cubes

4 very small peeled fresh shrimp (*koebi*), cut in half crosswise

4 sprigs of *mitsuba*

200 ml (7 fl oz) Shiro Dashi (page 126)

⅛ teaspoon fine sea salt

2 teaspoons sake

2 *sudachi*, halved (or 1 key lime, quartered)

Bring the *matsutake*, fish, shrimp, *mitsuba*, dashi, salt and sake to a simmer in a small saucepan over high heat. When you can smell the heady aroma of *matsutake* wafting up to you, quickly distribute the ingredients between 4 *dobin mushi* pots, pour in the dashi and serve immediately with a *sudachi* half resting on top of each pot.

Sobagaki Jiru

SOBAGAKI IN DASHI

These buckwheat 'dumplings' are often served with a sweet red bean sauce, but I find the savory version much more appealing. It is said that the method to make *sobagaki* is akin to making polenta, because of the constant stirring, and the fact that the mixture hardens up soon after it is done. *Sobagaki* can also be served with a dab each of grated daikon, ginger and wasabi as a garnish with the blanched greens, instead of the turnip, *yuba* and yuzu.

SERVES 4

1 small turnip with 1 cm (½ in) stem attached, quartered

2 large komatsuna leaves with stems

200 ml (7 fl oz) Happo Dashi (page 126), at room temperature

4 × 3 cm (1¼ in) squares of konbu leftover from making dashi

200 g (7 oz) Japanese buckwheat flour (*sobako*, page 280)

2 cm (¾ in) piece of fresh *yuba* (page 280), cut crosswise into quarters

4 strips of yuzu zest (5 mm × 3 cm/¼ in × 1¼ in)

Bring a medium pot of water to a boil. Blanch the turnip pieces for 2 minutes. Scoop out with a wire-mesh strainer and refresh under cold water to cool. Blot dry. Hold the komatsuna stems into the boiling water for 30 seconds, then drop them into the water and cook for another 30 seconds. Strain out and refresh under cold running water. Align on a clean dish towel and roll them up tightly to absorb moisture. Cut into 3 cm (1¼ in) lengths and stack them together in 4 even piles for serving. Keep the pot water simmering.

Distribute the happo dashi between 4 small lacquer bowls. Tuck a piece of konbu down the side of each bowl.

To make the *sobagaki,* put the *sobako* in a small saucepan and dip the bottom of the pan inside the pot of simmering water. Stir with a bamboo rice paddle for about 2 or 3 minutes, to warm the flour. Gradually add 120 ml (4 fl oz) boiling water while stirring continuously to emulsify. Increase the pace and vigorously work the mixture by bringing the mass against one side of the pan, while also folding over continuously, until a thick, sticky mass. Do not let the mixture form a tight ball, it should still be viscous. This will only take about 1 or 2 minutes, so work fast, because otherwise the mixture will harden and become unmanageable.

Immediately dollop a gravy ladle–sized blob of *sobagaki* into each bowl. Nestle the *yuba*, turnip and komatsuna next to the *sobagaki*, drape the yuzu strips over the top, and serve as a first course or mid-meal cleansing dish.

Soba Zushi

SOBA SUSHI ROLLS

A genius way to use up leftover soba noodles, these alternative sushi rolls are maybe more delicious than the traditional rice ones. This recipe is a riff on the country sushi rolls that grandmas still make in Japan, but are less and less made at home because of all the simmered components that usually are included. Here the ingredients are kept at a minimum for ease of execution.

SERVES 4

Pickled Ginger

2 × 2 cm (¾ in) fat knobs of ginger, peeled and sliced into fine rectangular pieces

½ teaspoon fine sea salt

75 ml (2½ fl oz) brown rice vinegar

50 g (1¾ oz) refined light brown Japanese sugar (*sanonto*, page 14)

2 medium shiitake, stems discarded, caps sliced 5 mm (¼ in) thick

100 ml (3½ fl oz) Kaketsuyu (page 127)

1 teaspoon refined light brown Japanese sugar (*sanonto*, page 14)

100 g (3½ oz) flowering brassica (*nanohana*, page 278)

2 sheets of best quality nori

125 g (4½ oz/1 cup) cooked soba noodles

1 tablespoon Sushi Su (page 128)

½ quantity of Dashi-maki Tamago (page 207), cut into 1 cm (½ in) batonnets

100 g (3½ oz) fresh picked crabmeat

To make the pickled ginger, massage the ginger with the salt in a medium bowl. Scrape into a sieve with all the lingering salt crystals and leave for 30 minutes. Blot off excess salt and moisture with spongy paper towels and return to the bowl. Bring the vinegar and sugar to a boil in a small saucepan. Remove from the heat and stir to dissolve the sugar. Pour the hot vinegar over the ginger and place a weight on the surface to keep the ginger submerged. Allow to return to room temperature before using.

Drop the shiitake into a small saucepan with the kaketsuyu and sugar and bring to a gentle simmer over low heat. Cook for 5–6 minutes and allow to cool to room temperature in the liquid. Drain.

Blanch the *nanohana* in boiling water for 3 minutes. Scoop out with a wire-mesh strainer and refresh under cold running water. Squeeze out excess water and chop roughly.

Lay the nori out on 2 bamboo rolling mats (*makisu*, page 275) with the shiny sides down and the nori striations horizontal to you. Lay the soba noodles across the bottom half of each nori piece and sprinkle with the sushi su. Add a tight line of tamago in the middle of the soba. Follow that with a fine line each of crab, shiitake and *nanohana*, pushing them up against each other so there is no open space. Use the *makisu* to roll up tightly, dipping your finger in the pickled ginger vinegar to wet the top edge of the nori to seal. Press together firmly to compact with the *makisu*, but don't overdo it. Be gentle.

Moisten a sharp knife with the ginger vinegar and cut each roll into 6 rounds. Serve 3 per person on rustic salad plates with a small stack of the pickled ginger.

Tororo Jiru Soba

SOBA WITH MOUNTAIN YAM DIPPING SAUCE

Unfortunately, mountain yam, also known as Chinese yam, can be challenging to source outside of Japan. Conventional yams are not the same. Mountain yams have brown tufted skin with snowy white viscous flesh that grates up to a lovely, slimy mass. Take care when grating it, because contact with mountain yam causes an immediate red, itchy rash, so use gloves, or wash your hands and forearms thoroughly with warm water and soap directly after grating. The red itchiness will quickly subside.

The homemade soba can also be served with Mori Tsuyu (page 127), chopped scallions (spring onions) and a dab of freshly grated wasabi, or with the Duck Broth Soup (page 118).

SERVES 4

Mountain Yam Dipping Sauce

625 ml (21 fl oz/2½ cups) Mori Tsuyu (page 127)

½ cup grated mountain yam (*yama imo*, page 277)

Soba

200 g (7 oz) Japanese buckwheat flour (*sobako*, page 280)

50 g (1¾ oz/⅓ cup) unbleached all-purpose (plain) flour

75 g (2¾ oz/½ cup) *uchiko* flour (page 281) or potato starch, for dusting

green nori powder (*aonori*), for serving

To make the mountain yam sauce, slowly stir the mori tsuyu into the grated yam until emulsified. Chill until ready to serve.

To make the noodles, combine the *sobako* and all-purpose flour together in a large bowl using your fingers. Measure 47% water into a cup with a spout: for 250 g (9 oz) combined weight of flour, that means about 120 ml (4 fl oz) water.

Sprinkle 100 ml (3½ fl oz) of the water over the flours in the bowl, and scissor your fingers through the flour until the water has been absorbed and the mixture is crumbly. Press the dough together with both hands to form a rough ball and transfer it to a large, flat work surface. Knead the dough for about 5 minutes, until smooth and pliable. This will take some elbow grease because the dough will be stiff, but don't flag or lose heart. Depending on the weather and the flours, the dough might want a bit more moisture. If the dough feels dry or continues to have cracks, dip your fingertips in the remaining water and rub it around the dough. Continue kneading and adding water if needed, until the dough achieves the desired consistency.

Form the dough into a 1 cm (½ in) thick disc and sprinkle with a small amount of *uchiko* flour. Using a long, thin rolling pin or dowel, roll the dough back and forth from the center into a 1.5 mm (1⁄16 in) thick rectangle. Dust the dough and work surface generously with the *uchiko* flour and flip the dough to make sure it is covered in flour.

Fold the dough in half lengthwise, then in half again to form a long, thin, folded log. With a fine, sharp knife, cut into thin noodles 1.5 mm (1⁄16 in) wide. Dust the noodles with more of the *uchiko*, unraveling the coiled clumps into long strands, and making sure some of the flour gets between the strands to prevent them from sticking together. If you are not cooking right away, gently gather handfuls of noodles and align straight in a wooden or plastic container. Cover and refrigerate for up to 2 days.

Bring a large pot three-quarters full of water to a rolling boil over high heat. Prepare a large bowl of cold water in the sink, and a medium bowl of ice water.

Gather the soba noodles up gently in two hands and drop into the boiling water. As soon as the water returns to a boil, cook the noodles for 60–90 seconds, depending on thickness. Scoop out the noodles with a wire-mesh strainer, plunge into the bowl of cold water, and run more cold water into the bowl for several minutes to rinse and remove starch. Scoop the soba out of the water and dip in and out of the bowl of ice water to shock.

Shake off and serve on noodle baskets, alongside small individual bowls of mountain yam dipping sauce garnished with a pinch of *aonori*.

Kamojiru Udon

DUCK BROTH SOUP WITH UDON

Kamojiru udon could be my family's hands-down-favorite noodle dish at Soba Ro and Ra over these last couple of decades. Also excellent with soba noodles instead of udon, which Kanji Nakatani served to much acclaim at Chez Panisse several years ago. Using homemade noodles elevates this dish to the superior, but good-quality dried noodles will make this a quick weeknight supper when you are low on time. A dollop of finely grated daikon is also a nice garnish for this soup to add a bit of fresh heat.

SERVES 4

Udon

25 g (1 oz) fine sea salt

500 g (1 lb 2 oz/3⅓ cups) Japanese udon flour (*hakurikiko*, page 280), plus extra for dusting

Duck Broth Soup

¼ small burdock (*gobo*, page 277) weighing about 50 g (1¾ oz), scrubbed

2 thin *negi* or 4 fat scallions (spring onions)

2 large shiitake, stems discarded, caps sliced 5 mm (¼ in) thick

handful of enoki mushrooms, weighing about 50 g (1¾ oz)

handful of shimeji mushrooms, weighing about 50 g (1¾ oz)

100 g (3½ oz) duck breast with skin, sliced 5 mm (¼ in) thick

360 ml (12 fl oz) Kaketsuyu (page 127)

180 ml (6 fl oz) Mori Tsuyu (page 127)

2 teaspoons finely grated ginger, for serving

To make the udon, stir 250 ml (8½ fl oz/1 cup) water into the salt in a small bowl to dissolve. Measure the flour into a large mixing bowl. Sprinkle in the salt water, scissoring your fingers through the flour until the dough finally holds together into a cohesive mass. Knead in the bowl or on your workspace until smooth and pliable. Allow the dough to rest for 1 hour to relax the glutens.

If rolling the dough with a rolling machine (*seimenki*, page 275), feed the dough through the rollers in pieces the size of large handfuls, and keep folding the dough in thirds over itself as you narrow the roller gap little by little. You should end up with 3 mm (⅛ in) thick sheets of dough, about 60 cm (2 ft) long. Cut on the udon or linguine setting of the rolling machine, and cut crosswise with a pizza cutter to make noodles about 30 cm (1 ft) long. Flour each bunch of noodles as you cut them so they do not stick together.

If rolling the dough by hand, roll the dough out into a rough oblong shape on a flat surface using a long dowel, approximately 75 cm (30 in) in length and 3 cm (1½ in) in diameter. Roll from the center out, periodically rolling the dough around the dowel to keep it from sticking to the counter. Once the dough is 3 mm (⅛ in) thick, roll it around the dowel, slide the dowel out, and gently flatten the roll of dough. Cut crosswise into 3 mm (⅛ in) wide noodles with a broad-bladed, razor-sharp knife. Toss with flour.

To make the soup, hold the burdock in your non-dominant hand and shave off small pieces with a sharp knife, cutting away from your body, as if sharpening a pencil by hand (*sasagaki*, page 276).

Cut the white parts of the *negi* crosswise into 2 cm (¾ in) pieces, and those pieces lengthwise into fine slices (*tanzaku-giri*, page 276). Finely chop the green parts to make 2 teaspoons for the soup, and slice the rest crosswise for 2 tablespoons of fine rounds to be used as a garnish.

Drop the burdock, shiitake, enoki, shimeji, white *negi* slices, chopped *negi* greens and duck into a medium saucepan with the kaketsuyu and mori tsuyu. Bring to a simmer over medium heat, then adjust the heat and cook gently for 2–3 minutes, until the vegetables and mushrooms are soft.

Bring a large pot three-quarters full of water to a rolling boil over high heat. Prepare a large bowl of cold water in the sink, and a medium bowl of ice water.

Gently gather up half of the udon noodles in two hands and drop into the boiling water. As soon as the water returns to a boil, cook the noodles for 2–3 minutes, depending on their thickness. You should no longer taste the raw flour. Scoop out the noodles with a wire-mesh strainer, plunge into the bowl of cold water, and run more cold water into the bowl for several minutes to rinse and remove starch. Scoop the udon out of the water and dip in and out of the bowl of ice water to shock. Shake off and mound on individual noodle baskets or a large dinner plate. Cook the other half of the noodles in the same pot of water, but prepare a fresh bowl of cold water for rinsing.

Serve the udon alongside small bowls of hot duck broth soup. Give each person a small saucer with a tiny mound of fine *negi* rounds and grated ginger to be added as desired. Dip the noodles little by little into the soup, and slurp.

ICHIRO'S MALT WHISKY

Chichibu, Saitama Prefecture

No section on Saitama prefecture would be complete without mentioning one of our most intriguing areas rich in food and artisans: the Chichibu mountains. In 2014, the village of Higashi-Chichibu joined nearby Ogawa-machi – famous for being a center of organic farming and craft beer, tofu and other traditional foods such as eel (*unagi*) – on the UNESCO Intangible Cultural Heritage list for *hosokawa-shi*, their indigenous Japanese paper.

In the early years of our marriage, we visited Chichibu often for the legendary soba, and to poke around an eclectic antique shop connected to a small craft museum, though in the intervening years the visits have tapered off.

Doing some work for Prime Minister Abe's office put me in contact with Seiji Watanabe, aka 'John', a quirky young man who happened to be the Chinese expert of the office. Periodically, 'John' would call me up to ask if I could host a Chinese dissident or exiled journalist or famous filmmaker, in order to demonstrate that farming life did not have to be dirty and dreary, as is the commonly held opinion in China.

These 'tours' sometimes included Chichibu Distillery – makers of Ichiro's Malt, a cult whisky difficult to obtain even in Japan. More of a bourbon aficionado, I had become particularly taken with Ichiro's Malt & Grain Blended Whisky (which makes sense, as blended whiskies are apparently more easily quaffable). As one of their least expensive versions, this whisky sells for an affordable US$55 in Japan, but US$100 and upwards abroad.

But on a recent visit I was captured by Ichiro's Malt & Grain Limited Edition Japanese Blended Whisky, which, unfortunately for me, was awarded 'World's Best Blended Whisky Limited Release' at the 2018 World Whiskies Awards, and now goes for the equivalent of US$1165 in Japan.

Ichiro Akuto is the owner of Chichibu Distillery, operated by his company Venture Whisky, and distilling whisky is a centuries-long tradition in the Akuto family. The family distillery was located in the city of Hanyu on the northeastern edge of Saitama prefecture. Historically, the family had been in the alcohol-brewing business since the 1600s, but the Hanyu Distillery was built by Ichiro Akuto's grandfather, Isouji Akuto, in 1941 during World War II. In the 1980s, the distillery purchased two pot stills to produce a Scotch style of whisky, but sadly gave up making whisky in 2000 due to financial issues. And in 2004, the pot stills and distilling equipment at the Hanyu Distillery were dismantled and the stock was to be dumped.

Ichiro Akuto negotiated purchase of these 400 casks, thereby rescuing his grandfather's Hanyu stock, and stored them in Fukushima prefecture until 2008. After graduating from brewery studies at university, Ichiro Akuto worked for Suntory before eventually joining his family's company. He also spent time in Scotland honing his craft. Ichiro Akuto established Venture Whisky in 2004 and about three years later built the Chichibu Distillery, completed in 2008. His is the only new whisky distillery to open in Japan since the 1970s.

Like so many Japanese products, Japanese whisky (mainly from large companies) has become the darling of the food and drink world, but maybe Ichiro's Malt is the first one to truly deserve that intense recognition. As a 21st-generation brewer, Ichiro Akuto has inherited centuries of know-how, but also built this business up through his own dedication to the craft, and he has been receiving accolades and winning awards ever since the release of the very first Ichiro's Malt from his family-owned Hanyu Distillery.

If you are a whisky professional and want to visit the Chichibu Distillery, it is only possible one day a year: the day before the Chichibu Whisky Festival in February. There are six tours for twenty people, and those 120 tickets for 2018 were sold out in five minutes. Put in perspective, this means that the five or six hours I have had the privilege of spending at Chichibu Distillery should last me a lifetime. This thought leaves me with a feeling of awe for their kindness and generosity in opening their doors for me once again, when I returned to gather more information for this book.

As an advocate of local food traditions, I am afforded unusual access, but all of us can enjoy Ichiro's Malt in whatever version we can afford by purchasing a bottle. And realistically, this might be the only chance to get to know and understand the marvel of what Ichiro Akuto is creating in Chichibu. Tasting surely means getting to know the chef or artisan, and the auspicious thing about whisky is that it is transportable, thus much easier to access than a chef's food in rural Japan.

When asked what sets their brewery apart, one of the workers at the distillery laughed and replied, 'We love whisky!' Of course the answer is far more complicated, and certainly has to do with the care and individual attention that each batch receives. This is the very definition of craft distillation, and that is what makes Ichiro's Malt a world-class whisky.

When asked what sets their brewery apart, one of the workers at the distillery laughed and replied, 'We love whisky!'

The mash tuns hold 2400 liters, of which 400 kilograms is a golden ratio of 20% husk, 70% grits and 10% flour, plus 1600 liters of hot water. In 2017, the distillery produced 60,000 liters of pure spirits. Although the majority of distilleries use stainless washback tanks, some employ Douglas fir (Oregon pine) washbacks during the critical few days of lactic fermentation. At Chichibu, the fermentation takes place over four days in Japanese oak (*mizunara*).

The company has their own cooperage for building these barrels slowly – it takes about one week for two coopers to create a few casks, but the coopers have other duties as well, so the production is not constant. To date, the Chichibu Distillery has eight washback tanks crafted from Hokkaido *mizunara*, and about 75 maturation casks from local Chichibu *mizunara*.

Distillation happens twice in two different tanks: after the first distillation, the alcohol is at 20%, with the batch made up of the head (too strong), the heart (which will be used for maturation), and the tail (too weak). The heart represents about 70% of the batch, about 200 liters. The head and tail will be transferred to a second tank, where they will go through a second distillation.

The Chichibu Distillery stores about 1200 casks of whisky for aging, but there are 4800 other casks stored off-site, for a total of 6000 casks by the end of 2018. The distillery uses many kinds of wooden casks, with about 50% bourbon barrels.

Due to intense popularity, production has had to increase exponentially in recent years, yet the attention to detail and dedication to the craft is still abundantly apparent in each bottle.

Soba Yokan Kuromitsu

BUCKWHEAT SQUARES WITH BLACK SUGAR SYRUP

Historically, Japanese did not serve dessert as we know it at the end of a formal meal, although small sweets and fruit became incorporated into the classic kaiseki meal in the early 19th century. Little squares set with gelatin, agar or kudzu are lovely and useful concoctions to provide a light, sweet bite at the end of a meal. Be careful not to buy the brown kudzu root supplements at health food stores. Look for the white variety available from macrobiotic or Japanese sources.

MAKES 8 SMALL SQUARES

40 g (1½ oz) Japanese buckwheat flour (*sobako*, page 280)

35 g (1¼ oz) well crushed kudzu powder (*kuzuko*, page 280)

200 g (7 oz) fine white Japanese sugar (*johakuto*, page 14)

4 tablespoons Japanese black sugar (*kurosato*, page 15), well crushed

4 tablespoons toasted soybean flour (*kinako*), for coating

Whisk the buckwheat flour, kudzu and white sugar together in a heavy medium pot and slowly add in 900 ml (30½ fl oz) water, while stirring continuously over medium heat for about 15 minutes to form a thick paste. At this point you might think the viscous paste is done, as it will be quite stiff and difficult to stir. However, keep cooking for 5 minutes more.

Scrape into a 10 × 20 cm (4 × 8 in) loaf pan and allow to cool to room temperature. Chill for at least 2 hours.

Stir 2 tablespoons water into the *kurosato* in a small saucepan and bring to a gentle simmer over medium heat, stirring constantly for about 1 minute to dissolve the sugar and thicken the mixture to a loose syrup. This syrup is called *kuromitsu*. Pool a teaspoonful of *kuromitsu* on individual saucers or small square ceramic plates.

Cut the buckwheat tofu into small squares and place side by side, but not touching, on a piece of parchment (baking) paper. Dust with the *kinako* using a sifter or fine sieve. Serve the squares on top of the *kuromitsu*.

SWEET SOBA DOFU

MAKES 8 SMALL SQUARES

15 g (½ oz/ ½ tablespoon) Japanese buckwheat flour (*sobako*, page 280)

15 g (½ oz/½ tablespoon) well crushed kudzu powder, (*kuzuko*, page 280)

150 g (5½ oz) fine white Japanese sugar (*johakuto*, page 14)

A savory version of soba dofu (page 68) is found on *zensai* plates at soba restaurants. Here this delicate sweet has just a hint of soba to close the meal on an understated note.

Mix the *sobako* and kudzu together in a small heavy saucepan. Slowly stir in 150 ml (5 fl oz) cold water, until completely emulsified. Heat over medium heat until it comes almost to a boil, stirring continuously to form a smooth paste. Stir vigorously with a flat wooden spoon, scraping the bottom, until the mixture is reduced a little, about 5%. Add the sugar and cook 2–3 minutes more, stirring, to melt the sugar. Scrape into a 20 × 10 cm (8 × 4 in) loaf pan and cool to room temperature. Chill at least 2 hours. Cut into small squares and serve as a subtle sweet bite at the end of a Japanese meal.

KINTOKI JELLY

Kintoki Zeri-

MAKES 8 SMALL SQUARES

150 g (5½ oz) medium-sized Japanese red beans (*kintoki mame*), soaked for half a day or overnight in plenty of cold water

150 g (5½ oz) refined light brown Japanese sugar (*sanonto*, page 14)

2 teaspoons powdered gelatin

1 teaspoon agar flakes

Little sweet squares made with buckwheat or red beans are ubiquitous at soba restaurants, and come in several different consistencies depending on the gelling agent. Here 'jelly' refers to a gelatinous square, not jelly as we know it in the West. Kanji Nakatani likes to add a small amount of agar to his gelatin preparations to give them a nice texture. If *kintoki mame* are unavailable, look for other round red beans such as domingo rojo, or use smaller azuki beans, but don't use kidney beans.

Drain the beans, put them in a heavy medium pot and cover generously with cold water. Bring to a boil over high heat and drain immediately. Repeat this step, then return the beans to the pot with 800 ml (27 fl oz) cold water. Bring to an almost boil over high heat, adjust to a gentle simmer and cook for 45 minutes, until the beans are easily squished between two fingers.

Place a sieve over a medium bowl and drain the beans through the strainer. Measure out 400 ml (13½ fl oz) of the simmering liquid and add to a medium saucepan with the sugar. Cook, stirring over low heat, until the sugar has completely dissolved.

Dissolve the gelatin and agar together in a small bowl with 2 tablespoons water. Let sit for 5 minutes to soften. Stir into the bean liquid and cook over low heat for 1–2 minutes, until the gelatin and agar have completely dissolved and the liquid has thickened. Fold the beans into the liquid and scrape into a 10 × 20 cm (4 × 8 in) loaf pan. Cool to room temperature. Chill for at least 2 hours or overnight before cutting into small squares.

BASIC RECIPES

Konbu Dashi

MAKES 1 LITER (34 FL OZ/4 CUPS)

20 cm (8 in) piece of konbu, weighing about 20 g (¾ oz)

Soak the konbu overnight in a medium pot with 1 liter (34 fl oz/4 cups) cold water. The following day, bring almost to a boil over medium heat. Scoop out the konbu and use for a second dashi or another dish, or discard. Remove the pot from the heat and let the dashi cool to room temperature.

Shiro Dashi

MAKES 750 ML (25½ FL OZ/3 CUPS)

20 cm (8 in) piece of konbu, weighing about 20 g (¾ oz)
60 g (2 oz) freshly shaved katsuobushi or *hanakatsuo* (page 16)

Soak the konbu overnight if possible, or at least for a few hours, in a medium pot with 1 liter (34 fl oz/4 cups) cold water. Bring almost to a boil over medium heat. Just before the water reaches boiling, remove the konbu. Stir in the katsuobushi and simmer for 10 minutes (increase the simmer time to 15 minutes if making larger batches). Strain through a sieve lined with muslin (cheesecloth) or an unbleached coffee filter. You can use the konbu and katsuobushi for a second dashi or another dish, or discard. Store the dashi refrigerated for 1–2 days, but best use as quickly as possible.

Happo Dashi

MAKES 180 ML (6 FL OZ)

180 ml (6 fl oz) Shiro Dashi (see above)
1 teaspoon fine white Japanese sugar (*johakuto*, page 14)
1 teaspoon fine sea salt
1 teaspoon mirin

Stir the dashi into the sugar, salt and mirin in a small saucepan to dissolve. Bring to a simmer over medium-high heat and remove from the heat immediately.

Variation 1

Stir 180 ml (6 fl oz) Shiro Dashi (see above) into 2 teaspoons salt and ¼ teaspoon mirin in a small saucepan to dissolve. Bring to a simmer over medium-high heat and remove from the heat immediately.

Variation 2

Add 1 teaspoon sake and a 5 cm (2 in) square of konbu to the simmering liquid. Remove the konbu after the dashi has cooled.

Kaeshi

MAKES ABOUT 1.5 LITERS (51 FL OZ/6 CUPS)

500 g (1 lb 2 oz) refined light brown Japanese sugar (*sanonto*, page 14)
50 ml (1¾ fl oz) mirin
1 liter (34 fl oz/4 cups) shoyu

Place the sugar in a heavy medium saucepan and stir in the mirin and shoyu. Bring almost to a boil over medium heat, and remove the pan immediately to a cool surface. Leave covered at room temperature for 1 week to develop flavor. Mix kaeshi with Shiro Dashi (see opposite) at different concentrations for Mori Tsuyu (see below), Kaketsuyu (see below) and Tentsuyu (see below). Stored in the fridge, kaeshi keeps for at least half a year.

Kaketsuyu

Mix Shiro Dashi (see opposite) with Kaeshi (see above) at a ratio of 11:1 (or 10:1 in the summer when you need more salt).

Mori Tsuyu

Mix Shiro Dashi (see opposite) with Kaeshi (see above) at a ratio of 3:1.

Tentsuyu

Mix Shiro Dashi (see opposite) with Kaeshi (see above) at a ratio of 4:1.

Tempura Batter

75 g (2¾ oz/½ cup) unbleached cake flour
125 ml (4 fl oz/½ cup) ice water

Put the flour in a medium mixing bowl, and use a pair of cooking chopsticks (*saibashi*, page 276) to quickly stir in the water. Do not overwork the batter – it should still have some small lumps. Use immediately.

Tama Miso

MAKES ABOUT 150 ML (5 FL OZ)

2 tablespoons refined light brown Japanese sugar (*sanonto*, page 14)
6 tablespoons white (*shiro*) miso
2 tablespoons brown rice (*genmai*) miso
1 tablespoon sake
2 tablespoons Kaketsuyu (see above)

Stir the sugar into the misos in a small saucepan. Add the sake and kaketsuyu and stir until emulsified. Bring to a simmer over low heat and cook, stirring, for 3–5 minutes, until thickened a little and fragrant.

Dengaku Miso

MAKES ABOUT 150 ML (5 FL OZ)

4 tablespoons white (*shiro*) miso
4 tablespoons brown rice (*genmai*) miso
2 tablespoons refined light brown Japanese sugar (*sanonto*, page 14) or mirin
4 tablespoons Shiro Dashi (see opposite)

Stir the misos, sugar or mirin, and dashi together in a small saucepan and bring to a simmer over low heat, stirring continuously. Cook until slightly thickened and glossy.

Goma Miso

MAKES ABOUT 90 ML (3 FL OZ)

4 tablespoons Dengaku Miso (page 127)
2 tablespoons Japanese gold sesame paste
1 tablespoon gold sesame seeds, roasted and ground (optional)

Mix the dengaku miso with the sesame paste and sesame seeds (if using).

Sumiso

MAKES ABOUT 90 ML (3 FL OZ)

4 tablespoons Tama Miso (page 127)
2 tablespoons rice vinegar
1 tablespoon Kaketsuyu (page 127)
1 tablespoon refined light brown Japanese sugar (*sanonto*, page 14)
¼ teaspoon Japanese mustard powder mixed with ¼ teaspoon water

Stir the ingredients together in a small saucepan. Bring to a gentle simmer over low heat, stirring continuously to dissolve the sugar and soften the vinegar's acidity.

Nihaizu

1 part rice vinegar
2 parts Happo Dashi (page 126)

Bring the vinegar to a simmer in a small saucepan over medium heat. Immediately remove from the heat and stir in the dashi.

Sanbaizu

1 part rice vinegar
3 parts Happo Dashi (page 126)

Bring the vinegar to a simmer in a small saucepan over medium heat. Immediately remove from the heat and stir in the dashi.

Sushi Su

MAKES ABOUT 400 ML (13½ FL OZ)

300 ml (10 fl oz) rice vinegar
100 g (3½ oz) fine white Japanese sugar (*johakuto*, page 14)
1 teaspoon fine sea salt

Bring the vinegar, sugar and salt to a simmer in a small saucepan over medium heat. Remove from the heat immediately and leave to cool.

Ponzu

MAKES ABOUT 1.2 LITERS (41 FL OZ)

300 ml (10 fl oz) rice vinegar
50 g (1¾ oz/¼ cup) refined light brown Japanese sugar (*sanonto*, page 14)
500 ml (17 fl oz/2 cups) shoyu
500 ml (17 fl oz/2 cups) Shiro Dashi (page 126)
150 g (5½ oz) freshly shaved katsuobushi or *hanakatsuo* (page 16)

Bring the vinegar to an almost boil in a medium saucepan. Remove from the heat and stir in the sugar to dissolve. Add the shoyu and dashi. Bring to a simmer over medium–high heat. Remove from the heat and immediately stir in the katsuobushi. Let sit for 30 minutes before straining and using. Stored in the fridge, ponzu keeps for 1–2 months.

Momiji Oroshi

MAKES 125 ML (4 FL OZ/½ CUP)

150 g (5½ oz) daikon
1 tablespoon Japanese chili powder (*ichimi togarashi*, page 19)

Grate the daikon on a circular ceramic grater (*oroshiki*, page 275) or sharp-toothed grating plate (*oroshigane*, page 275). Drain naturally for 10 minutes in a fine sieve set over a small bowl. Reserve the dripped out juices. Transfer the daikon to a bowl, stir in the *ichimi togarashi* and taste. If the daikon seems too dry, rehydrate by slowly stirring back in some of the daikon juices. Use within 2 hours of being made.

Okaka

2 small handfuls of freshly shaved katsuobushi or *hanakatsuo* (page 16)
1 tablespoon shoyu

Toss the katsuobushi with the shoyu and use as a garnish for grilled vegetables.

Cabbage and Komatsuna Gelée

MAKES ABOUT 1 LITER (34 FL OZ/4 CUPS)

2 large green cabbage leaves
2 large napa (Chinese) cabbage leaves
8 komatsuna or 16 spinach leaves
750 ml (25½ fl oz/3 cups) Happo Dashi (page 126)
1 tablespoon powdered gelatin

Blanch the green cabbage for 3 minutes, the napa cabbage for 2 minutes and the komatsuna for 1 minute (if using spinach, blanch for 30 seconds) in a large pot of boiling water. Refresh each under cold water after you scoop them out and squeeze out excess water. Chop each finely, squeeze again, and strew across the bottom of a 20 cm (8 in) square pan.

Warm the dashi over low heat, and stir a small spoonful of the dashi into the gelatin in a small bowl. Scrape the dissolved gelatin back into the dashi and cook, stirring, for 1 minute, then pour over the greens in the pan. Cool to room temperature, chill to set, and spoon out as the base for seafood salads (the gelée will be spoonable, not cuttable).

OSECHI RYORI: NEW YEAR FOOD

Contrary to popular belief, the 'traditional' Japanese New Year food, *osechi ryori*, is not eaten all over Japan. Certain pockets around the archipelago (such as Suzu in Ishikawa prefecture) do not have this custom, but instead focus their energies on special foods for other times, such as funerals or weddings. But the stark reality is that all of these food traditions are eroding at an alarming pace.

Already in 1988, the year I arrived in Japan, preparing *osechi ryori* was on the wane, yet the custom of visiting close friends and relatives January 1st, 2nd and 3rd was still firmly in place in the countryside. Ten years later the visits had all but stopped. Fewer and fewer people had a family farmhouse to return to, and modern house design does not encourage visitors. Certainly no one would think of walking into a modern house and announcing themselves with a robustly shouted '*Gomen kudasai!*' ('Pardon y'all!') without knocking. Entrance doors are locked on modern houses. Modern houses are shut up tight like drums, unlike the farmhouse, which allows a free flow of air between outside gardens and inside rooms.

One oft-encountered explanation for the custom of preparing *osechi ryori* is that people were not supposed to use fire to cook during the first three days of the New Year, except to prepare *ozoni*, the traditional soup used to serve pounded rice 'cakes' (mochi). Also shops were not open during the immediate days following New Year's Eve; without refrigeration, families needed foods that would keep for several days. Before New Year, all members of the family (including the men) cooperated on a big year-end clean. Farmhouses are large and dusty; papered wooden-framed doors and shoji screens were meticulously cleaned or repapered. A damp cloth was taken to every surface. In modern Japan, people live in airtight houses, so this big cleaning has become less a way of life.

With the advent of refrigeration, and the fact that stores never seem to close, the need or desire to prepare *osechi ryori* has weakened. Nonetheless, many families hold to their own made-up assortment of traditional holiday foods that they put together each New Year. In our house, my mother-in-law always made at least two varieties of sweet simmered beans, as well as *kuri kinton* (mashed sweet potato with chestnut). Somewhere in the first few years after I married my Japanese farmer husband almost three decades ago, my mother-in-law gave up preparing the quintessential sticky-sweet, darkly-shoyu-flavored dried fishes called *tazukuri* that seemed inseparable from New Year.

Most likely the lack of enthusiasm among the younger members of the family outweighed the time it took to cook.

More and more, families around Japan are relying on bought *osechi ryori* boxes, and even my mother-in-law ordered a tiered set from our local convenience store one year – to the tune of 10,000 yen (about US$90). Department store *osechi* sets range from around 13,000 to 43,000 yen (US$117–387) and typically serve a family of two to four. And for around 650,000 yen (US$5850), well-heeled families can enjoy *osechi ryori* packed in stacked lacquer boxes (*jubako*) prepared by Kitcho, a venerable old Japanese restaurant in Kyoto.

Since we cook our own food, and I am not a fan of bento-style foods, I had never been tempted to purchase *osechi ryori*. A few New Years ago, however, I ordered an *osechi* set for the first time because I intended to write about the custom and needed photos for this book. Our close friend Kanji Nakatani ('Kanchan') prepares somewhere near a hundred *osechi* sets each year at Soba Ro (page 61). Not presented in the traditional tiered lacquer boxes, the foods are nestled in square or round deep-sided ceramic plates commissioned from local potter Isao Kimura (page 82). Each year, Kanchan incorporates new dishes into an assortment of orthodox *osechi* preparations to create a unique platter. And each *osechi* set is accompanied by a pack of freshly rolled, uncooked soba noodles and a container of dipping sauce for *toshikoshi soba*: the first soba of the year, partaken on the eve of December 31st to usher in the New Year with good luck. That year, Kanchan's *osechi* included fish terrine, mashed sweet potato with chestnut (*kuri kinton*) for prosperity, shrimp dumplings, sweet miso–grilled Spanish mackerel, simmered abalone with dashi gelée, braised beef tendons, chicken loaf, sweet yuzu paste, grilled duck breast, chicken liver, sweet simmered beans (golden, flower, and black) for health, *dashi-maki tamago* (page 207), home-cured gray mullet eggs (*karasumi*) for fertility, boiled shrimp (resembling the bent shape of an old man to signify longevity), and a sprig of kumquats (*kinkan*) for prosperity and to keep the *osechi* fresh.

As it happened that year, I was heading to the United States on a midnight flight, leaving New Year's Eve in Japan and arriving New Year's Eve in California. Having run out of time to enjoy dinner with my family before taking my train to the airport, I packed an unglamorous *osechi* bento into a plastic box and ate it at the airport. Washed down by a glass or two of champagne in the JAL lounge, it was the perfect meal. Each morsel of food complemented the next, and I wished I had packed more.

These *osechi* sets prepared by Soba Ro go for 20,000 yen (US$180), almost twice what the least-expensive *osechi* sets command, but you get to keep the Isao Kimura plate. And while certainly an extravagance, I am tempted to order one again.

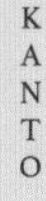

L'Effervescence
Tokyo

SHINOBU NAMAE

Shinobu Namae, part poet, part chef, is all genius. With 12K followers on Instagram, he might be one of the most followed Japanese chefs – especially noteworthy are his photos of visits to artisanal producers across Japan. Every chef I know who is headed to Japan hangs on Namae's Instagram feed, and when Noma staged a 5-week pop-up in Tokyo, Namae was their sourcing guru. But don't be fooled into thinking he is a trendy glitterati chef, because despite his almost movie-star good looks, Namae could be one of the nicest chefs in the business. This is not merely surface niceness turned on for customers or the media, as Namae is selfless, generous and caring to his very core. And that shows through in his soulfully whimsical food. Eating at L'Effervescence when Namae is in-house is akin to a religious experience, and one I mostly prefer to enjoy alone.

Namae, a sought after chef, is consistently invited to the top world food events such as Noma's MAD Symposium, the Culinary Institute of America's Worlds of Flavor, and Slow Food's Terra Madre. Stints as sous chef at Michel Bras' Toya Japon in Hokkaido and Heston Blumenthal's Fat Duck in Berkshire readied Namae for his position as executive chef of L'Effervescence, which opened in 2011, the year of the devastating Tohoku earthquake that resulted in a massive tsunami on the Sendai coast. Like many of us, the horror of the tragedy affected Namae and his team deeply, and it caused Namae to rethink his priorities, and his plans for the future of his restaurant.

As an innately compassionate person, Namae is extremely empathetic and can intuit the feelings of those around him, be they diners in the restaurant or staff in the kitchen or front of house. Every day he has a kind word or piece of advice for the members of his team. And Namae values his suppliers deeply, from the farmers, to the fishermen, to the hunters, to the artisanal food producers. He visits these suppliers often, on a rotating basis, and genuinely engages with their processes in a knowledgeable and respectful way. This is not always true for other chefs who buzz about Japan with media trailing after them, recording their visits to producers, often sadly bungling the information and thus disrespecting the artisans.

Namae values his suppliers deeply, from the farmers, to the fishermen, to the hunters, to the artisanal food producers.

Despite a typical rocky first year, L'Effervescence earned its first Michelin star in 2011, and its second in 2015. Consistently ranked high on Asia's 50 Best Restaurants list sponsored by San Pellegrino, L'Effervescence was ranked 12th in 2017 and 20th in 2018, and in 2018 also became the first winner of the Sustainable Restaurant Award.

Several years ago, Namae volunteered to assist me at a cooking event I was staging in the countryside near my home. I did not know what to make of the offer, since Namae is obviously an impeccably trained chef who also happens to be the executive director of his restaurant. Namae arrived with Yasushi Ozaki, the Tokyo editor who had introduced the two of us. No ego present, Namae set to mincing and prepping, and eventually to cooking the meat over charcoal outside. I will never forget his mild, unobtrusive assistance in the kitchen, and experienced it once again when he came for mochi pounding at our house the day following our visit to Terada Honke (page 164).

We have grown into an easy friendship, and though our recent schedules have not been conducive to meeting up in person, we keep in touch via email and social media. At this writing, my burgeoning desire to visit L'Effervescence and Namae is taking hold. The longing for his uniquely modern and creative food cannot be denied – French in origin, Japanese at heart, yet with added complexity from the elements of fermentation – Namae's food is profoundly personal and in some way life-altering.

Namae does not just put lip service to his brand. When it came time to give L'Effervescence a facelift, Namae chose traditional artisans from across Japan to add authenticity and honesty to the design construction. Selecting such artisans certainly stretched the budget, but the result is stunning and reflects the value put on environment as well as on craftsmanship, similarly found in fine old Japanese houses and exquisitely constructed tearooms. Outward simplicity belies the unique or carefully sourced materials, such as stone, wood, metal and traditional plaster wall surfacing.

Namae has a degree in political science from Keio University (Japan's equivalent to Yale), but ended up cooking instead, and this rarefied background shows in his cerebral yet sensitive approach to food. By all appearances, Namae is at the top of his game, though I would venture to say that we will see more and more evolutions from him as the years unfold.

'Kakusei': Seppu, Kawahagi, Kujo Negi, Mi-do Guranita

'AWAKENING': CÈPE PURÉE, FILEFISH AND NEGI FOAM WITH MEAD GRANITA

The complex layers and textures in the 'Awakening' are brought into relief by the surprise spritz and coldness of the mead granita and yuzu. There are many components to this recipe, so in a sense, it should be viewed as five recipes under the guise of one. And, depending on the size of your serving glass, you could very well end up with extra of each component. Do not worry – each piece is just as delicious on its own as it is put together into this stunning first bite. If cèpes are out of your reach, substitute shiitake.

SERVES 8

Cèpe Purée

1 teaspoon unroasted sesame oil

1 tablespoon unsalted butter

50 g (1¾ oz) shallots, thinly sliced

500 g (1 lb 2 oz) cèpes (porcini mushrooms), wiped clean and thinly sliced

150 g (5½ oz) may queen (or yukon gold or similar creamy-style) potatoes, peeled and thinly sliced

½ teaspoon flaky sea salt

To make the cèpe purée, heat the sesame oil and butter in a large frying pan over medium–low heat, until the heat is beginning to rise from the bottom of the pan and the butter has melted. Scrape in the shallots and cook slowly, stirring occasionally, until they have sweetened completely and are yellowed and translucent. Drop in the cèpes and continue cooking slowly until they have cooked through and all of their liquid has dissipated. Add the potato and continue cooking until very soft and the slices are falling apart. Transfer the mixture to a food processor or blender and process to a smooth purée with the salt. Cool to room temperature and chill until ready to serve.

Sherry Vinegar Gelée

140 ml (4½ fl oz) Pedro Ximenez sherry vinegar, such as El Majuelo Vinagre de Jerez

2 tablespoons shoyu

3 tablespoons granulated sugar

¾ teaspoon fine sea salt

10 g (¼ oz) leaf gelatin

Mead Granita

125 ml (4 fl oz/½ cup) mead

125 ml (4 fl oz/½ cup) organic apple juice

1 cup liquid nitrogen (optional)

Filefish

50 g (1¾ oz) skinless fillet of filefish (*kawahagi*), plus its liver

fine sea salt, weighing 1.1% of the fish fillet (about a pinch)

1 tablespoon extra-virgin olive oil

60 ml (2 fl oz/¼ cup) mirin

Kujo Negi Foam

2 small *kujo negi* or 4 fat scallions (spring onions), white parts only

unroasted sesame oil

1 medium egg, at room temperature

100 ml (3½ fl oz) strained tomato juice (squeezed from 2 large tomatoes)

scant 2 teaspoons fine sea salt

1 teaspoon finely chopped chives, for serving

1 teaspoon finely slivered yuzu zest, for serving

To make the sherry vinegar gelée, warm the vinegar, shoyu, sugar and salt over low heat until the sugar has melted. Remove from the heat. Soak the gelatin in 125 ml (4 fl oz/½ cup) water until softened, then drain (discarding the water) and slide it into the warm sherry mixture. Stir until the gelatin has completely melted. Pour into a 10 cm (4 in) square pan or mold to set. Cool to room temperature, chill for about 30 minutes, then break up to make spoonable for serving.

To make the mead granita without liquid nitrogen, pour the mead and juice into a shallow metal or plastic container and freeze for 30 minutes. Remove from the freezer and run through the forming ice crystals with a fork. Return to the freezer and repeat at 30-minute intervals until completely flaked and icy.

If making the granita with liquid nitrogen, you can do it just before serving. Mix the mead and apple juice together in a stainless medium bowl. Wearing protective glasses, pour the liquid nitrogen (which should be stored in a properly vented glass-lined thermos) directly over the liquid in the bowl and wait until the smoke clears.

To prepare the filefish, cut the fillet at a diagonal into 4 mm (⅛ in) slices and then into a 4 mm (⅛ in) dice. Toss with the salt in a small bowl, mix in the olive oil, and marinate for 30 minutes. Cover and store in the fridge until needed.

Heat the mirin in a small saucepan and bring to a simmer over medium–low heat. Simmer for 30 seconds to burn off the alcohol, then set aside to cool.

Set up a small steamer and place the filefish liver on a plate inside. Steam for 1–2 minutes, until warmed through. Pass through a fine sieve (*uragoshi*, page 275) to remove any hard tendrils. Flavor the liver with a few drops of the cooled mirin, or to taste. Use the remaining mirin for another dish.

To make the *kujo negi* foam, put the *negi* on a plate and cook in the microwave for 3 minutes until soft. Weigh the softened *negi* and measure out 30% of its weight in unroasted sesame oil. Drop the *negi* and oil into a blender and pulse to purée. Measure out 30 g (1 oz) of the purée into a medium saucepan and set aside.

Boil the egg for 5 minutes, cool under cold running water and peel. Drop into a small mixing bowl and process to a smooth purée using an immersion hand blender. Dribble in 130 ml (4½ fl oz) of unroasted sesame oil while blending to make a mayonnaise-like emulsion. Measure out 40 g (1½ oz) of this sauce and stir it into the *negi* purée in the saucepan. (The unused sauce can be used as mayonnaise in other dishes.) Gradually stir in the tomato juices, salt and 200 ml (7 fl oz) water until completely incorporated. Warm slowly over low heat until the ingredients in the pan reach 50°C (120°F). Remove from the heat and beat until frothy with the immersion hand blender. Use only the foam.

Spoon a 2 cm (¾ in) layer of cèpe purée in the bottom of 8 pretty shot glasses (about 2 heaping tablespoons in each). On top of that, dot in a thin layer of sherry vinegar gelée (about 1 teaspoon each). Place a small amount of the marinated diced filefish and its liver purée across the gelée, and sprinkle with the chives and half of the yuzu zest. Top with a healthy dollop of *kujo negi* foam – at least a 2 cm (¾ in) layer, shaped in a lovely round cloud protruding from the glasses.

Spoon the granita into the bottom of 8 chilled glasses (ideally of the roly-poly variety). Garnish with the remaining yuzu zest. Set one of each glass on each plate and serve immediately.

'Shoshu-ni': Hamo no Age-yaki to Nyusan Hakko Saseta Ko-rurabi, Bi-tsu, Amaebi no Kyarameru to Sanshou no Oiru

'IN THE EARLY AUTUMN': PIKE EEL ON BEET PURÉE, PICKLED KOHLRABI, SHRIMP CARAMEL AND SANSHO OIL

This dish speaks to me on so many levels, and is as classically whimsical as Namae. Be aware that the pickled kohlrabi will take at least two days to make. Leftover components of the dish can be incorporated into other meals put together on the fly.

SERVES 8

Pickled Kohlrabi

500 g (1 lb 2 oz) kohlrabi

flaky sea salt

Beet Purée

300 g (10½ oz) beets (beetroot), peeled and sliced 5 mm (¼ in) thick

1½ tablespoons unroasted sesame oil (or 10% of the weight of the cooked beets)

Shrimp Caramel

300 g (10½ oz) small shrimp (*amaebi*) in their shells

50 g (1¾ oz) Japanese black sugar (*kokuto*, page 15)

¼ teaspoon flaky sea salt

55 g (2 oz) cold unsalted butter, cut into small pieces

Sansho Oil

4 tablespoons fresh green *sansho* berries, or ¼ teaspoon powdered green *sansho*

60 ml (2 fl oz/¼ cup) unroasted sesame oil

Vinegar Sauce

60 ml (2 fl oz/¼ cup) Iio Jozo Fujisu red label or other best quality rice vinegar (page 14)

½ teaspoon well crushed kudzu powder (*kuzuko*, page 280)

'Fried' Pike Eel

1 small pike eel (*hamo*) weighing about 500 g (1 lb 2 oz), cleaned, butterflied, center bone removed

250 ml (8½ fl oz/1 cup) unroasted sesame oil

sansho leaves (page 19), for garnishing

Make the pickled kohlrabi at least 2 days in advance. Peel the kohlrabi well and slice it into fine rounds about 3 mm (⅛ in) thick. Cut these rounds into 6 mm (¼ in) strips similar to tagliatelle pasta. Weigh the kohlrabi, and calculate 2% salt (about 1 teaspoon). Massage the salt into the kohlrabi in a large bowl, then vacuum seal. Alternatively, pack into a sterilized jar and fill the gap between the kohlrabi and the lid with a leak-proof plastic bag containing water, so the surface of the kohlrabi is not exposed to air. Leave in a warm spot (about 20°C/70°F) and allow to sour naturally for at least 2 days. Beyond 1 week, store the kohlrabi in the refrigerator to slow fermentation, and use within 1 month.

To make the beet purée, vacuum seal the beet slices (or pack inside a resealable freezer bag, unsealed) and place on a plate. Set up a steamer over rapidly boiling water and cook the beets for 20 minutes, until soft. Purée with the oil in a blender or food processor until smooth.

To make the shrimp caramel, heat a large dry frying pan over medium–high heat. Once hot, sauté the shrimp, stirring, until the shells are bright pink. Add 500 ml (17 fl oz/2 cups) water and the black sugar and simmer for 30 minutes over medium–low heat. Strain, discarding the solids. Pour the liquid into a small saucepan and simmer down for about 5 minutes, until syrupy. Remove from the heat and stir in the salt, and about 1 tablespoon of the butter at a time, adding the next tablespoon after the previous one has melted.

To make the *sansho* oil, finely chop the *sansho* berries (if using) with a sharp knife. Heat the oil in a small saucepan over medium–low heat until rippling but not smoking, about 180°C (350°F). Dump in the *sansho* berries or powder and cover with a lid. Remove from the heat and allow to cool, thus infusing the oil with *sansho*. Strain the oil, discarding the solids.

To make the vinegar sauce, bring the vinegar to a boil in a small saucepan, then remove from the heat immediately. Stir a little into the kudzu in a small bowl to dissolve it. Scrape back into the hot vinegar and stir off heat to thicken slightly.

To prepare the pike eel, make small cross cuts about 3 mm (⅛ in) deep through the flesh side to slice through the minute bones. Cut crosswise into 3 cm (1¼ in) pieces and set these side by side in a large flat sieve (*uragoshi*, page 275), skin side down. Pour boiling water over the pieces for 30 seconds. Pat dry, and thread 2 bamboo skewers through each piece to keep them flat (insert each skewer from the bottom of one edge, up through the middle, then back down through the bottom of the opposite edge). Thread as many pieces as will fit onto each pair of skewers.

Place a rack on top of an oven tray and lay the skewers next to each other on the rack. Heat the oil in a small saucepan until very hot, about 200–220°C (400–430°F). Ladle the oil carefully over both sides of the pike eel to 'fry'.

Working in an imaginary vertical line on 8 salad plates, pool 1 tablespoon of beet purée towards the top of the line, and another towards the bottom of the line. Drizzle each plate with 1 teaspoon of warmed shrimp caramel, ½ teaspoon of vinegar sauce and a few drops of *sansho* oil. Remove the just-'fried' pike eel from the skewers and set 3 pieces, skin side down, along each line. Strew each plate with a tablespoon of pickled kohlrabi and garnish with a few *sansho* leaves torn off the stem. Serve immediately.

Tofu Sawa- Kuri-mu

SOUR CREAM TOFU

L'Effervescence first makes sour cream in-house with cream and yogurt, and then mashes it with pressed tofu. The tofu is sourced from Tsuki no Tofu, located across the way from Terada Honke brewery (page 164) in Chiba prefecture, and is made from organic heirloom soybeans and mineral-rich well water.

At the restaurant, this luscious tofu-flavored sour cream is served with tangy fermented country bread made at their bakery, Bricolage Bread & Co., a collaboration with Ayumu Iwanaga from Le Sucre-Coeur bakery on the outskirts of Osaka. It would be equally lovely as a raw dip for seasonal crudités or as an accompaniment to smoked fish. The recipe makes quite a big quantity, but as this takes no more effort, and the result is so deliciously versatile, it makes sense to do a generous portion. At L'Effervescence they make batches of double this amount – feel free to do the same.

MAKES 750 G (1 LB 11 OZ/3 CUPS)

500 ml (17 fl oz/2 cups) cream

450 g (1 lb) plain yogurt

150 g (5½ oz) *momendofu* (page 279) or Japanese-style soft block tofu

½ tablespoon flaky sea salt

extra-virgin olive oil, for serving

Stir the cream into the yogurt slowly, until incorporated. Scrape into a yogurt maker, cover and set at 45°C (115°F) for 6 hours.

Line a large sieve with a large piece of muslin (cheesecloth) and place it on top of a bowl. Scrape the yogurt mixture into the cloth, fold to close, and set a firm but gentle weight across the top to gradually press out the whey. Refrigerate overnight with the weight in place. The next morning, you should have 625 g (1 lb 6 oz) sour cream and about 335 ml (11½ fl oz) whey.

Put the tofu in a fine sieve set over a bowl to catch the drips, and place a small heavy saucepan on top to press out excess moisture for at least 20 minutes, until 100 g (3½ oz) of tofu remains.

Beat the sour cream, tofu and salt in a medium bowl with an immersion hand blender until well emulsified. Spoon into small bowls and drizzle with a little olive oil.

'Samusa to Tomoni':
Seikogani to Satsuma
Imo no Su-pu,
Shirako Age

'WITH THE COLD': SEIKO CRAB AND SWEET POTATO SOUP WITH FRIED COD MILT

Cod milt is rich, especially when fried, but it adds balance to the briny crab and shares a wildness with the boar caramel. Sweet potatoes are the perfect canvas for all of these flavors in the bowl, and the salt-pickled lemon finishes the dish with a bright note on the tongue.

You need less than one salt-pickled lemon, but it never makes sense to put up a tiny batch of pickles, so I recommend salting at least four lemons. Use them to garnish any dish that benefits from a spark of lemon. The remaining boar caramel can also be used as a small flavor addition to other dishes. And if boar does not suit your fancy, use pork.

SERVES 8

Salt-pickled Lemon

4 small lemons

4 tablespoons flaky sea salt

Boar Caramel

2 kg (4 lb 6 oz) boar shin meat (or substitute pork)

2 tablespoons Japanese black sugar (*kokuto*, page 15)

Fried Cod Milt

240 g (8½ oz) cod milt (*shirako*) – about 6 pieces

fine sea salt

3 tablespoons unbleached cake flour

3 tablespoons unroasted sesame oil

1 small lemon, for zesting

Seiko Crab and Stock

90 g (3 oz) fine sea salt

2 live seiko (or other) crabs, weighing about 250 g (9 oz) each

Sweet Potato Soup

800 g (1 lb 12 oz) yellow-fleshed sweet potatoes, scrubbed

120 g (4½ oz) unsalted butter

¼ teaspoon flaky sea salt

1 liter (34 fl oz/4 cups) whole (full-cream) milk

400 ml (13½ fl oz) cream (35% fat)

1.2 liters (41 fl oz) crab stock (see above)

Make the salt-pickled lemon at least 2 weeks in advance. Cut 4 deep vertical slits through the peel of each lemon. Working over a bowl to catch any errant grains, rub 1 tablespoon of salt into the cuts of each lemon. Push the lemons into a jar just big enough to hold them. Scrape in any fallen salt. Add water to the top of the lemons and store in the fridge for at least 2 weeks. Soak 1 lemon in cold water for 1 hour to remove salt before using.

To make the boar caramel, bring 4 liters (135 fl oz/16 cups) water and the shin meat to a simmer in a large heavy pot over medium–high heat. Cook at a gentle simmer for 6 hours, until reduced to about 1.25 liters (42 fl oz/5 cups) stock. Strain and discard the solids.

While the boar stock is cooking, prepare the milt by rinsing it in cold water, then soaking it for 6 hours in water containing 2% salt (i.e. 10 g/2 teaspoons salt to 500 ml/17 fl oz/2 cups water).

Stir 600 ml (20½ fl oz) of the finished boar stock into the black sugar in a small saucepan and place over medium heat. Cook at a lively simmer for about 15 minutes, until large bubbles form and the liquid is syrupy and reduced by half.

To cook the crabs, bring 3 liters (101 fl oz/12 cups) water and the salt to a boil in a large stockpot over high heat. Drop in the crabs and cook for 20 minutes. Drain and cool. Pull off the backs of the crabs and reserve for making stock. Place the bodies on a thick wad of newspaper and whack with a rubber mallet or meat tenderizer. Remove as much meat as possible from the bodies, legs and claws, and toss the picked meat together so the different types are evenly distributed. Do not discard the shells. Store the meat in the fridge. About 1 hour before serving, measure out 8 heaping teaspoons of crabmeat and allow it to return to room temperature. Use the remaining meat in a salad or to garnish another soup.

To make the crab stock, dump backs, shells, and other leftover crab pieces into a large stockpot and add 4 liters (135 fl oz/16 cups) water. Bring to a boil over high heat and immediately adjust to a gentle simmer. Cook for 3 hours to extract all the crab flavor. Strain.

To make the sweet potato soup, preheat the oven to 250°C (480°F). Prick the sweet potatoes through their skins and roast on the middle rack of the oven for 30 minutes, until soft. Scoop the flesh from the skins while still warm and mash in the butter and salt.

Heat the milk and cream together over medium–low heat until almost simmering. Process the sweet potato in batches in a blender with the warmed milk and cream and 200 ml (7 fl oz) water until a smooth purée. Scrape into a medium stockpot and stir in the crab stock.

Remove the milt from the salt water and cut it into 4 cm (1½ in) portions. Bring a medium pot of water to a boil over medium–high heat and blanch the milt pieces for 2 minutes. Scoop out with a wire skimmer and drain on spongy paper towels. Cool to room temperature, then blot dry gently. Sprinkle the bottom of a flat pan with 2 tablespoons of the flour and place the milt in the pan. Sprinkle the remaining 1 tablespoon of flour over the milt and roll gently to coat generously.

Heat the oil in a large frying pan over medium heat. Sauté the milt for about 2 minutes until golden brown on all sides, shaking the pan back and forth to roll the pieces and encourage heat distribution. Skim the milt out from the oil and drain on paper towels. Shave a generous sprinkling of lemon zest over the fried milt using a microplane.

Cut the soaked pickled lemon into a 5 mm (¼ in) dice. Heat the sweet potato soup. Ladle the hot soup into 8 wide shallow bowls. Set 3 pieces of milt into each bowl, and add 1 heaped teaspoon of crabmeat, pinched in a couple of mounds. Strew each with ½ teaspoon chopped lemon and drizzle each with a scant teaspoon of boar caramel.

'Teiten': Kabura to Paseri, Kinto Hamu, Buriosshu

'A FIXED POINT': FOUR-HOUR CARAMELIZED TURNIPS WITH PARSLEY SAUCE

It is counterintuitive that these small turnips can cook for four hours and yet still hold their shape and be succulent. Surely, this is the wonder of sous vide. Finished with a vibrant parsley sauce, this might be one of the simplest yet longest running dishes on the menu at L'Effervescence. You will end up with extra sauce – drizzle on pasta or salt-grilled fish.

SERVES 4

4 small turnips with 2 cm (¾ in) stem intact, weighing about 100 g (3½ oz) each

1 small bunch flat leaf (Italian) parsley, stems removed

1 heaping tablespoon well crushed kudzu powder (*kuzuko*, page 280)

180 ml (6 fl oz/¾ cup) unroasted sesame oil

flaky sea salt

1 small slice of brioche, cut into minute dice

2 cm (¾ in) cube of Iberian ham, cut into minute dice

1 tablespoon unsalted butter

a few parsley leaves, for garnishing

Shave each turnip into a beautifully perfect shape weighing 85 g (3 oz). Vacuum seal each individually and cook sous vide (page 272) for 4 hours. Cool in a bowl of ice water for 20 minutes.

Blend the parsley in a mini-prep food processor with 4 tablespoons water until smoothly puréed. Scrape the parsley water into a sieve lined with muslin (cheesecloth) set over a bowl. Bring the edges of the cloth together and twist tightly to squeeze out the parsley liquid. Discard the solids.

Stir 3 tablespoons water into the kudzu in a very small saucepan. Heat, stirring over low heat, until thickened and viscous. Scrape into a small mixing bowl and blend with an immersion blender to 'liquefy'. Slowly add the expressed parsley water, blending continuously until emulsified. Continue blending, and add the sesame oil in a thin stream until incorporated into a thick, dark green sauce. Season with a few generous pinches of salt.

Dry the brioche in a small dry pan over low heat, covered, for about 2–3 minutes until crispy. Slide into a small bowl and dry the ham in the same way. Add to a different small bowl and crumble the dried ham with your fingers.

Remove the turnips from the vacuum bags and halve lengthwise. Sprinkle a pinch of the salt on the cut faces. Preheat the broiler (grill). Heat the butter in a large heavy frying pan over high heat until sizzling and starting to brown. Sear the turnips face down in the brown butter for about 30 seconds, until the cut sides are golden. Set the turnips, cut-side up, on an oven pan. Sprinkle the cut sides with a few more pinches of salt and grill 10 cm (4 in) from the heat for about 1 minute, until crisped.

Drizzle a thin line of parsley sauce down the middle of 4 salad plates. Make a small pile of the brioche croutons and crumbled ham in the middle of the line. Nestle 1 half turnip, face up, on top of the croutons. Set another half on top, face down and slightly askew, so that the top turnip is a little lower on the line. Garnish with parsley leaves and serve.

'Utsukushi Aki ni Kakomarete': Hato no Aburi-yaki, Asari no Ju, Satoimo, Poronegi, Torebisu no Kareha

'BEING CAUGHT IN A BEAUTIFUL AUTUMN': GRILLED PIGEON, CLAM, TARO, LEEKS, DRIED TREVISO

The treviso leaves are meant to evoke the dead leaves of autumn and add a playful note to this serious plate. Namae uses briny clams instead of salt here for seasoning the leek sauce, which juxtaposes nicely with the pigeon. Small mallard duck also works well instead of pigeon.

SERVES 8

Clam and Leek Sauce

1 tablespoon unroasted sesame oil

250 g (9 oz) trimmed leeks, finely sliced

100 g (3½ oz) small clams (*asari*), scrubbed and soaked in several changes of cold water

½ tablespoon well crushed kudzu powder (*kuzuko*, page 280)

Vinegar Reduction

300 ml (10 fl oz) red-wine vinegar

2 tablespoons Japanese black sugar (*kokuto*, page 15)

Begin the clam and leek sauce the day before. Heat the oil in a medium frying pan over medium–low heat and sauté the leeks slowly until translucent. Stir in 100 ml (3½ fl oz) water and simmer for 2 minutes to soften the leeks a bit more. Purée in a small food processor, scrape into a plastic or metal container, and freeze overnight.

To make the vinegar reduction, stir the vinegar into the black sugar in a small saucepan and bring to a simmer over medium–low heat, stirring continuously until the sugar is dissolved. Cook at a lively simmer until the liquid has reduced by 90%, to about 2 tablespoons.

Sprinkle the boned pigeon halves with sea salt on all sides and keep in the refrigerator. Place the pigeon bones and vegetables in a medium stockpot and add 4 liters (135 fl oz/16 cups) water. Cook at a gentle simmer for 3 hours. Strain.

Pigeon and Sauce

2 pigeons, cut in half, breast and rib bones removed, wings removed (bones and wings reserved for stock)

2 pinches flaky sea salt, plus 1 teaspoon extra

1 small carrot, sliced 2 cm (¾ in) thick

1 small onion, quartered

1 small celery stalk, sliced 2 cm (¾ in) thick

225 g (8 oz) unsalted butter

250 g (9 oz/1⅔ cups) unbleached cake flour

125 g (4½ oz) pigeon livers, hearts and gizzards

4 small taro roots, scrubbed

3 tablespoons unroasted sesame oil

1 medium leek, cut into 5 cm (2 in) pieces

2 medium *matsutake*, brushed clean, bases trimmed

a couple of pinches of flaky sea salt

8 treviso (radicchio) leaves, dried in a dehydrator or under a hot sun

Heat the butter in a heavy medium pot over medium–high heat until bubbling and dark golden brown. Dump in the flour and stir to a smooth roux. Keep cooking, scraping the roux across the bottom of the pan, until the raw flour aroma dissipates. Remove from the heat.

Bring 500 ml (17 fl oz/2 cups) of the pigeon stock to a boil. Stir in the pigeon innards off the heat, and immediately purée in a blender until smooth. Scrape into a medium saucepan and heat slowly over low heat until the stock reaches 70°C (160°F) and is warm to the touch. Stir in the teaspoon of salt and 1½ tablespoons of the vinegar reduction and cook for another 1–2 minutes, until the flavors have intensified. Pass through a fine sieve and whisk the stock slowly into the roux over low heat to form a smooth sauce. Warm gently before serving.

To finish the clam and leek sauce, place the clams in a small saucepan with 100 ml (3½ fl oz) water. Cover and bring to a simmer over medium–high heat. Cook for 3 minutes, until the clams have opened. Skim out the clams and slide them into a sieve set over a bowl to catch the drips. Use the clams in another dish. Strain the broth, including the drips, through muslin (cheesecloth) to remove any sand, and set aside.

Take the leek out of the freezer and wrap it in a piece of muslin (cheesecloth). Squeeze the bundle over a small bowl, rubbing the leek to extract as much liquid as possible.

Combine 100 ml (3½ fl oz) clam broth and 50 ml (1¾ fl oz) leek juice in a small saucepan. Scoop out ½ tablespoon of the liquid and smash it into the kudzu in a small bowl until smooth. Bring the liquid in the saucepan to a simmer and scrape in the emulsified kudzu. Simmer for 30 seconds–1 minute to thicken slightly to a silky sauce.

Preheat the oven to 250°C (480°F). Wrap each taro tightly in aluminum foil and place directly on a rack in the middle of the oven. Roast for 10 minutes, until heated through and half softened. Slice off the skins with a sharp paring knife, cut in half lengthwise, then cut crosswise into 12 mm (½ in) thick half moons.

Heat 2 tablespoons of the sesame oil in a large heavy frying pan over medium–high heat. Once starting to shimmer, quickly lay the taro pieces side by side in the pan. Cook for 1 minute on each side, until golden brown. Remove the pieces to a paper towel–lined pan with a pair of tongs or a spatula.

Vacuum seal the leek pieces (or alternatively, place in a resealable freezer bag and partially seal). Microwave for 4 minutes until softened. Remove from the bag and cut into 5 mm (¼ in) rounds. Heat the remaining 1 tablespoon of oil in a small frying pan over medium–low heat and sauté the leek for 2 minutes, until translucent and confit-like.

Tear the *matsutake* into long strips and place in a metal pan. Scorch lightly with a butane blowtorch or salamander. Sprinkle with the salt.

Grill the pigeon halves over low embers, or in a broiler (grill) 10 cm (4 in) from the heat, for 5 minutes on each side. Let the pigeons rest for 5 minutes before cutting the breast meat on a diagonal, 1 cm (½ in) thick. Whack the thighs in half diagonally through the bone.

Swirl 60 ml (2 fl oz/¼ cup) of warmed pigeon sauce in a haphazard pattern on 8 plates. Place 4 pieces of fried taro and 2 teaspoons of sautéed leeks here and there on each plate. Nap with 1 tablespoon of warmed clam and leek sauce, and lay 2 slices of pigeon breast and half a thigh on each plate. Strew with a few strips of *matsutake* and a small handful of torn dried treviso leaves.

'Toke-au': Jukusei Kuri to Yama Budo no Mon Buran, Buru-chizu no Merenge, Ramu Aisu

'MELTING TOGETHER': AGED CHESTNUT AND MOUNTAIN GRAPE MONT BLANC, BLUE CHEESE MERINGUE, RUM ICE CREAM

Each part of this spectacular dessert could be used on its own as a more simple sweet bite. The astringent skin–braised chestnuts are unusual in that they are treated to soften bitterness, and served with their astringent skins intact. At L'Effervescence, Namae brushes beet concentrate over one half of each chestnut tuile to introduce a bright contrasting color on the plate.

SERVES 8

Rum Ice Cream

230 ml (8 fl oz) whole (full-cream) milk

scant 2 tablespoons granulated sugar

generous 1 tablespoon artisanal Japanese sugar (*wasanbon*, page 15)

½ vanilla bean

3 small egg yolks, at room temperature (about 40 g/ 1½ oz)

1 tablespoon dark rum

Mountain Grape Sorbet

75 g (2¾ oz) granulated sugar

400 g (14 oz) mountain grapes or small flavorful purple wine grapes

50 ml (1¾ fl oz) fresh lemon juice

25 g (1 oz) mild honey

To make the rum ice cream, pour the milk into a heavy medium saucepan and stir in the sugars. Scrape the seeds out of the vanilla bean and drop them, along with the pod, into the milk. Heat over medium–high, stirring with a wooden spoon, until the sugars have melted and the milk is hot but not simmering. Whisk the egg yolks in a small bowl, and add a ladleful of milk to the yolks to warm. Scrape back into the pan of milk and cook, stirring, over medium heat until the mixture has thickened and coats the back of the spoon. Stir in the rum and let cool to room temperature before chilling for several hours. Freeze with an ice cream maker or Pacojet according to its instructions.

To make the grape sorbet, stir 150 ml (5 fl oz) water into the sugar in a small saucepan and place over medium heat, stirring, just until the sugar melts. Allow the syrup to cool.

Blue Cheese Meringue

175 g (6 oz) Fourme d'Ambert blue cheese, or other semi-hard blue cow's cheese

250 g (9 oz) Fromage Blanc

150 ml (5 fl oz) cream (35% fat)

3 small egg whites, at room temperature (about 80 g/ 2¾ oz)

100 g (3½ oz) granulated sugar

Almond Meringue

75 g (2¾ oz) almond powder (ground almonds)

75 g (2¾ oz) confectioners' (icing) sugar

7 small egg whites, at room temperature (about 195 g/ 7 oz)

60 g (2 oz) granulated sugar

Astringent Skin–Braised Chestnuts and Tuiles

500 g (1 lb 2 oz) chestnuts with brown skins intact

350 g (12½ oz) light brown Japanese cane sugar (*kibizato*, page 15)

Chestnut Butter Cream

100 g (3½ oz) Astringent Skin–Braised Chestnuts, at room temperature

2 tablespoons unsalted butter, at room temperature

½ teaspoon dark rum

Marron Cream

500 g (1 lb 2 oz) chestnuts, steamed for 20 minutes and peeled

500 ml (17 fl oz/2 cups) whole (full-cream) milk

½ teaspoon fine sea salt

125 g (4½ oz) artisanal Japanese sugar (*wasanbon*, page 15)

Vacuum seal the grapes with 100 ml (3½ fl oz) of the syrup and simmer for 30 minutes in a medium pot of water. (Alternatively, place in a resealable freezer bag and clip one side of the bag onto the edge of the pot, but leave the other side open to release steam.)

Set a fine flat sieve (*uragoshi*, page 275) over a large bowl and empty the grapes into it. Push through the sieve to capture all the juices and discard the solids. Measure out 425 ml (14½ fl oz) of the grape liquid into a medium mixing bowl. Stir in another 75 ml (2½ fl oz) of the syrup and 300 ml (10 fl oz) water. Stir the lemon juice into the honey in a small bowl until emulsified, and add to the grape juice. Chill, then freeze with an ice cream maker or Pacojet according to its instructions.

To make the blue cheese meringue, preheat the oven to 60°C (140°F). Drop the blue cheese and fromage blanc into a food processor and pulse to amalgamate. Slowly pour in the cream while pulsing until the mixture becomes a creamy paste. Do not over process.

Beat the egg whites on high speed in a medium mixing bowl until soft peaks have formed. Gradually beat in the sugar to a stiff meringue. Carefully fold in the creamy cheese mixture, and spread in a thin layer on a large baking sheet lined with parchment (baking) paper. Place in the low oven for 8 hours to dry. Break the cooled meringue into small pieces (leftovers can be sprinkled on ice cream or eaten as is).

To make the almond meringue, preheat the oven to 135°C (275°F). Whisk the almond powder and confectioners' sugar together to make *tant pour tant* (the classic base for macarons). Beat the egg whites in a large mixing bowl on high speed until soft peaks form. Gradually add in the sugar, beating until the meringue is stiff. Gently fold in the *tant pour tant*, taking care not to deflate the whites. Form into 3 cm (1¼ in) balls on a paper-lined baking sheet. Bake in the middle of the oven for 1 hour to dry. Break into small pieces for serving.

To make the astringent skin–braised chestnuts, drop the chestnuts into a medium pot and cover with cold water. Bring to a boil, then drain, discarding the water. Repeat another 3 times to remove astringency, but on the last time, keep cooking the chestnuts until soft, about 10 minutes after coming to the last boil. Stir in the sugar, adjust to a simmer and cook for 10 more minutes. Remove from the heat and allow to cool in the syrup. Drain and break up into small pieces.

To make the tuiles, preheat the oven to 160°C (320°F). Process about a cup of the astringent skin–braised chestnuts to a paste. Drop very small spoonfuls of the paste on a paper-lined baking sheet, smoothing into very thin rectangles of 2 × 4 cm (¾ × 1½ in). Bake in the middle of the oven for about 10 minutes.

To make the chestnut butter cream, pulse the astringent chestnuts, butter, and rum together in a small food processor to make a smooth cream.

To make the marron cream, bring the chestnuts, milk and ¼ teaspoon of the salt to a simmer in a medium pot and cook over medium–low heat until soft. Smash through a fine flat sieve set over a bowl to make a rough purée. Return the chestnut mixture to the pot, stir in the sugar and remaining salt, and cook over medium–low heat, stirring, to melt the sugar and evaporate excess liquid until the purée balls up in the pan.

Scatter some pieces of almond meringue on chilled dessert plates. Add a few small dollops of chestnut butter cream and a heaping tablespoon of icy grape sorbet here and there. Strew some pieces of astringent skin–braised chestnut and blue cheese meringue around each plate and top with an attractive mound of marron cream. Add a couple of chestnut tuiles and finish with an oval of rum ice cream.

Shared by Zacchari Touchane,
Sowaryu Tea Ceremony Secretariat
(formerly of L'Effervescence)

TEA PHILOSOPHY AT L'EFFERVESCENCE

During the tea ceremony, we believe in '*ichi za kon ryu*', the shared feeling of participating in a tea ceremony by having one mind set, one atmosphere, and building new relationships among the participants. We want the guests to be part of our collective experience so they understand where their food is from: who picked, cooked and served it. Sharing a mutual place builds new bonds. Through this sharing, guests come to value the food, the service and the originality of what is L'Effervescence.

At L'Effervescence, the tea is served tableside. We had some carts custom-built for us. We do a style of tea ceremony known as *bon-temae*, using a tray to hold all necessary utensils. We use an iron teakettle rather than the proper iron water pot (*kama*). This particular style has been adapted for house service.

We bow once at the table and start the tea ceremony. Though talk is permitted, we usually do not talk. We perform the tea ceremony, serving the main guest first. A second guest can be served and then so on.

Just before the tea service, small *mignardises* and the 'World Peace' (L'Effervescence original peanut milk) are served, to be enjoyed with the tea.

Utensils used in the ceremony

Obon: tea tray

Chawan: teacup

Chakin: linen cloth

Chasen: bamboo whisk

Chashaku: tea scoop

Chaki: tea caddy with matcha

Binshiki and *tetsubin*: iron tripod and iron teakettle

Kensui: receptacle for used water

La Bonne Table
Tokyo

KAZUNARI NAKAMURA

Kazunari Nakamura gently plucks up a tiny delicate flower with a pair of fine, long-handled tweezers, and places it ever so precisely into a space between the baby greens mounded on the plate. The flowers have joined small pieces of roasted, pickled and fresh vegetables for one of the best simple salads I have ever eaten. This says a lot, since salad is my favorite food, and I frequent Chez Panisse, the world's best restaurant to eat salad. Nakamura-san's face is in repose, almost as if in a state of meditation; his focus is solely on this one salad. For me, this is the moment when we have a window into his soul as chef.

Nakamura-san has a mild demeanor, which leads one to assume that he is shy or reserved. And perhaps, at heart, he is. But talking about food, his eyes light up and his whole demeanor transforms. At La Bonne Table, the chef and the cooks bring out and explain the food to the tables. When Nakamura-san delivers my food personally, I am honored and almost breathless with expectation, because I know his words will bring the food alive. His manner of delivery, as well as his self-deprecating laugh, are endearing.

A warm smile and kind eyes are clear indicators of his beautifully sensitive approach to food. Nakamura-san's flavors are always vibrant and clear, never muddied or overbuilt. Every component on the plate has a reason to be there and makes absolute sense. The fish and vegetables are hyper-seasonal, the meat is responsibly raised, thoughtfully sourced, and this so-called French cuisine has its roots firmly in Japanese classical techniques. This might be the best French neo-bistro meal in the world.

A warm smile and kind eyes are clear indicators of his beautifully sensitive approach to food.

Nakamura-san studied cooking at trade school – which may not be the obvious path to becoming an exceptional chef – but there is something special about him, an intangible element that might be easily overlooked if one does not have an attuned palate. Recognizing Nakamura-san's stewardship of the pristine ingredients he sources is essential for appreciating his sensitive approach to Japanese food through the lens of France.

Nakamura-san has been cooking professionally for over fifteen years in Tokyo-based French restaurants, including two years as sous chef at L'Effervescence under the mentorship of Shinobu Namae (page 132). Nakamura-san may not have any Michelin stars at La Bonne Table, but I would wager that some of the best food in Tokyo is coming out of his hands. The promise he shows with his personal touch to this new wave Franco–Japonaise cuisine bodes well for his rising reputation. And I have never eaten a meal at La Bonne Table when Nakamura-san was not at the helm, so clearly he is immensely dedicated to his metier. I wonder when he has time for a life, but am grateful, because eating at La Bonne Table is a perfect example of 'eating the chef' with his gentle, considered, ingredient-driven food.

And, perhaps unusually, although his pastry team executes the desserts, Nakamura-san is the conceptual artist behind them. They are never overdone, and in contrast, never simple, but always delicious. I can go either way on dessert at the end of a meal, but look forward with great anticipation to the seasonal fruit creations at La Bonne Table (such as the tangerine dessert on page 160). And somehow I always find room for the signature *takoyaki* (page 162), a molten chocolate cake *trompe l'oeil* version of the ubiquitous octopus balls sold from itinerant food stalls at festivals.

Genboku Shiitake Tsutsumi

ROASTED SHIITAKE STUFFED WITH YUZU MISO, ONION AND WALNUTS

These might be the tastiest little bites that I have ever eaten. Just one per person is served at La Bonne Table, always with a glass of sake, but I surely could eat at least four. Finely slivering the flavorful yet tough shiitake stems renders them softly chewy and deliciously edible.

The yuzu miso is inspired by *yubeshi*, a traditional dried yuzu sweet that, when well made such as by Yubeshi Nakaura-ya in Wajima, can be spectacular. While only one miso-stuffed yuzu is called for in this recipe, since the yuzu is hung outside to dry for one and a half months, it makes great sense to make at least three at a time.

A variation stuffing for these mushrooms is a mixture of three tablespoons of ground boudin noir (blood sausage) with one heaping tablespoon of finely chopped walnuts. After roasting, sprinkle the shiitake with a pinch each of yarrow leaf and finely chopped *narazuke* (chayote pickled in sake lees).

SERVES 4

Yuzu Miso

3 medium yuzu or 2 small round lemons

125 g (4½ oz) brown rice (*genmai*) miso

3 tablespoons finely chopped roasted peanuts

8 medium shiitake

2 tablespoons extra-virgin olive oil, plus extra for roasting

6 tablespoons finely chopped onion

2 tablespoons finely chopped walnuts

2 small sprigs of yarrow leaves (or substitute dill)

To make the yuzu miso, cut out a circle in each yuzu stem end to expose the flesh inside and create a lid. Scoop out all the flesh and membrane with a small spoon and place in a small piece of muslin (cheesecloth). Twist up the ends and squeeze the juice into a small bowl.

Drop the miso, peanuts and yuzu juice into a small food processor and pulse to a smooth paste. Stuff the mixture back into the 3 hollowed-out yuzu and replace the stem ends. Make a cradle for each one from kitchen twine and hang outside under the eaves away from direct sunlight to dry for 45 days.

Spoon the mixture from all of the yuzu into a small container – it will be dry and crumbly. Discard the tough hollowed-out yuzu. The mixture keeps for several months, if stored in the refrigerator.

Pare off the tips of the shiitake stems. With the stems upright, use a sharp knife to finely slice the stems into fine strands that remain attached to the cap.

Heat the olive oil in a small frying pan over low heat. Once warm, scrape in the onion and slowly sauté for about 5 minutes, stirring occasionally, until translucent, golden and confit-like.

Preheat the oven to 220°C (430°F). Arrange the shiitake, cap-side down, on a lightly oiled oven pan and roast for 3 minutes in the middle of the oven. Smash a spoonful of yuzu miso into one-third of each roasted shiitake cap, scraping it with a small spoon from the stem to the cap. Scrape in a spoonful of onion confit into another third of each cap, and walnuts into the remaining third. Roast again for 3 minutes. If not browned or sizzling sufficiently, cook under the broiler (grill) for an additional 1 minute.

Sprinkle each shiitake with a pinch of yarrow and serve 2 per person, burning hot as an appetizer.

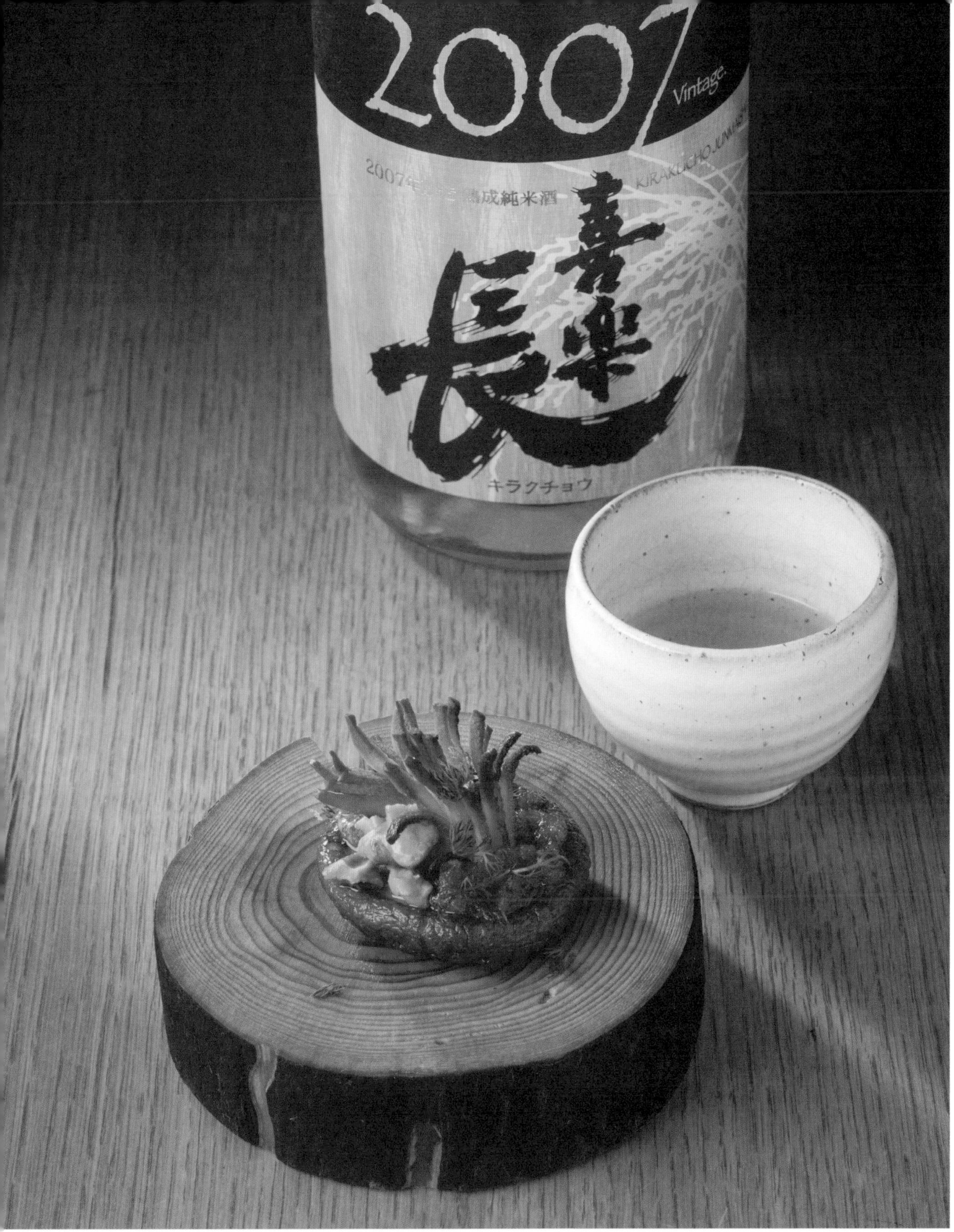
2007
Vintage.
喜楽長
キラクチョウ

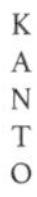

Sarada Karamanshi Doresshingu

FIELD SALAD WITH CALAMANSI VINAIGRETTE

The thought put into treating each small component of this seasonal salad almost brings me to tears. Some of the vegetables are roasted and warm, some are raw, so each bite is a delightful surprise. The dressing is just a light film so don't be tempted to add more. Calamansi (also known as calamondin) is a thin-skinned small green citrus with tart orange flesh. Commonly used in the Philippines, it is similar in taste to Japanese *sudachi* or *kabosu*. The best calamansi vinegar is produced by Huilerie Beaujolaise and is available through various mail order sites around the world.

SERVES 4

50 ml (1¾ fl oz) extra-virgin olive oil, plus extra for roasting

25 ml (¾ fl oz) calamansi vinegar, or other bright citrus vinegar such as *sudachi* or *mikan*

1 teaspoon flaky sea salt

4 × 5 cm (2 in) ends of very fine burdocks (*gobo*, page 277), scrubbed

1 small red pepper (capsicum), sliced

4 small shiitake, quartered

1 small piece of watermelon radish, finely sliced with a mandoline

1 baby turnip, finely sliced with a mandoline

4 micro carrots, with 1 cm (½ in) of tops

4 handfuls of baby salad mix

handful of edible flowers

Whisk the olive oil into the calamansi vinegar in a small bowl until emulsified. Stir in the salt and taste.

Preheat the oven to 200°C (400°F). Rub the burdock, red pepper and shiitake lightly with a little oil and roast on an oven pan for 3 minutes. Cool.

Put the roasted vegetables, raw vegetables, and baby salad greens and flowers into 3 separate bowls. Toss each with a little of the dressing so the ingredients are just lightly coated and glistening, not overwhelmed or drenched.

Mound the greens and flowers on 4 salad plates. Using a pair of chopsticks or kitchen tweezers, poke roasted vegetables into any small openings and add the raw vegetables in a haphazard fashion. Serve immediately.

Itoyoridai,
Yuzu Bu-ru Buran

SNAPPER WITH YUZU BEURRE BLANC

Served as a first course at La Bonne Table, this dish is light yet rich with the beurre blanc. The acid balance comes from the yuzu and tomato and brings the whole plate together beautifully. Cooking in the bamboo steamer gently infuses the fish with an almost imperceptible hint of bamboo.

SERVES 4

6 oval cherry tomatoes, halved lengthwise

1 large clam (*hokkigai*) or 6 firm medium clams, flushed with several changes of cold water

125 ml (4 fl oz/½ cup) white wine

8 tablespoons cold unsalted butter

1 teaspoon yuzu (or Meyer lemon) juice, plus 1 teaspoon finely slivered zest

4 small snapper fillets, skin on, weighing about 60 g (2 oz) each

¼ teaspoon flaky sea salt

1 Belgian endive leaf, sliced crosswise into 1 cm (½ in) strips

8 small sprigs of dill

8 small sprigs of chickweed (*hakobe*)

Preheat the oven to 150°C (300°F). Spread the tomatoes, cut-side up, on a small oven pan and roast for 20 minutes, until slightly whitened and half dry.

Bring the clam in its shell and the white wine to a boil in a small covered saucepan and cook until the clam opens and is cooked through. Pluck the clam out of the liquid and cut the meat into 1.5 cm (½ in) cubes. Discard the shell.

Strain the clam liquid through a fine sieve into a small saucepan and simmer until reduced to ½ tablespoon. Off the heat, whisk in 2 tablespoons of the butter. Return to low heat and continue to whisk in 1 tablespoon of butter at a time, adding the next tablespoon as the previous one has just melted. Stir in the yuzu juice and keep barely warm, or remove from the heat and reheat briefly before serving.

Fill a large wok one-third with water, bring to a boil and place a bamboo steamer inside the wok. Lay the snapper fillets on a plate that will fit inside the steamer and sprinkle on both sides with the salt. Set inside the steamer, adjust the heat to a lively simmer and steam for 2½ minutes, until the fillets are cooked through.

Spread 2 generous tablespoons of sauce in the middle of each of 4 salad plates. Distribute the endive between the plates, scattering artfully. Place the snapper fillets on top of the beurre blanc. Strew each plate with 3 or 4 pieces of clam, 3 tomato halves, and 2 sprigs each of dill and chickweed. Garnish with a pinch of yuzu zest and serve.

Kamasu, Kabocha, Mitsuba So-su

FRIED BARRACUDA WITH KABOCHA PURÉE AND MITSUBA SAUCE

Nakamura-san has great sense when building a plate – never too complicated. But there are always complementary elements, resulting in a perfect marriage each time. Each recipe method often includes a provocative, delicious little component that is well worth absorbing into one's repertoire. Here the fish skin is scorched for a crispy texture, while the flesh side is brushed with a light batter before frying. And the salt-pickled yuzu zest adds a compelling spark that lingers on the tongue after each bite. Take note that the yuzu zest needs one week to pickle.

SERVES 4

Salt-pickled Yuzu Zest

1 teaspoon flaky sea salt

6 tablespoons julienned yuzu (or Meyer lemon) zest

1 small kabocha (pumpkin), weighing about 250 g (9 oz)

4 tablespoons unsalted butter

1 teaspoon flaky sea salt

2 large bunches *mitsuba*

100 ml (3½ fl oz) Clam Broth (page 159)

4 barracuda fillets, skin on, weighing about 50 g (1¾ oz) each

2 tablespoons rice flour

neutral oil such as canola, safflower or peanut for deep-frying

6 tablespoons salmon roe freshly removed from the sac, rinsed in salt water

Make the salt-pickled yuzu zest 1 week or more in advance. Massage the salt gently into the zest and pack in a small jar. Leave in a cool, dry place for 1 week before using. Keeps for several months in the refrigerator.

Preheat the oven to 200°C (400°F). Halve the kabocha, cutting down through the stem end with a heavy knife. Scoop out the seeds and thready pulp and discard. Wrap each half tightly with aluminum foil, place on an oven pan and roast in the oven for 1 hour.

Scrape the kabocha flesh away from the skin and drop into a medium stainless bowl. Discard the skin. Mash the butter and salt into the kabocha to make a smooth purée. Keep warm by placing the bowl over a saucepan of barely simmering water.

Reserve about 16 small sprigs of the *mitsuba* for garnish, and roughly chop the rest. Pulse in a blender with the clam broth (just barely reaching up to the top of the leaves) to emulsify then purée to a smooth sauce. Mash through a fine sieve to remove any remaining pieces of leaf or stem.

Grill (broil) the barracuda skin without cooking the flesh in a salamander or with a butane blowtorch.

Whisk 1 tablespoon water into the rice flour to make a smooth batter. Heat 8 cm (3¼ in) of oil in a heavy medium saucepan over medium–low heat until rippling. Drip a little batter into the oil to check the heat: if hot enough, the batter will immediately form a ball and bounce back up to the surface (the oil should be slightly lower in temperature than for tempura). Paint the flesh side of 2 barracuda fillets with the batter, and slip into the oil. Fry for 1 minute, until golden brown and just cooked through. Drain on a paper towel–lined cooling rack. Repeat with the remaining 2 fillets.

Spread 60 ml (2 fl oz/¼ cup) of the warm kabocha purée into a circle on the left side of each of 4 salad plates. Place a hot barracuda fillet on the purée and spoon a pool of *mitsuba* sauce to the right of the kabocha and fish. Dollop a heaping tablespoon of salmon roe into the center of the *mitsuba* sauce and garnish with a pinch of salt-pickled yuzu zest and a few *mitsuba* leaves.

Kiku Imo Su-pu,
Age Saba

JERUSALEM ARTICHOKE SOUP WITH GRILLED MACKEREL

The textures in this soup are surprising, yet satisfying, and each bite is slowly savored while a feeling of comfort washes over. Since no butter or cream are used in the soup, the flavor is intense and clear.

SERVES 4

Clam Broth

100 g (3½ oz) small clams (such as *asari*), scrubbed and soaked in several changes of cold water

1 tablespoon sake

500 g (1 lb 2 oz) Jerusalem artichokes, scrubbed

2 tablespoons unroasted sesame oil

4 large komatsuna or bok choy leaves, stems removed

4 center pieces of mackerel fillet, skin on, weighing about 30 g (1 oz) each

¼ teaspoon flaky sea salt

neutral oil such as canola, safflower or peanut for deep-frying

To make the clam broth, place the clams in a small saucepan and add 500 ml (17 fl oz/ 2 cups) cold water and the sake. Cover and bring to a lively simmer over medium–high heat. Cook for 3–5 minutes, or until the clams have opened. Scoop out the clams with a wire-mesh skimmer and use them in another dish. Strain the broth through a piece of paper towel or an unbleached coffee filter to remove sand particles.

Do not peel the Jerusalem artichokes. Cut half of one into 1 cm (½ in) cubes and set aside. Cut the remaining Jerusalem artichokes crosswise into fine slices. Drop the slices into a medium pot, and add the sesame oil and 250 ml (8½ fl oz/1 cup) of the clam broth. Bring to a boil over medium–high heat, then adjust to a lively simmer. Cook for about 20 minutes, until the slices are completely soft. Purée in batches in the blender until smooth. Pass through a fine sieve back into the clean pot and keep warm on the lowest heat possible (using a flame tamer if you have one).

Fill a medium saucepan with water and bring to a boil. Blanch the komatsuna leaves for 30 seconds (or 1 minute for bok choy). Drain and refresh under cold running water until cool to the touch. Shake off excess water and pat dry in a clean dish towel. Chop roughly.

Sprinkle both sides of the mackerel with the salt. Place on a rack set over an oven pan and grill for 2 minutes on each side under a preheated broiler (grill), 10 cm (4 in) from the heat.

Heat 5 cm (2 in) of oil in a small heavy saucepan over medium heat. Once hot but not smoking, deep-fry the reserved Jerusalem artichoke cubes for about 2 minutes, until golden brown and crispy. Drain on paper towels.

Ladle 60 ml (2 fl oz/¼ cup) of the soup into 4 wide shallow soup bowls and set a grilled piece of mackerel in the middle of each bowl. Garnish with the blanched greens and fried Jerusalem artichoke. Serve steaming hot.

Mikan, Howaito Chokore-to Mu-su, Matcha no Bisukui

WHITE CHOCOLATE BOMBE, TANGERINE, MATCHA BISCUIT

Winter is citrus season, so make this during the cold months. Tangerines are a type of mandarin, but you can use others such as clementines. The important point is to source very small citrus that is both sweet and sour. The fine slices covering the exterior hide a complex interior. This is a spectacular dessert.

SERVES 4

Tangerine Granita

60 g (2 oz) mild honey

300 ml (10 fl oz) potato shochu

300 ml (10 fl oz) fresh tangerine juice

White Chocolate Mousse

335 ml (11½ fl oz) whole (full-cream) milk

1 tablespoon granulated sugar

4 medium egg yolks, at room temperature (about 65 g/2¼ oz)

335 g (12 oz) white chocolate, finely chopped

800 ml (27 fl oz) cream

Matcha Biscuit

95 g (3¼ oz) almond powder (ground almonds)

25 g (1 oz) matcha powder

40 g (1½ oz) unbleached all-purpose (plain) flour

175 g (6 oz) granulated sugar

10 medium egg whites, at room temperature (about 320 g/11½ oz)

40 g (1½ oz) unsalted butter, melted and cooled

4 small tangerines, skin cut off with a sharp knife, sliced into fine rounds

2 tablespoons potato shochu

4 nasturtium flowers, for garnishing

1 marigold flower, for garnishing

white chocolate, for garnishing

To make the tangerine granita, spoon the honey into a medium mixing bowl and slowly whisk in the potato shochu until well emulsified. Stir in 300 ml (10 fl oz) water and the tangerine juice, and pour into a rectangular plastic or stainless container. Place in the freezer. After 1 hour, remove from the freezer and scrape with a fork to create large ice flakes. Repeat every 30 minutes until the granita is completely flaked.

To make the white chocolate mousse, heat the milk and sugar over medium heat in a small saucepan until the sugar has dissolved. Stir the egg yolks together in a small mixing bowl to break up. Ladle in a quarter or so of the milk to warm the yolks, then scrape back into the pan of milk. Heat, stirring continuously, until the mixture slightly thickens and coats the back of the wooden spoon (you are making crème anglaise). Remove from the heat. Once the crème anglaise is no longer burning hot and has cooled down to a bit above body temperature, about 40°C (105°F), stir in the white chocolate until completely melted. Chill.

Beat the cream for about 7 minutes, until very stiff but not granular. Gradually fold in the chilled white chocolate crème anglaise to form a light and fluffy mousse.

To make the matcha biscuit, preheat the oven to 165°C (330°F). Whisk the almond and matcha powders, flour, and 95 g (3¼ oz) of the sugar together in a small mixing bowl. Beat the egg whites in a medium mixing bowl until soft peaks form. Beat in the remaining 80 g (2¾ oz) of sugar slowly until the mixture forms a stiff meringue. Carefully fold in the dry ingredients, sprinkling about a quarter at a time over the meringue so as not to deflate. Once incorporated, drizzle in the butter and gently fold in until well emulsified. Scrape the mixture into a 20 cm (8 in) square pan lined with parchment (baking) paper. Bake for 9 minutes in the center of the oven. Cool on a rack for 5 minutes before removing from the pan and allowing to come to room temperature directly on the rack.

Place the matcha biscuit on a flat surface and spread a 2 cm (¾ in) layer of the mousse across the top. Cut into perfect circles with a 9 cm (3½ in) ring mold. Slide a thin spatula under each biscuit and transfer to a dessert plate. Cover the mousse with the tangerine slices, overlapping them in an attractive fashion. Brush with shochu. Top with a heaping tablespoon of tangerine granita and garnish with a few torn pieces of nasturtium flower, some marigold petals and a grating of white chocolate. Serve immediately.

Chokore-to no Takoyaki

MOLTEN CHOCOLATE 'TAKOYAKI'

Takoyaki are batter-based octopus balls sold at stalls at every festival and street fair around Japan. They are served with a dollop of mayonnaise and a sprinkling of green nori powder. Here the ball is made with a chocolate batter and oozes warm chocolate when bitten into. The mayonnaise is replaced with crème anglaise, and the nori with dried mint.

MAKES 24

Crème Anglaise

250 ml (8½ fl oz/1 cup) whole (full-cream) milk

1½ tablespoons granulated sugar

2 medium egg yolks, at room temperature (about 35 g/1¼ oz)

'Takoyaki'

75 g (2¾ oz) unsalted butter, softened, plus extra for the pan

75 g (2¾ oz/⅓ cup) granulated sugar

40 g (1½ oz) chocolate (55% cacao), melted and cooled

2 large eggs, at room temperature

½ tablespoon unsweetened cocoa powder

¼ teaspoon baking powder

75 g (2¾ oz/½ cup) unbleached cake flour

dried mint, for garnishing

To make the crème anglaise, heat the milk and sugar in a small saucepan over medium–low heat until the sugar dissolves. Whisk the egg yolks together in a small mixing bowl. Add a ladleful of the milk to warm the yolks, then scrape back into the pan of milk. Heat, stirring continuously, until the mixture slightly thickens to coat the back of a wooden spoon. Transfer the crème anglaise to a pitcher or jug. (Leftovers can be stored in the refrigerator for up to 1 week.)

To make the *takoyaki*, beat the butter and sugar until light and creamy. Add the melted chocolate and eggs, beating them into the butter until smooth and emulsified. Beat in the cocoa, baking powder and flour until well incorporated.

Preheat the oven to 180°C (350°F). Lightly butter a *takoyaki* pan and add batter to fill each hole. (Alternatively, use mini ramekins.) Cook in the middle of the oven for 15 minutes. Unmold and serve hot, 1 per person, with ½ teaspoon of crème anglaise drizzled over the top of each ball and a small sprinkle of the mint.

TERADA HONKE

Bose Peninsula, Chiba Prefecture

In October 2016, I traveled to Australia for the first of what has now become a regular schedule of visits. I make the 9-hour trip for two reasons: first, to promote my books, and second, to introduce people to the incredible artisanal Japanese products about which I am passionate, and to which I am deeply committed.

My first trip was planned due to a liaison with Fino Foods, a Brisbane- and Sydney-based purveyor of well-chosen artisanal foods for restaurants and quality retailers. Dedicated to sharing the best of Japan, I teamed up with Michael Dalton, visionary owner of Fino Foods, to do just that. Having experienced how difficult it is to get artisanal products into the Japanese food distribution chain in the United States, Dalton's proactive stance was refreshing and energizing. I threw my hat in the ring, and Australia might have the best line-up of honest, well-made Japanese ingredients of any country outside of Japan.

In the fall of 2016, I was four years in to the promotion of my first two books, with scores of dinners under my belt, though up to that point only in the US. For each of these collaboration events, I always brought the important Japanese ingredients. However, sourcing sake had been a constant issue. I found that many of the sakes I tasted had lost approximately 30% of their integrity in transit, and so I set about finding responsible sake importers. I did: Wine of Japan (New Jersey), Floating World Sake (New Mexico) and World Sake Imports (US/UK). But what I came to realize was that the palate for sake in the US was not at all mine. The sakes that people seem to enjoy there are too powerful, too big, too much. I had resigned myself to this peculiar proclivity, but was disappointed nonetheless.

On that first trip to Australia (and all subsequent ones), I did several collaboration dinners at top restaurants with Fino's support. One of the first dinners was with Mat Lindsay at Ester in Sydney. Mat asked his pal Matt Young, of Black Market Sake, to work up a sake pairing for the dinner. As was typical of these collaboration events, I spent most of the time on the floor, talking with the diners.

Sake consumption is declining in Japan, but thankfully rising outside of it, and as a champion of artisanal Japan, I have an inherent duty to promote sake as well as food. I knew I would

not have time to taste all the sakes that night, so I asked for a small glass of the two sakes on the list that I knew and loved: Terada Honke's Daigo no Shizuku and Kidoizumi Shuzo's Hakugyokuko, both from Chiba prefecture. And those tastes dropped me in my tracks, because both sakes tasted exactly as they do in Japan. Beyond that, the choices themselves touched me. Both sake houses are well known, though perhaps Kidoizumi has a wider reach, while Terada Honke has a dedicated cult following.

A 150-year-old brewery, Kidoizumi Shuzo tends towards well-balanced, elegant sakes very much in line with my typical preference. On the other hand, Daigo no Shizuku is a wild, unpasteurized sake with lightly acidic back notes, which, despite my penchant for sakes that fall in the 'close to water' category, happens to be one of my all-time favorites.

Still stupefied by the thoughtful, eclectic selection of beautiful sakes, and of the meticulous care obviously given to them, I heard that Matt Young was in the house that night. Boldly accosting him at the bar where he was eating, I thanked him from the bottom of my heart for the critically important work he was doing. And thus began a mutually supportive relationship that has grown over the years – mostly by email – but occasionally in person.

Terada Honke has been brewing sake for over 345 years, since 1673. And for the last five generations, the brewer at Terada Honke was not a son of the Terada family, but rather the husband of a daughter of the family. In this ancient Japanese custom, parents adopt the son-in-law, who then assumes the family name. As adopted son (*mukoyoshi*), he is now in line to take over whatever business the family operates, and is carefully groomed to do so. One of the most well known sakes made by Terada Honke is Gonin Musume (Five Daughters) – a reference to this unusual unbroken lineage of adopted son-in-laws.

Masaru Terada, husband of Satomi Terada, is the 24th-generation brewer at Terada Honke. Several points set this centuries-old brewery apart from most other sake houses. Thanks to Satomi's father, Keisuke Terada, who was the previous brewer, Terada Honke has been making sake naturally for over sixty years, and is now using only local organic rice.

Rice-planting season is in the late spring in their area of Chiba, an off-time for brewing sake. During these months of hiatus, the brewery workers put great effort into testing and cultivating heritage rice varieties to use in their sake. And since 2016, Terada Honke exclusively uses koji spores that have propagated naturally and live on the walls of the brewery (*kura*) and propagating room (*koji muro*). They make their sake following the ancient *kimoto* method, whereby a mother (*shubo*) is created from rice koji, rice and deep well water. These three ingredients are mashed together in a large low tub by a handful of workers

wielding long-handled mallets. They work in unison, singing a deep-throated ancient song, which imparts a joyous feeling to the work and the mash, and ultimately to the sake.

I have visited Terada Honke three times over the last several years, and each time have been overwhelmed by Masaru and Satomi's generosity. A few years ago, I made the trip out to the Boso Peninsula with Sandor Ellix Katz (*The Art of Fermentation*), Shinobu Namae (L'Effervescence, page 132) and Robbie Swinnerton ('Tokyo Food File', *The Japan Times*). Despite being two days before New Year's Eve (Japan's version of our western Christmas), Masaru spent at least three hours with us, chatting, showing us the inner workings of the brewery, tasting sake and enjoying lunch. Lunch was an eclectic yet utterly delectable macrobiotic spread cooked by Satomi, eaten in their cavernous Edo period rice storage house, renovated for receiving visitors several years back.

I have had two other occasions to enjoy Satomi's food, and each time I linger on each bite, savoring it carefully, wondering how she has prepared the dish. Satomi's unerring approach and clarity of flavor is impressive and speaks to me viscerally. As a cook who puts much thought and care into my own food, always with the aim for the ingredients to shine and the dishes I prepare to be honestly delicious, I deeply appreciate Satomi's food and look forward to eating it again, as much as I look forward to once again tasting the uniquely delicious sakes produced by Masaru and his team at Terada Honke.

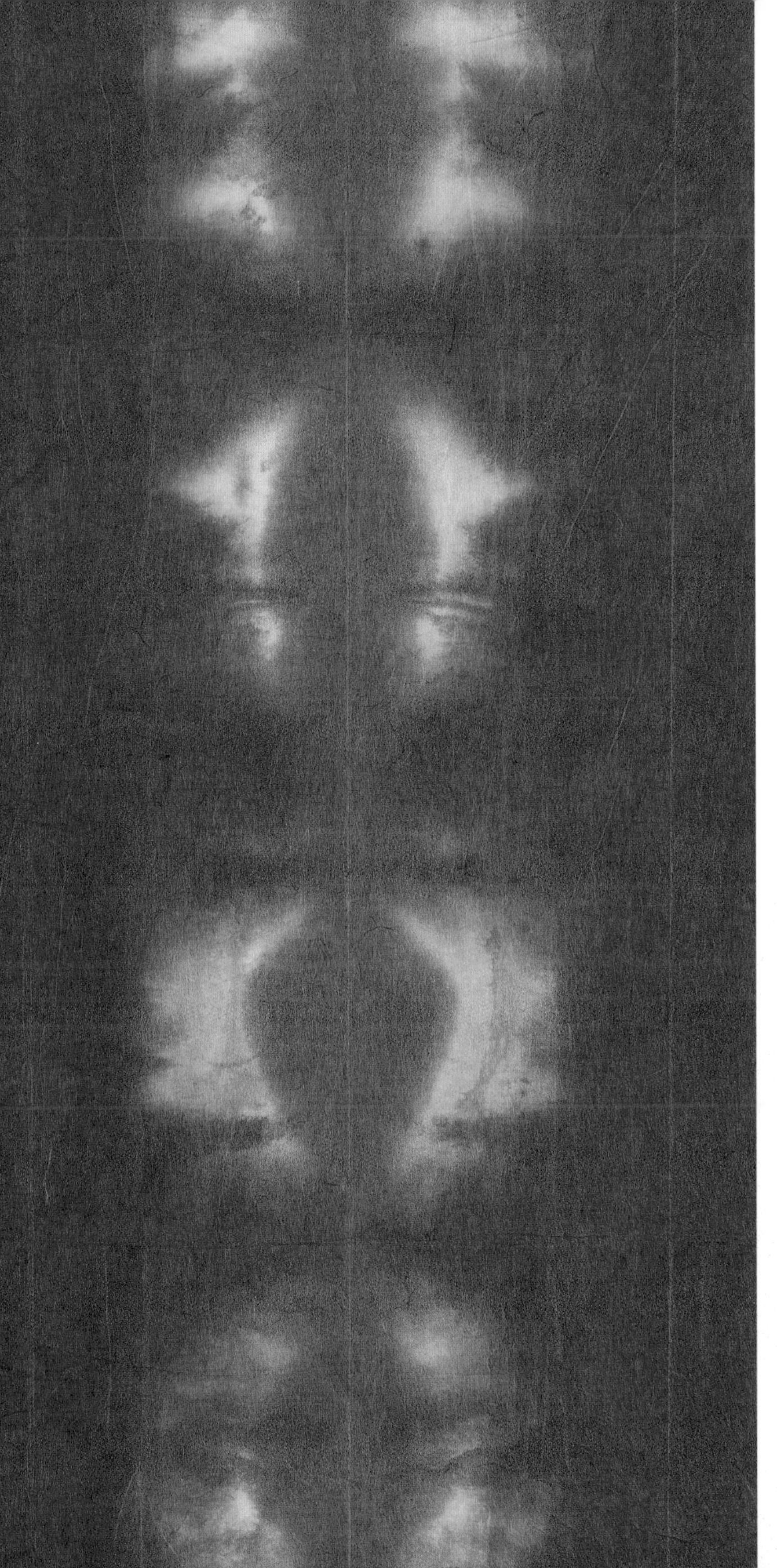

北陸

HOKURIKU

Noto Peninsula

THE NOTO BLACKSMITH

Sparks fly off the metal as 3rd-generation blacksmith Katsuji Hoshiba pokes the steel into the 700–800°C (1290–1470°F) fire fueled by Noto wood charcoal, before placing it on his anvil for pounding a total of fifteen times. Most other knife makers use coke, but charcoal is one of the Noto Peninsula's important local products and there is a long history of its use by local artisans, as well as in daily life.

Extending northward into the Sea of Japan, Noto Peninsula is one of the few places in Japan that has successfully hung on to traditional building materials and long-standing ways, which have defined the area for centuries. As we wound our way along the coastal road spanning the entire peninsula, on my very first visit to Noto in 2011, I was awestruck by the authentic feel of the countryside and the lack of depressingly crappy pre-fab structures. Still an anomaly in my mind, the best theory I have mustered up is that Noto has an abundance of raw materials such as diatomaceous earth for building, and trees for wood and charcoal. This theory cannot be too far off, since the United Nations designated parts of Noto as Globally Important Agricultural Heritage Systems (GIAHS), for its 'agriculture, forestry and fishery industries as well as human livelihoods'.

One of those industries is blacksmithing. The Noto blacksmith must become a master of ten types of forestry, fishery and culinary blades, and he will spend fifteen years apprenticing to become skilled in his craft. Today, only one traditional forge remains on Noto and wider Ishikawa prefecture: Fukube Kaji, now headed by 4th-generation son Kentaro Hoshiba, assisted by his ever-proficient wife, Yuka. Yuka showed such self-confidence at our first meeting and on all subsequent occasions that I mistook her for the daughter of the family.

Upon joining the workforce as a young man, Kentaro initially split his time between the Noto town hall and the family blacksmith shop and forge, but has now stepped into his father's footsteps as the head of the business. While currently still honing his craft before becoming a master blacksmith like his father, Kentaro brings other qualities to the table, and has started a mobile blacksmith shop in a van, plying his family's wares across the length and breadth of the Noto Peninsula. And these days, due to a marked decrease in people's abilities to care for tools, their workroom also has a constant backlog of knives, scythes, hoes and axes tagged for repair on the shelves. The repairs take up so much of Katsuji Hoshiba's time that he is only able to craft a few hand-hammered knives per month, and it was a great favor to me that he agreed to work at the forge the day we came to photograph.

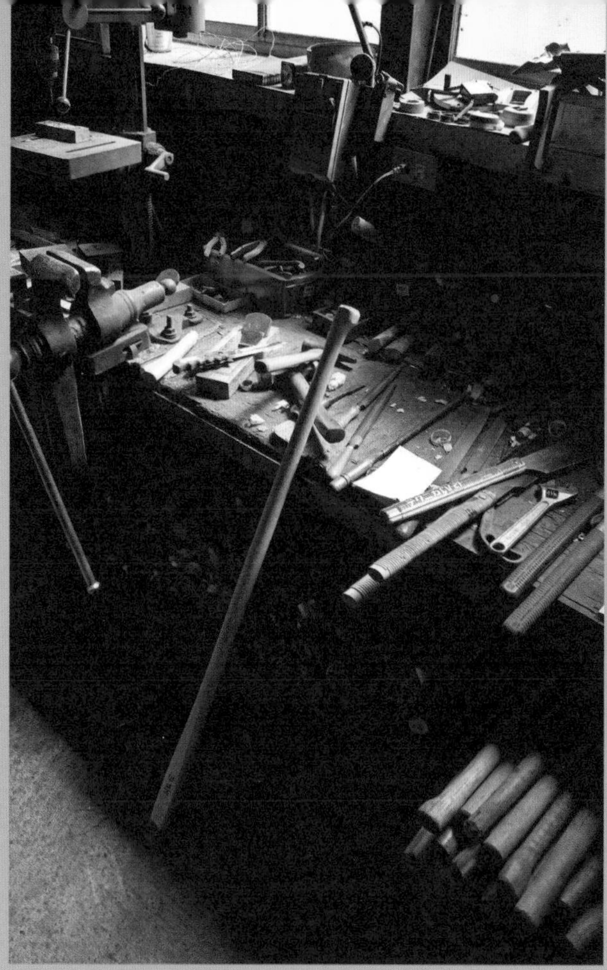

irrevocably captivating me. I bought two: one magnificent, hand-hammered, carbon-steel *magiri*, and an elegant squid knife (*ikasaki*) that I knew would be put to good use. Having finally gotten over being intimidated by cleaning and cutting squid for sashimi, I now relish the task – especially when their gut sacs are plump with the slightly bitter, creamy, coral-colored gastric fluids – exquisite when folded into raw squid strips and served as an accompaniment to sake (*sake no sakana*).

I return to Fukube occasionally, and each visit I linger over the cases, resisting the urge to buy, but never able. Recently I selected two boar-skinning knives as presents for my husband and a friend. It is the unexpected that often catches my eye. I would love to take a few of the well balanced, light-in-the-hands, razor-sharp hoes home to Saitama, but the airline might object to the blades.

People are heading to Japan in droves, and buying a cool Japanese knife or two is certainly on the top of many people's lists. But a fair number of the Japanese knives I see in restaurant kitchens outside of Japan are unnecessarily ornate or etched with swirl markings on the blade, and sadly, little do the cooks know that their so-called artisanal Japanese knives are actually made of pressed steel rather than the far superior hand-hammered blue steel. Master blacksmith Katsuji Hoshiba's opinion of these common, pressed knife blades: 'weak'.

Several years ago, enjoying mid-morning 'coffee time' around the family table at Yuyado Sakamoto (page 172), while picking Shinchan Sakamoto's brains, Shinchan's eyes widened in an 'aha' moment and he began describing a knife that he loved: his *magiri*. The story unraveled further and he excitedly asked his wife, Mihoko, to fetch the knife to show me the actual specimen. Apparently, he had had an even more special *magiri*, but had given it to a girl because she was 'so cute'. We laughed ruefully at his folly while examining the *magiri* he still possessed.

A *magiri* is a thick, flat, double-edged knife that curves to a point at the tip. It is the one knife carried by every fisherman, because it will free him when caught in a tangled net, and also doubles as a fish-gutting knife. I may never need to cut my way out of a fishing net, or even gut a fish on the fly, but the story evoked a romantic notion of the sea, and Shinchan's enthusiasm was infectious. I, too, had to have one. Mihoko rang up the shop, and after a typical late lunch at Sakamoto, we made the 30-minute drive to the town of Noto to visit Fukube Kaji.

Our daily kitchen knives and farm tools are from Hitoshi Matsunaga and his father, blacksmiths in the small country town of Annaka in a neighboring prefecture, so I had no specific need for additional knives. But there was something about the fishermen's knives at Fukube that held a special allure,

THE LOCAL STORE: DRY GOODS AND HARDWARE

Japan was 90% agrarian before World War II, a mere eighty years ago. This simple fact still resonates in modern Japan, creating a marked dichotomy between the traditional and the Now.

Many vestiges of the rural way of life remain, evidenced by the artisanal foods and crafts still produced today. Although now joined by convenience stores, 'family restaurants' (chain restaurants), supermarkets, chain hardware stores and 'home centers', small shops still dot the landscape in the form of tiny restaurants and thoughtfully stocked establishments such as the dry goods store (*kanbutsu-ya*) and the hardware store (*kanamono-ya*). Sadly, the attrition rate of these small establishments is high and their survival is threatened.

In our medium-sized town of 15,000, we have several Cainz Home 'home centers' now selling more and more of their proprietary brand products, but no traditional hardware store. By good fortune, an expertly staffed, impressive local hardware store is located in Kodama-machi, the next town over. Chihara Hardware is stocked with actually useful, professional supplies for local carpenters and home cooks, unlike the prettily packaged items for amateurs that line the shelves and walls of the local chain store. It is depressing, though, that there is no comparing the traffic between the two stores. There is also no comparison between the personal service and the breadth of knowledge of the staff at Chihara Hardware. Or the personal greetings and warm smiles rather than the perfunctory, automatic bark of '*irashaimase*!' ('welcome' without the 'well') that 'greets' one at chain stores.

Several years ago, our Edo period storage house burned to the ground. The horror of that night still lingers; the building was located directly adjacent to our house, mere meters away. The flames licked towards our exterior mud walls, yet the house did not burn. Piled high with boxes and lined with shelves containing small farm tools, our storage house also held summer screen doors custom-made by the traditional door maker (*tateguya-san*), our hollowed-out tree trunk for pounding mochi (*usu*), and my drying equipment for umeboshi.

When June was coming around that year, I stopped by Chihara Hardware to see if I could order another umeboshi set-up or two: consisting of a wooden stand with an oversized bamboo rack. These pieces are last vestiges of farm life – now replaced by plastic – so no longer available. Perceiving my crestfallen demeanor, the Chihara staff brainstormed a solution. They remembered a local guy who might have the pieces I was seeking to replace. Once tracked down, the gentleman agreed to sell me two sets for the equivalent of about US$45, and even rigged them up with strapping so that the stands would stay securely in place when splayed open. I keep one set in our garage and one set at my school (our former home), hedging my bets in case we have another fire. And every time I haul a set out, I am thankful for that local guy and for Chihara Hardware.

Another important, though even more rare, shop is the *kanbutsu-ya*: the dry goods store. In this case, we are speaking of a purveyor of dried fish or dried sea-related foods, the essential building blocks of traditional Japanese cuisine. With no *kanbutsu-ya* in sight, our local fish market is the best choice to purchase these products in our area, and the supermarket the last choice. The person who chooses the products for the shelves should have expert knowledge and insight – absolutely not the case with supermarkets.

Beyond the fish market, staffed with fish mongers skilled in selecting sea-related products, is a rough-and-ready fish wholesaler (*sakana tonya*) such as Kotobuki-ya located on the outskirts of Tsukiji market, or Shirai Shoten, a drop-dead-gorgeously appointed, 80-year-old *kanbutsu-ya* in the town of Nanao on the Noto Peninsula.

Introduced by Shinichiro and Mihoko Sakamoto, I travel ninety minutes each way to reach Shirai Shoten when visiting Yuyado Sakamoto in Noto's Suzu town. The edifice of the shop is reminiscent of a traditional, thick-walled storage building. Inside, the shelves and refrigerators glow softly, cast in an almost golden aura. The packaging is understated, artistic, stunning in its very wabi-sabi simplicity. I want to buy one of everything and never leave without several shopping bags full of fish- and sea-related ingredients of the highest level. There may be no rival to Shirai Shoten in Japan. Shirai-san personally visits far-flung areas such as Rausu, Rishiri and Hidaka in Hokkaido for konbu, and Ariake Bay in Kyushu for nori – two of the most important sea-related ingredients in Japanese cuisine. And he sources the very best (repeat, best) locally produced Noto foods, such as air-dried fish, fresh seaweeds and fish sauce.

The shop also makes a handful of classic Japanese foods in-house. Candied herring (*nishin no ame daki*), konbu rolls (*konbu maki*) and soybeans simmered with konbu (*konbu mame*) are all cooked slowly in old-fashioned iron pots for five to six hours each day. Only Japanese ingredients are used, including 1-year-aged Hidaka konbu, a hint of Noto fish sauce, local soy sauce, and coarse light brown Japanese sugar (*zarame*).

Shirai Shoten encourages a physical visit to the shop to touch, smell and see the goods, and does not offer online sales. Their knowledge and advice is crucial in making your selections, so a visit goes beyond cultural enrichment, and is well worth the travel to get there. If the town of Nanao is out of your reach, Shirai Shoten also has a shop in the city of Kanazawa – a popular destination for foreign travelers.

It's all about connecting. Because we tend to be disconnected by the very nature of our work. Whether we work at home or at an office, alone or with others around us, there is a sense of autonomy in how we work, even as part of a team. Community in the old-fashioned sense belongs largely to a time gone by, though certainly does exist in remote pockets here and there in the world. I live in a rural environment, but cook and write at my small immersion English school with the preschoolers screaming around me. My adult connection comes through my occasional interactions with shopkeepers – their pleasure at seeing me, our easy conversation. Experts are there for the mining of information and advice, and I could spend hours in their presence.

And in Japan, my message to young housewives or disenfranchised office workers is to take some time to patronize the local *kanbutsu-ya* and *kanamono-ya* before these treasures of materials and information are lost forever. Buying from a skilled professional means high quality at reasonable prices. The knowledge gained and the human contact offer a sense of warmth and a feeling of being valued and appreciated that is no longer part of the marketplace today, but was once a given element of community interplay.

SHINICHIRO SAKAMOTO

Yuyado Sakamoto
Suzu-shi, Ishikawa Prefecture

A cult-favorite hot-spring inn for food people and artists, located forty-five minutes by car or bus from the town of Wajima on the Noto Peninsula, Yuyado Sakamoto could be the most wabi-sabi inn in Japan.

Driving up, the inn is surrounded by pink-flowered *sakura* trees in spring and fiery-leafed maple trees in autumn, expressly planted to celebrate the changing seasons. You part the stunning low-hanging hemp curtain (*noren*), and enter a vast entry hall with a stone basin where water lilies float. The gleaming lacquered floors beyond the entrance beckon you into a structure where inside and outside are almost seamless. With unusually reflective, compelling local food, and soothingly spare traditional architecture, Sakamoto is a destination not to be missed.

As for the hot spring: that is the water piped nightly into one of Sakamoto's breathtaking bathtubs – red lacquer or grey granite, a choice determined by the number of guests that day.

Unlike most Japanese inns, you will not be served a huge tray groaning with small dishes (many of which are not made in house). Shinichiro Sakamoto and his wife, Mihoko, make all their food, as well as the pickles, preserves and smoked fish. Soba is hand rolled each day and treated with the respect it deserves: it is never cooked until the guests finish their previous course, since the aroma of soba is ephemeral, and the just-cooked texture of the noodles paramount. The Sakamotos put much thought into their methods: rice is flushed with icy cold, continuously running water for three hours before soaking and cooking over a gas-fired system used only for rice and noodles. The cooked rice is not fluffed, but turned out onto a flat wooden tub (*handai*) untouched, then covered with a damp piece of muslin cloth. Each dish is deceptively understated, yet exquisitely flavored. At the end of the meal, grilled rice balls and a small dish of pickles leave you replete, but never overstuffed, conducive for a good night's sleep. And the following morning's Japanese breakfast might be the best you will ever taste.

I had heard about the Sakamotos and their inn for years from my editor pal, Kim Schuefftan: they only operate during certain times of year, they only take a few guests at a time, they take days off when they feel the need. Hard to picture such an operation being successful, but then, success is also measured in quality of life. And one thing has become abundantly clear to me over the years that I have gotten to know Shinichiro and Mihoko Sakamoto – their lives follow a sensible, unhurried rhythm, no matter how busy they are. I emulate and absorb that peaceful flow each time I am among them, and hope that I can somehow follow suit in my own life. To date, that has not happened, but our friendship has deepened and transitioned from tentative to profoundly comfortable. There is never a time in my life that I am not planning my visit to Sakamoto.

The land itself was where Shinichiro Sakamoto's parents ran a *tojiba* – a kind of hot-spring respite where local people could take a day of 'vacation' from their life and, after enjoying the baths, have some food and drink. The current inn was designed by Shinji Takagi to have the look and feel of a traditional

Buddhist temple where priests typically dwell. The design of the structure embodies the Japanese aesthetic where inside and outside are symbiotic. The communal wooden sink area is open to the elements year round, a concept that is both astonishing and unexpected, since in winter the ground is blanketed with deep snowdrifts. The two wood-burning stoves mitigate the fact that one wall of the dwelling is completely open to the outside, with only a roll-down rattan screen to shield the house from the wind and precipitation. There is a high-ceilinged room below two small guest rooms, punctuated by a traditional ash-pit hearth (*irori*) with low embers to warm the room during the winter. It is here that guests enjoy their dinners, or view the cherry blossoms lit up at night in the spring.

On my first visit to Sakamoto, I ate alone. The classic, deceptively simple cuisine touched me in a way that other food seldom had in Japan. There was an element of honesty, yet an incredible hidden complexity that almost confounded me. The food was deeply contemplative, and this fact almost brought me to tears.

Now, over eight years later, Sakamoto is like my second home. I go when I can, and have taken many visitors. I have countless photos, hours of video footage, and copious notebooks filled with scratchings in a mixture of English and Romanized Japanese. There is probably a whole book to be written between the inn's food for paying guests, and the *makanai* ('family meal', page 208). But for now, we must be content with the twenty-odd guest dishes and few family meals and breakfast dishes that appear in this book.

On each visit, I see that Mihoko Sakamoto, an aficionado of foreign languages, is getting better and better at English as the number of foreign guests filtering through increases. When we are alone in the kitchen, Mihoko practices her English with me, and we laugh at her mistakes and mine. I send wine on ahead, we let down our hair during 'family meal' (and after), with me writing notes and hanging on every word that Shinchan utters. But Mihoko is the backbone of the kitchen, and does much of the prep. She also prepares the family meals – breakfast, lunch and dinner every day – along with expertly brewed coffee paired with local cakes for the mid-morning break.

Shinichiro Sakamoto (aka 'Shinchan') is the creator of the dishes for the inn. He ponders considerably on what he does and how he builds a dish using classical technique, while also bringing extensive travel and life experiences to the table.

In high school, Shinchan broke several vertebrae in a trampoline accident, and his movements are still slow and painful. Previously, he had dreamed of apprenticing at a Japanese sweet maker (*wagashi-ya*), but due to the need for exceptional dexterity to create hand-carved *wagashi*, this was not to be. Of necessity, his dream shifted to become a traditional Japanese cook (*ryori-nin*), and to that end, he set out to find an apprenticeship. However, no matter how many doors he knocked on, not one restaurant or temple would take him on due to his mobility limitations.

Shinchan gave up finding a mentor, and instead began eating out around Japan. And he eventually began traveling to Spain and Korea with his wife to experience foreign cuisines as well. Shinchan became a self-taught chef, and influences from these travels now appear here and there in his own traditional Japanese cooking. Several years ago, Tsuyoshi Miki, chef-owner of famed (now closed) Jean Moulin in Kobe, told Shinchan that learning in an experiential fashion, rather than doing an apprenticeship, had shaped his cooking into the interesting, delicious, multi-leveled phenomenon that it is today.

In spring of 2016, I brought Edward Lee with a crew from Zero Point Zero Films (the production company that used to film Anthony Bourdain's material). They were filming *Fermented*, a documentary, and I assisted on the Japan leg. Although the footage taken at Sakamoto eventually did not make the cut, after dinner Edward commented, 'The food is so simple, yet so complex,' and mused, 'Maybe I am doing too much to my food?' While I cannot speak to that, I can agree with the observation about complex simplicity. And contrary to the eating experience at many other Japanese inns, the food here comes one dish at a time, and does not overwhelm. I am always grateful for the Sakamotos being so uniquely attuned to their guests, and wish other tasting menus had the same mindfulness.

Aji no Nuta

HORSE MACKEREL WITH SWEET MISO

Nuta is a sweet miso sauce often served on silky steamed *negi* (Japanese 'leek'), which might also include clam. Here Shinichiro Sakamoto naps it alongside vinegared shiny fish, thus creating a lovely juxtaposition between the sweet vinegar and the sweet mustardy miso.

SERVES 4

1 tablespoon coarse light brown Japanese sugar (*zarame*, page 15)

2½ tablespoons rice vinegar

3 very fresh (sashimi-grade) skinless fillets of horse mackerel (*aji*), weighing about 100 g (3½ oz) each

¾ teaspoon fine sea salt

4 tablespoons white (*shiro*) miso

⅛ teaspoon Japanese mustard powder mixed with ⅛ teaspoon water

1 tablespoon Katsuobushi Dashi (page 202)

1 teaspoon freshly squeezed ginger juice

1 small bunch fine chives (*konegi*), cut into 4 cm (1½ in) lengths (halved lengthwise if thick)

In a medium bowl, stir ½ tablespoon of the sugar into 2 tablespoons of the vinegar to dissolve.

Cut the horse mackerel into 2 × 4 cm (¾ × 1½ in) pieces and sprinkle with ½ teaspoon of the salt. Leave for 10 minutes, then rinse under cold running water. Swish the fish pieces around in the sweetened vinegar for a few seconds, but not longer. A fresh taste is good here. Lay side by side on a piece of spongy paper towel to drain.

Drop the miso into a small bowl and whisk in the remaining ½ tablespoon sugar and ½ tablespoon vinegar, the mustard, dashi, ginger juice and remaining ¼ teaspoon salt to make a smooth paste.

Arrange the fish pieces in attractive cascading stacks in 4 small bowls. Spoon a dollop of the *nuta* miso on top of each stack, and stand a 6 mm (¼ in) thick bunch of thread-like chives against the fish.

Ninjin, Shiitake to Seri no Shira-ae

CARROT, SHIITAKE AND SERI IN SMASHED TOFU

Smashed tofu treatments (*shira-ae*) are versatile in that they can contain either raw or blanched vegetables, and are flavored with any of the following ingredients: toasted ground sesame seeds (white or gold), miso (white, country-style, brown rice or barley), mirin or sugar, and possibly some yuzu for brightness. Here, the skin (*yuba*) that is freshly skimmed off soy milk replaces the tofu, and a light hand is used in the seasoning for a sweetly gentle treatment. *Konnyaku*, a firm yet gelatinous ingredient made from the devil's tongue corm, appears in various dishes at Yuyado Sakamoto to add an appealing chewy texture.

SERVES 4

100 g (3½ oz) fresh *yuba* (page 280), or substitute *momendofu* (page 279) or Japanese-style soft block tofu

1 tablespoon white sesame seeds, finely ground

2 teaspoons coarse light brown Japanese sugar (*zarame*, page 15)

½ teaspoon *usukuchi shoyu* (page 9)

½ small carrot weighing about 50 g (1¾ oz), scrubbed

small handful of Japanese wild parsley (*seri*, page 18) or thick cress

50 g (1¾ oz) *konnyaku* (page 279), finely julienned

1½ tablespoons shoyu

1 tablespoon sake

¼ small dried red chili (*chile japones*, page 278), torn into small pieces

1 medium shiitake, stem removed

Finely chop the *yuba*. Or, set the tofu (if using) in a fine sieve set over a bowl and place a weight on top to drain off excess water for 20 minutes. Smash the tofu in a Japanese grinding bowl (*suribachi*, page 275). Fold the sesame, ½ teaspoon of the sugar and the *usukuchi shoyu* into the *yuba* or tofu until well incorporated.

Bring a medium pot of water to a boil over high heat. Drop the carrot into the water and cook for 5–7 minutes, until soft. Scoop out, shake off, and dry in a clean dish towel. Dip the *seri* or cress in and out of the boiling water, and refresh under cold running water. Pat dry in a dish towel. Blanch the *konnyaku* in the boiling water for 1 minute, then scoop out and blot dry. Finely dice the carrot, and cut the *seri* into 1 cm (½ in) pieces.

Drop the *konnyaku* into a small saucepan and bring to a simmer with the remaining 1½ teaspoons sugar, shoyu, sake and chili. Remove from the heat and let cool to room temperature. Drain, and discard the liquid.

Grill the shiitake cap in a dry cast-iron frying pan over medium–low heat for 2–3 minutes on each side, until lightly browned and fragrant. Cool, and slice finely.

Fold the carrot, *seri*, *konnyaku* and shiitake into the *yuba* or tofu mixture. Mound into 4 small lacquer bowls and serve.

Goboten

BURDOCK-FILLED FISH CAKES

Burdock root seems to be rising in popularity outside of Japan, and non-Japanese farmers are growing it as well. Because of its brownish hue, this dish is not the most beautiful, but it is tasty so should not be overlooked. Shinichiro Sakamoto uses a fish called *megisu*, a relative of sardine local to the Noto Peninsula, but any good-tasting white fish will be fine.

MAKES 4

1 tablespoon fine sea salt

20 cm (8 in) piece of burdock (*gobo*, page 277), the bottom thick part, weighing about 100 g (3½ oz)

300 g (10½ oz) very fresh, boneless, skinless white fish fillets, diced

1 teaspoon sake

1 teaspoon freshly squeezed ginger juice

1 teaspoon country-style miso (*inaka miso*, page 12)

1 teaspoon coarse light brown Japanese sugar (*zarame*, page 15)

2 tablespoons grated mountain yam (*yama imo*, page 277)

1 tablespoon potato starch

neutral oil such as canola, safflower or peanut, for deep-frying

Bring a medium pot of water to a boil over high heat and add the salt. Scrub the burdock with a stiff vegetable brush and cut into 4 × 5 cm (1½ × 2 in) pieces. Simmer for 2–3 minutes, depending on the thickness of the burdock. The center should still be hard. If the *gobo* is too soft, the *goboten* will not be tasty. Drain and cool.

Mash the fish in a Japanese grinding bowl (*suribachi*, page 275) with a wooden pestle (*surikogi*, page 275), or pulse in a food processor until it forms a paste. Mash or pulse in the sake, ginger juice, miso, sugar, mountain yam and ½ tablespoon of the potato starch until well combined.

Toss the burdock pieces in the remaining ½ tablespoon potato starch to aid in adhesion of the fish paste.

Set a small bowl of oil next to your workplace to oil your fingers slightly. Smooth a quarter of the fish paste around each piece of salt-simmered burdock. Leave a bit of burdock peeking out at the top, and form into oblique oval-shaped cakes, setting each one on a sheet of waxed paper as you go.

Prepare a thick pad of newspapers next to the stove and line with paper towels. Fill a medium pot halfway up with oil and place over medium heat. Once hot, slide the fish paste–enrobed burdock pieces into the oil. Fry, turning frequently with cooking chopsticks, until golden brown on all sides. When the bubbling oil has quietened, they are done. Remove from the oil with a metal skimmer, drain on the paper towels, and serve immediately.

Tomato to Teba Saki no Wan

GRILLED CHICKEN WINGS AND TOMATO IN CLEAR BROTH

Chicken wings tend to have more skin than meat, but when grilled can form the base for a lovely light broth. The tomatoes lend background notes of acid to give balance to the dish. Sakamoto uses 'fruit tomatoes', a variety of sweet tomato popular in Japan. And if you do not have access to *seri*, substitute a mild cress.

SERVES 4

4 chicken wings without the drumettes attached, weighing about 200 g (7 oz) in total

2 tablespoons *shio koji*

4 medium tomatoes

300 ml (10 fl oz) Katsuobushi Dashi (page 202)

¼ teaspoon freshly squeezed ginger juice

¼ teaspoon mirin

¼ teaspoon fine sea salt

1 or 2 drops of shoyu

4 large sprigs of Japanese wild parsley (*seri*, page 18), for garnishing

Toss the chicken wings in the *shio koji* and marinate at room temperature for 1–2 hours.

Preheat the broiler (grill). Arrange the chicken wings on a rack set over an oven pan and place under the broiler about 10 cm (4 in) from the heat. Cook for 2 minutes on each side, until sizzling and the chicken skin is speckled brown.

Core the tomatoes and score an 'X' into their bases. Pass a butane blowtorch over the skin of the tomatoes, to wrinkle a bit and blacken slightly.

Bring the dashi to a simmer in a medium saucepan over medium heat with the ginger juice, mirin, salt and shoyu. Nestle in the tomatoes (unpeeled) and the chicken wings and simmer gently for 30 minutes, until the tomatoes are soft and the broth is subtly infused with the chicken. Taste the broth and add salt if needed – it should be delicately salty. Dip the *seri* sprigs in and out of the broth to blanch.

Place a tomato and chicken wing side by side in each of 4 small lacquer soup bowls. Ladle enough broth (about 50 ml/1¾ fl oz) to come halfway up the sides of the chicken and tomato. Drape a *seri* sprig across the top and serve piping hot.

Ishidai no Sashimi Kureson-zoe

STRIPED BEAKFISH SASHIMI WITH CRESS

Although cress is not a typical garnish for sashimi, Shinichiro Sakamoto likes to use it because it is seasonal and grows abundantly around their house. The densely dark soy sauce they serve with sashimi is Kadocho shoyu from the Yuasa area of Wakayama prefecture, the birthplace of soy sauce in Japan. If you do not have access to fresh wasabi, make do with the cress as your spicy foil to the rich fish. Also, feel free to substitute other fresh white sashimi fish from your locale, and tamari for the Kadocho shoyu.

SERVES 4

200 g (7 oz) very fresh fillet of striped beakfish (*ishidai*), bones and skin removed

2 teaspoons freshly grated wasabi

large handful of wild cress leaves

2 teaspoons Kadocho dark shoyu

Cut the fish on the diagonal into 5 mm (¼ in) slices. Curl 5 slices into the bottom of each of 4 small, elegant ceramic bowls. Dab ½ teaspoon wasabi on top of the fish, and nestle a pluche of cress to one side. Serve each with ½ teaspoon of dark shoyu in small saucers.

Takenoko-ni

DASHI-SIMMERED BAMBOO SHOOT

Bamboo shoots are like corn. They are best fresh-boiled after a quick dash from the field. Dig up bamboo shoots. Peel and cook within thirty minutes of digging up. Also, timing is everything since bamboo shoots need to be served as soon as they are simmered in their slightly salty flavoring dashi. Here, because the bamboo is so fresh, it is cooked raw, rather than parboiled and soaked overnight in rice bran.

SERVES 4

1 small, freshly dug bamboo shoot, weighing about 300 g (10½ oz)

4 tablespoons brown rice (*genmai*) miso

15 cm (6 in) piece of konbu, preferably Rausu

600 ml (20½ fl oz) Katsuobushi Dashi (page 202)

1 teaspoon fine sea salt

2 tablespoons sake

1 tablespoon mirin

small sprig of young *sansho* leaves (page 19)

Peel the bamboo shoot and slice crosswise into 2 cm (¾ in) thick rounds.

Whisk 1 liter (34 fl oz/4 cups) water slowly into the miso in a medium pot until emulsified. Bring to a boil with the konbu over high heat. Drop the slices of bamboo shoot in and cook for 30 minutes. Leave to cool in the cooking liquid.

Working back about 90 minutes before you want to serve, drain the bamboo shoot. Place in a heavy medium pot and add the dashi, salt, sake and mirin. Bring the heat up slowly over medium heat and cook at a gentle simmer for a little over 1 hour, until soft all the way through. Serve hot, family style, in an attractive ceramic bowl with a sprig or two of *sansho* leaves.

Kasago no Ara no Nitsuke

SWEET SHOYU-SIMMERED ROCKFISH WINGS

Nitsuke is perhaps one of the most well loved, easy fish preparations in Japan, but also one of the most poorly executed due to over seasoning or a heavy hand with the sugar. Balance and timing are essential, and Shinichiro Sakamoto is a master of both. And melting a portion of the sugar in the bottom of the pan will impart a lovely caramelization to the fish.

SERVES 4

4 rockfish (*asago*) collars with wings attached, weighing about 600 g (1 lb 5 oz) in total

1 teaspoon fine sea salt

3 tablespoons coarse light brown Japanese sugar (*zarame*, page 15)

400 ml (13½ fl oz) sake

15 cm (6 in) piece of konbu

2 tablespoons julienned ginger

2 small dried red chilies (*chile japones*, page 278), torn into small pieces

1 garlic clove, thinly sliced crosswise

60 ml (2 fl oz/¼ cup) shoyu

Set the fish collars in a large bowl, sprinkle with the salt, and pour hot water over to cover. Let sit for 10 seconds to aid removal of the scales and any lingering odors. Drain. Rub off the scales with your thumbs and rinse the wings well with cold water.

Put 2 tablespoons of the sugar in a medium saucepan and place over low heat to melt. Nestle the fish collars into the pan and add the sake. It should reach about halfway up the fish. Bring to a simmer over medium–high heat, then add water to just cover the fish. Drop in the konbu, ginger, chili, garlic, shoyu and remaining 1 tablespoon of sugar. Place a drop lid (*otoshibuta*, page 275) or piece of parchment (baking) paper on top and bring to a brisk simmer. After about 20 minutes, remove the drop lid and skim off any scum that has accumulated. Replace the drop lid and continue simmering for about 10 minutes more, until the liquid has reduced by two-thirds. Serve hot.

Ishiru no Yaki Onigiri

FISH SAUCE–GRILLED RICE BALLS

The trick here is to not lose patience. Crisping up the surface slowly is the key to success. Low-ember charcoal is the best method for cooking these, but grilling under the broiler or in a cast-iron pan is also possible.

MAKES 8

1 quantity of Japanese Rice (page 205)

2 tablespoons Japanese fish sauce (*iwashi* or *saba ishiri*; or *hata hata shottsuru*, page 13)

1 tablespoon toasted sesame oil

Turn the cooked rice out into a flat wooden tub (*handai*, page 275) or onto a large wooden board and sprinkle 1 tablespoon of the fish sauce over the top. Cut and turn the rice with a rice paddle to distribute the fish sauce evenly and help the rice to absorb the liquid.

Add the remaining 1 tablespoon of fish sauce to a small bowl. Wet the palms of your hands with the fish sauce, and form 8 fat triangular rice balls by cupping and shaping the rice between your palms. The palm of your bottom hand should form one side of the triangle, and your top hand should form the other two sides by creating a cupped upside-down 'V'. Brush the rice balls lightly on all sides with the sesame oil.

Prepare low-ember charcoal, such as in a Japanese tabletop brazier (*shichirin*, page 275). Alternatively, preheat the broiler (grill), or a cast-iron frying pan over low heat.

Place the rice balls over the charcoal, or 15 cm (6 in) from the heat in the broiler, or in the frying pan. Grill for 7–8 minutes on each side, until crisped. Best warm, but also good at room temperature. No nori needed.

Nanohana no Kobujime

KELP-WICKED NANOHANA

Kelp-wicking is a common method to cure raw fish to be served as sashimi (page 78). The konbu firms up the flesh of the fish so the texture becomes appealingly tight with a hint of chewiness. Here, leafy greens benefit from having their moisture slowly sucked out by the konbu, while infusing them with a hint of the sea. Serve alongside Fish sauce–grilled Rice Balls (see above), for lunch or at the end of an evening meal.

SERVES 4

½ small bunch flowering brassica (*nanohana*, page 278), or soft rapini (broccoli rabe)

15 cm (6 in) piece of konbu, preferably Rausu

2 tablespoons white sesame seeds, warmed

Bring a medium pot of water to a boil over high heat. Hold the *nanohana* stems in the boiling water for 30 seconds. Drop in and cook for 2–3 minutes more, depending on toughness. The *nanohana* should soften but not become mushy. Drain and refresh under cold running water. Pat dry and cut into pieces the same width as the konbu. Align side by side along the length of the konbu. Once the konbu is pliable, roll from one of the short ends into a fat log, and wrap tightly in plastic wrap. Refrigerate overnight.

Cut the *nanohana* into 3 cm (1¼ in) lengths and mound on small pickle plates with a healthy spoonful of the sesame seeds alongside.

WAJIMA AIR-DRIED FISH

As I strolled down the canopied booth–lined morning market street of Wajima, friendly faces called out greetings; I have become a bit of a champion of the town's local fish sauce and other fermented products. In recent years, there are fewer wrinkled countrywomen selling their wares, but a fresh crop of grandchildren has been slowly taking over some of the stalls. There is hope for the future of Wajima sea products such as air-dried fish (*himono*), fish fermented in rice bran (*nukazuke*), and fish sauce (*ishiri*, *ishiru*).

Though most of the small fish-processing operations are located in the cramped warren of streets in Fugeshi area, the Minamidani home stretches along a curve in the residential hills above Wajima City Hall. In another incarnation, their home was an upscale Japanese restaurant run by Yoshie Minamidani's father, and is an elegant whitewashed structure with dark wooden posts and beams.

Despite our late arrival, Yoshie Minamidani greets us casually with a wide smile that brightens her pretty face. She is friendly, approachable, and all too willing to show us their operation. However, our lateness has held up the drying process, and her husband Toshiaki is anxious to get the last fish into the drying cage. The cage is an ingenious structure akin to a shelved closet with netting rather than wood paneling as the walls and floor. The structure sits under an overhang, thus protected from direct sun, and is adjacent to a bluff, which provides air currents. Moving air is the key to being able to produce the best dried fish: you need a location where the air passes freely and consistently, 'so the flesh becomes taut and the flavor concentrated,' according to Yoshie Minamidani.

As spring arrives, typically the locals stop air-drying fish until the fall because the weather is too warm. The day we visited in early April was probably the last day that Yoshie and Toshiaki would be using their outside drying chamber. But since the couple makes their living selling dried fish all year round, they will move the drying operation into a temperature-controlled, humidity-free room with fans simulating the sea breeze to buffet the fish.

Wajima is a middle-sized port on the western side of the Noto Peninsula, with about 200 fishing boats going out when weather

permits. Each day at 5 pm, the loudspeaker system announces if weather will make setting out of harbor dangerous or not. When conditions are fair, the boats motor out after midnight and bring in their catch before dawn. The fish is unloaded at the docks and auctioned off in place. From there, wholesale vendors sell the fish to restaurants, inns, small market vendors, and fish-processing people such as the Minamidani couple. Buying from this short chain ensures that the fish seen at the Wajima morning market or on tables around Wajima each day came in fresh the day it is served or treated for drying and fermenting.

As for air-dried fish (*himono*, which roughly translates as 'dried things'), the salting process generally happens in the early afternoon right after the market closes at noon and the vendors have sold their dried fish from the day before. Each producer varies slightly in their salting method. Yoshie learned from her paternal grandmother and thus follows a method that involves a moderate sprinkling of salt or souse in soy sauce and no rinse before hanging. She leaves the fish in the salt or soy sauce for one hour before hanging or drying on racks. Smallish fish remain whole and are threaded through the mouth and gills for hanging. Medium-sized fish are gutted and splayed, butterfly-like, while larger fish are filleted – both are laid on drying racks stretched with netting. The fish will be taken in in the morning and brought to market to be sold as *himono* or, specifically, semi-dried fish known as *ichiyaboshi* (one night dried).

Yoshie Minamidani's eyes lit up when she spoke of her grandmother, though a note of sadness crept into her voice at her loss. Her morning market education began with helping her grandmother while still only in elementary school. After junior high graduation, Yoshie chose to attend high school at night, and spent her mornings manning their booth at the Wajima morning market with her grandmother. And now her husband and mother support Yoshie in this family endeavor. Her husband assists with treating the fish, and her mother backs Yoshie up at the market, allowing Yoshie to do a little bit of everything. As the face of their business, Yoshie has a global, approachable demeanor. While she does not have English skills, she has people skills, and interacted easily with the foreign crew I brought to photograph her air-dried fish operation.

Good news for all of us living in Japan is that Yoshie and her husband are willing to pack up their air-dried fish and send it to Japanese addresses via one of our very convenient delivery companies. This style of air-dried fish keeps four days in the fridge or about a month in the freezer. It is sold by the 'plate', an 18 × 20 cm (7 × 8 in) plastic receptacle that is used for display at the market. A plate typically holds about five or so pieces, and the price varies from 500 to 1000 yen (US$4.50 to $9), depending on the fish. With the inevitable decline in purchasing from individual vendors due to the shift to supermarket shopping, perhaps the future of this local production lies in our hands.

Though not particularly convenient for urban dwellers, cooking air-dried fish over low-ember charcoal is quite spectacular. Alternatively, grilling under a low flame works well, or even on a frying pan lined with parchment (baking) paper. Begin cooking the fish with the skin side closest to the heat source (i.e. skin up for grilling, skin down for stovetop cooking), but cook both sides lightly until the natural oils bubble up a bit and the surface of the fish develops some light browning. While air-dried fish is typically served at breakfast or lunch, it makes a tasty accompaniment to drinks before dinner.

Nama Yuba Sashimi

YUBA SASHIMI

SERVES 4

175 g (6 oz) fresh *yuba* (page 280)

1 teaspoon freshly grated wasabi

1 teaspoon shoyu

Yuba is the creamy skin that is skimmed off soy milk while heating it to make tofu, so very little is produced naturally each day. Some tofu makers such as Hodo Foods in Oakland, California, have opted to meet demand by producing *yuba* separately from the tofu-making process.

Yachi Tofu, on the outskirts of Wajima in Ishikawa prefecture, has been delivering tofu by motorbike in the environs since 1945. Since they are a small operation, they only produce about two to three packs of *yuba* per day, of which at least two weekly are promised to Sakamoto. Yachi *yuba*, like Hodo Foods Kumiage Yuba, is unctuously scoopable, suitable as is for *shira-ae* (page 279), or for dolloping into a crab and miso *nabe* (one-pot dish). Here it is simply adorned with a bit of freshly grated wasabi and a drop or two of shoyu.

If the *yuba* is not easily spooned up, cut it crosswise into 1 cm (½ in) pieces. Scoop the *yuba* into 4 small lacquer bowls. Dab on wasabi and dribble in a small amount of shoyu. Serve as a small bite with a beautifully clear, elegant sake.

Kani Miso to Fuyu Negi

CRAB MISO WITH WINTER NEGI

SERVES 4

2 small crabs weighing about 200 g (7 oz) each, freshly boiled

1 egg yolk, at room temperature

2 tablespoons sake

2 tablespoons brown rice (*genmai*) miso

2 thin winter *negi* or fat scallions (spring onions), white parts only, cut into 4 cm (1½ in) lengths

Technically, crab 'miso' in Japanese means the creamy, coral-colored substance adhering to the insides and backs of crabs, easily spooned up when breaking down a freshly boiled crab. Hauntingly bitter, this pungent delicacy is the crab's digestive gland, the hepatopancreas. In this version of crab miso, actual miso is blended into the crab 'miso' for an intriguing little salty bite before dinner. Sakamoto uses female snow crabs for this dish.

Pull off the backs of the crabs and harvest the rusty orange, soft 'miso' from the inside backs and stomach areas. Pick the meat out of the shells (the yield should be about 100 g/3½ oz, or 25% of the total weight of the crabs).

Smash the crabmeat, crab 'miso', egg yolk, sake and miso together in a small saucepan. Cook, stirring continuously over low heat for 3–5 minutes, until fragrant. Cool to room temperature before serving a small spoonful per person in individual sake cups, garnished with a piece of the *negi*.

Ebi Imo–ni

SIMMERED SHRIMP POTATOES

SERVES 4

2 small shrimp potatoes or taro roots, weighing about 150 g (5½ oz) in total

300 ml (10 fl oz) Katsuobushi Dashi (page 202)

½ teaspoon salt

½ tablespoon mirin

½ teaspoon finely diced yuzu (or Meyer lemon) zest, for serving

Shrimp potatoes, so named because of their curved shape and horizontal striations, are a relative of taro. They are in season in Japan from the beginning of October to the middle of November. The taut texture of the simmered potatoes balances well against the creamy *yuba* and salty crab miso when served together on a *zensai* tray as a bite with sake before dinner. The middle pieces of shrimp potato have the best flavor, so serve those first.

Peel the shrimp potatoes or taro roots and cut into 1.5 cm (½ in) thick rounds. Drop into a medium saucepan and add the dashi, salt and mirin. Bring to a simmer over medium–high heat, adjust to a gentle gurgle and cook for 30 minutes, until soft in the center and the flavoring liquids have been mostly absorbed.

Spoon a little of the liquid into 4 small bowls and serve hot, one middle piece per person, sprinkled with a bit of yuzu zest.

Zaru Soba

SOBA WITH FRESH WASABI

Shinichiro Sakamoto believes that soba is like *shojin* sashimi. '*Shojin*' means 'temple', referring to the traditional Zen Buddhist style of eating, which eschews meat, fish and dairy. One should eat soba like sashimi: dab a little wasabi on the noodles and dip a teeny corner into the densely shoyu-flavored dipping sauce (*tsuyu*). Sakamoto makes *kyuwari* soba (nine parts buckwheat flour to one part all-purpose flour) rather than the *nihachi* style (eight parts to two) of Soba Ra (page 61).

SERVES 4

Soba

225 g (8 oz/1⅔ cups) Japanese buckwheat flour (*sobako*, page 280)

25 g (1 oz) unbleached all-purpose (plain) flour

75 g (2¾ oz/½ cup) *uchiko* flour (page 281) or potato starch, for dusting

2 teaspoons freshly grated wasabi

4 small maple leaves, for garnishing

Soba Tsuyu (page 203)

Make and cook the soba noodles using the basic method on page 117.

Arrange small portions of freshly cooked noodles on 4 flat bamboo baskets (*zaru*), each one set on top of a salad plate to catch drips. Dab a little wasabi onto each maple leaf and place on top of each pile of soba. Ladle 50 ml (1¾ fl oz) of tsuyu into individual lacquer cups or ceramic *soba choko*. Serve immediately.

Hasu Tenpura

LOTUS ROOT TEMPURA

Make this juicy, crunchy tempura when lotus root is at its best, as the weather turns cold in the early winter. The fresher the root, the faster it will cook. Although available throughout the year, lotus roots are in season in the cold winter months. At that time, their starch is low and the flesh is juicy, making them well worth the wait.

SERVES 4

15 cm (6 in) piece of lotus root, medium thick

50 g (1¾ oz/⅓ cup) cake flour

neutral oil such as canola, safflower or peanut, for deep-frying

½ teaspoon flaky sea salt

Peel the lotus root and slice off the browned ends. Cut the root crosswise into 4 slices 3 cm (1¼ in) thick.

Spoon the flour into a medium bowl and stir in 60 ml (2 fl oz/¼ cup) cold water with a pair of cooking chopsticks (*saibashi*, page 276) to make a thin batter, but do not overwork. There should still be small lumps.

Heat 10 cm (4 in) of oil in a medium pot over medium heat. Once hot but not smoking, dip the lotus slices into the tempura batter to coat, and slip them into the oil. Fry for 3–4 minutes, until golden brown and the bubbling has largely subsided. Blot dry on paper towels and sprinkle with the salt. Serve 1 slice per person as a burning hot bite.

Kijihata to Kan-buri no Sashimi

RED-SPOTTED GROUPER AND WINTER AMBERJACK SASHIMI

On the Noto Peninsula, red-spotted grouper (*kijihata*) – the two pieces standing up in front of the bowl – is called *namera bachime*. And winter amberjack (*kan-buri*) is in season from November to January when the cold-water fishing is allowed, and is plentiful around the Toyama coast to the east of the peninsula.

SERVES 4

100 g (3½ oz) very fresh boned and skinned red-spotted grouper (*kijihata*) fillet, sliced for sashimi

100 g (3½ oz) very fresh boned and skinned winter amberjack (*kan buri*) fillet, sliced for sashimi

large handful wild cress leaves

2 teaspoons freshly grated wasabi

2 teaspoons dark shoyu, such as Kadocho from Wakayama prefecture

Place two or three slices of each kind of fish per person in small individual bowls, on a bed of fresh cress leaves dug out from under the snow. Add a healthy pinch of freshly grated wasabi and serve with a small saucer of the full-flavored shoyu.

Kobako-gani to Kohaku Namasu

SNOW CRAB WITH SWEET-VINEGARED DAIKON

Crab marries well with vinegar treatments, and here the daikon and carrots are marinated in lightly sweetened vinegar softened with dashi. Substitute any medium-sized fresh crab, and if working with whole crabs, use the extra legs and body meat for another dish.

SERVES 4

3 tablespoons rice vinegar

1 teaspoon coarse light brown Japanese sugar (*zarame*, page 15)

2 tablespoons Katsuobushi Dashi (page 202)

5 cm (2 in) piece of daikon, scrubbed

½ small carrot, scrubbed

½ teaspoon flaky sea salt

½ teaspoon finely slivered yuzu zest

12 small legs of female snow crabs (*zuwaigani*) that have been boiled in salted water

Stir the vinegar into the sugar in a small bowl to dissolve. Add the dashi.

Slice the daikon into fine ribbons (*tanzaku-giri*, page 276), and finely julienne the carrot. Slide them into a medium mixing bowl, massage the salt in lightly, and leave to macerate for 10 minutes. Squeeze the daikon and carrot firmly by handfuls to express out as much liquid as possible, dropping as you go into a clean bowl. Toss with the yuzu zest and vinegar dressing.

Serve 3 crab legs per person with a mound of the sweet-vinegared daikon and carrot (*namasu*) as a light first course.

Hasumushi

SILKY SIMMERED LOTUS BALLS

Japanese chefs will tell you that the test of a chef's mettle is the *wanmono* – a soup or simmered course served in a lidded lacquer or ceramic bowl. The delicate broth and presentation of ingredients are essential to create a 'wow' moment when the diner opens the lid of the bowl. Shinichiro Sakamoto hated the idea of *wanmono*, because the chef is supposed to carve vegetables into pretty shapes for these dishes. The waste incurred in this cutting was abhorrent to him. As the years went by, he developed his own style of *wanmono*, without waste, and now serves a version at every meal.

He also takes advantage of the local *matsutake* when they are in season, because their end is near. Rampaging boars dig them up and scatter the mushroom spores, thus disturbing the natural habitat, and many pines are succumbing to blight. Heartbreaking to imagine no *matsutake* on the Noto Peninsula, but that is the reality. In the autumn of 2018, Sakamoto was only able to access enough *matsutake* for a few meals, leaving regular customers devastated. Here, in the spirit of no waste, Sakamoto takes advantage of the flavorful *matsutake* stems.

SERVES 4

200 g (7 oz) lotus root

2 medium egg whites, at room temperature

pinch of fine sea salt

8 gingko nuts, shelled

50 g (1¾ oz) grilled river eel (*unagi*), finely diced

400 ml (13½ fl oz) Katsuobushi Dashi (page 202)

½ teaspoon coarse light brown Japanese sugar (*zarame*, page 15)

¼ teaspoon flaky sea salt

½ teaspoon freshly squeezed ginger juice

1 teaspoon well crushed kudzu powder (*kuzuko*, page 280)

50 g (1¾ oz) julienned *matsutake* stems, or 1 teaspoon freshly grated wasabi

Peel and grate the lotus root on a metal-toothed grater (*oroshi kin*, page 275). Stir the egg whites and fine salt into the lotus until well incorporated. Fold the gingko nuts and *unagi* into the mixture. Pat into 4 balls of 5 cm (2 in) and place on a dinner plate. Set the plate inside a bamboo steamer.

Bring a large wok, one-third full with water, to a boil over high heat. Place the steamer in the wok over the water and steam for 12–15 minutes, until the lotus balls are set. Carefully remove the plate from the steamer and tip the juices into a medium saucepan with the dashi, sugar, flaky salt and ginger juice. Spoon a few teaspoons of the pan liquids into the kudzu in a small bowl, and stir to dissolve. Bring the dashi mixture to a gentle simmer and stir in the kudzu. Cook, stirring for 3–5 minutes, until silky smooth.

Place 1 ball in each of 4 deep soup bowls (if possible, ones with lids) and ladle in the thickened dashi. Garnish with the *matsutake* or wasabi and serve immediately as a first course.

Koyadofu to Yasai no Nimono

DASHI-SIMMERED KOYADOFU WITH VEGETABLES

Koyadofu (freeze-dried tofu), when reconstituted, has a spongy texture that soaks up simmering liquids. The roots of this quintessential temple food are in a version made in the mountains of northern China over a millennium ago. Due to issues of spoilage and difficulties in transport for fresh tofu, a temple at Mount Koya in Wakayama prefecture in southeastern Japan developed a way to dry frozen tofu using heat around the year 1225. Eventually, the heat-drying method was replaced by sun-drying in the 15th century. Modern production of *koyadofu* uses baking soda or ammonia to speed up the water-absorption rate, so it then needs to be soaked in several changes of cold water to leach out those additives. Source additive-free *koyadofu* from organic stores or online. You will have more greens than needed for this recipe, so use them for another meal.

SERVES 4

4 × 8 g (¼ oz) pieces of freeze-dried tofu (*koyadofu*)

700 ml (23½ fl oz) Katsuobushi Dashi (page 202)

3 tablespoons sake

4½ tablespoons coarse light brown Japanese sugar (*zarame*, page 15)

2 tablespoons *usukuchi shoyu* (page 9)

4 small carrots, scrubbed

1 small bunch komatsuna (page 278) or spinach with stems

7 tablespoons shoyu

1 teaspoon mirin

¼ teaspoon Japanese mustard powder, mixed with ¼ teaspoon water

4 × 1.5 cm (½ in) squares of *konnyaku* (page 279)

4 small shiitake, stems discarded

4 medium *hon shimeji* (page 279) or other shimeji mushrooms

1 tablespoon finely slivered ginger

2 small dried red chilies (*chile japones*, page 278), torn into small pieces

1 teaspoon white sesame seeds, warmed

Place the *koyadofu* in a small rectangular container and pour hot tap water into a corner of the container (avoiding the *koyadofu*) until the *koyadofu* is covered with water. Once cooled and reinflated, after about 10 minutes, lift each piece out carefully with a spatula, and discard the water. Return the *koyadofu* to the container and add cold water to cover. Leave for 5 minutes, remove the *koyadofu* and discard the water. Repeat 2 more times. After the last cold water bath, squeeze the *koyadofu* ever so gently to express water, and carefully nestle the pieces into a medium saucepan.

Add 200 ml (7 fl oz) of the dashi, 2 tablespoons of the sake and 1 tablespoon of the sugar. Place a drop lid (*otoshibuta*, page 275) or piece of parchment (baking) paper on top, and bring to a simmer over medium–low heat. Remove the drop lid, swirl in 1 tablespoon of the *usukuchi shoyu*, and take the pan off the heat. Allow the *koyadofu* to come to room temperature in the liquid.

Slice off the tops and trim the very bottoms of the carrots. Carve both ends into pleasingly rounded shapes. Blanch for 3–5 minutes in a medium pot of rapidly boiling water until half cooked. Scoop the carrots out, but leave the pot of water on medium–low heat. Place the carrots in a small saucepan with 150 ml (5 fl oz) of the dashi, the remaining 1 tablespoon of sake, and ½ tablespoon of the sugar. Set a drop lid or piece of parchment paper over the carrots and bring to a simmer over medium–low heat. Cook the carrots for 2 minutes to absorb sweetness, then stir in the remaining 1 tablespoon of *usukuchi shoyu* and cook for 1 minute more, until soft. Cool in the simmering liquid.

Curl the komatsuna or spinach into a wire-mesh strainer and plunge into the almost boiling water, to cook the komatsuna for 1 minute or the spinach for 30 seconds. Refresh under cold running water until cool to the touch. Squeeze well. Add 2 tablespoons of the shoyu to a medium mixing bowl and swish the squeezed greens around in the shoyu. Squeeze again, and unfurl across a cutting board. Cut into 2 cm (¾ in) lengths. Align in a small rectangular container. Stir another 2 tablespoons of the shoyu and the mirin into the mustard paste in a small bowl. Add 100 ml (3½ fl oz) of the dashi and pour over the greens. Cover until serving. Keeps for 3 days if stored in the refrigerator.

Make fine cross cuts about 5 mm (¼ in) deep into the top of each square of *konnyaku* to create hedgehog-like bristles. Bring the pot of water back to a boil over high heat and blanch the *konnyaku* for 5 minutes to remove any odors. Drain. Nestle the *konnyaku*, shiitake and shimeji in a small saucepan. Add the remaining 250 ml (8½ fl oz/1 cup) of the dashi, and the ginger, chilies and remaining 3 tablespoons of sugar. Set a drop lid or piece of parchment paper on top and simmer over medium–low heat for 5 minutes. Remove the drop lid briefly, swirl in the remaining 3 tablespoons of shoyu, and simmer for 3 minutes more to absorb flavor. Cool in the simmering liquid.

Lay a drained carrot to one side in each of 4 shallow lacquer bowls. Set 1 shiitake and 1 shimeji across the middle of each carrot. Place 1 piece of *konnyaku* next to the mushrooms. Sprinkle each *konnyaku* piece with ¼ teaspoon of the sesame seeds. Gently drape a piece of *koyadofu* against the *konnyaku*, curving it a little to add dynamism to the plating. Squeeze a bundle of dressed greens, 1 cm (½ in) thick, and lean against each piece of *koyadofu*. Serve this dish towards the end of a meal, as a light vegetable course to fill the tummy.

Daikon to Hoshi Nishin no Amazake-zuke

AMAZAKE-PICKLED DAIKON AND DRIED HERRING

Amazake is a naturally sweet, often homemade drink fermented from rice koji, cooked rice and water. Typically, it has grains of rice still floating in it, though commercial versions are often emulsified. Be careful to read the ingredients as some *amazake* contains sake lees (*kasu*), sweeteners or preservatives. A natural one made only from rice is the better choice here, unless you make your own.

This pickle requires five full days of salt-pickling for the daikon and four days of soaking for the dried herring, so plan ahead. Hundreds of years ago when the seas were full of fish, herring was plentiful. And in the spring when spawning, the water was cloudy white from the sperm. The herring were caught and cleaned, boned and de-headed, and hung splayed in the sun to dry. This style of dried herring is called *migaki nisshin*. Salt-dried cod (*shiodara*) can also be used – either Japanese or western.

MAKES ABOUT 800 G (1 LB 12 OZ)

400 g (14 oz) daikon, scrubbed (not peeled)

16 g (½ oz) flaky sea salt, or 4% the weight of the daikon

2 dried herring fillets (*migaki nishin*)

rice bran (optional)

½ small dried red chili (*chile japones*, page 278), cut into fine rounds

1 tablespoon julienned carrot

2 tablespoons finely julienned softened konbu

1 tablespoon finely slivered yuzu (or Meyer lemon) zest

Amazake

150 g (5½ oz) Japanese white rice

200 g (7 oz) rice koji

Cut the daikon crosswise into 6 cm (2½ in) thick rounds. Cut each piece lengthwise into 10 slabs. Sprinkle with the salt, weight, and leave for 5 days in a cool dark place.

From the second day, begin to soak the dried herring fillets in rice bran water (3 tablespoons of rice bran mixed with 500 ml/17 fl oz/2 cups water), or alternatively in rice washing water, changing the water every day.

On the fourth day, make the *amazake*. Follow the directions for Japanese Rice (page 205), but use 175 ml (6 fl oz) water, and cook for 8 minutes. Once the rice has cooled to body temperature, gently cut in the koji with a rice paddle (*shamoji*, page 275) or chopsticks. Stir in 250 ml (8½ fl oz/1 cup) water, scrape into a yogurt maker and leave to culture at 55°C (130°F) for 2 days.

On the sixth day, when 5 days have elapsed from starting the daikon, drain the herring and cut crosswise into 3 cm (1¼ in) lengths. Drain the daikon. Toss the daikon, herring, chili, carrot, konbu and yuzu zest with 300 ml (10 fl oz) of the *amazake*. The pickle is now ready to eat, but keeps for 1 month or more stored in a well-sealed container in the refrigerator.

Kinkan Shiroppu-ni

KUMQUATS IN SYRUP

Although originally transplanted from China, kumquats have been cultivated in Japan for centuries. They are a winter fruit. Plucked fresh from the tree and popped into your mouth whole, kumquats make a bright citrus snack on the go. But kumquats are also often simmered in syrup for a simple dessert, since fruit lends itself so well to the end-of-the-meal bite for traditional Japanese menus.

MAKES ABOUT 12

250 g (9 oz) kumquats

100 g (3½ oz) coarse light brown Japanese sugar (*zarame*, page 15)

2½ tablespoons mirin

2½ teaspoons *usukuchi shoyu* (page 9)

Wipe the kumquats and poke about 6 small holes in each one with a toothpick. Pop the kumquats into a medium saucepan, fill with water to cover, and bring to a boil over medium–high heat. Drain.

Measure the sugar into the empty saucepan and stir in 500 ml (17 fl oz/2 cups) water, the mirin and *usukuchi shoyu*. Add the kumquats and bring to a simmer over medium–high heat. Adjust the temperature to very low and cook for at least 1 hour, until the kumquats have softened and the liquids have reduced to a thick syrup. Cool and store refrigerated in a jar or covered container for up to several weeks.

Shinichiro Sakamoto

BASIC RECIPES

Katsuobushi Dashi

MAKES 400 ML (13½ FL OZ)

15 cm (6 in) piece of konbu, preferably Rausu
large handful of shaved katsuobushi (*hanakatsuo*, page 16)

Soak the konbu in 500 ml (17 fl oz/2 cups) cold water in a medium saucepan overnight. The next day, bring to an almost boil over medium heat. Remove from the heat and pluck out the konbu. Allow the konbu dashi to cool for 3–5 minutes before stirring in the katsuobushi. Let sit for 5 minutes, then strain through a sieve lined with muslin (cheesecloth).

Katsuobushi Dashi – Variation 1

MAKES 900 ML (30½ FL OZ)

4 large handfuls of thick cut katsuobushi (*ara-kezuri*)

Bring the *ara-kezuri* to a simmer in 1 liter (34 fl oz/4 cups) cold water over medium heat. Let sit for 5 minutes, then strain through a sieve lined with muslin (cheesecloth).

Niboshi Dashi

MAKES 800 ML (27 FL OZ)

6–8 Roasted Niboshi (see below)
2 × 5 cm (2 in) squares of konbu, preferably Rausu

Soak the roasted niboshi and konbu in 1 liter (34 fl oz/4 cups) cold water in a saucepan overnight. Bring to a simmer the next morning, then remove from the heat and strain.

Roasted Niboshi

MAKES 1 CUP

1 cup sun-dried *niboshi* (page 16)

Preheat the oven to 150°C (300°F). Pinch off the heads, break the bodies in half, and pinch out the guts of each dried fish. Scatter them on an oven pan as you work. Roast in the middle of the oven for 5 minutes, until slightly browned in spots. Do not blacken. Cool and store in a glass jar. Keeps for several months or more. Pinching off the heads and guts of *niboshi* and roasting them before using takes off any unpleasant smells sometimes associated with dried fish. This is a signature Sakamoto method.

Kaeshi

MAKES APPROX. 1.5 LITERS (51 FL OZ/6 CUPS)

1.26 liters (42 fl oz/5 cups) double-brewed shoyu (*saishikomi shoyu*, page 10)
360 ml (12 fl oz) mirin
140 g (5 oz) coarse light brown Japanese sugar (*zarame*, page 15)

Bring 900 ml (30½ fl oz) of the *saishikomi shoyu* to a simmer in a heavy medium pot with the mirin and sugar. Cool to room temperature and add the remaining 360 ml (12 fl oz) *saishikomi shoyu*. Store in glass bottles. Keeps for more than 6 months. Since heating shoyu destroys some of the fermentation nuances, Sakamoto adds in some unheated *saishikomi shoyu* at the end to give the kaeshi a fresh feeling.

Soba Tsuyu

Mix Katsuobushi Dashi – Variation 1 (page 202) with Kaeshi (page 202) at a ratio of 5:2.

Roasted Red Chili Powder

Preheat the oven to 130°C (265°F). Spread dried red chilies (*chile japones*, page 278) out on an oven pan and roast for 3–5 minutes, keeping a close eye on them, and turning every minute or so until starting to color. Lower the temperature to 120°C (250°F) and continue to roast, turning and checking closely for about 10 minutes, until the chili aroma is prevalent. Cool, remove the tops and about half or more of the seeds, and grind to a powder with a spice grinder. This powder can be used in place of *ichimi togarashi* (page 19) but is spicier, so be warned.

Brown Rice

MAKES 5 CUPS, ABOUT 900 G/2 LB

540 ml (18 fl oz) measure of Japanese brown rice (about 450 g/1 lb)

Rinse the rice well and soak overnight in 600 ml (20½ fl oz) cold water in a pressure cooker. Bring to a rapid boil over high heat, then adjust to medium and cook for 10 minutes. Adjust to low and cook for 15 more minutes. Let sit for 10 minutes before fluffing and serving.

Japanese Rice

Yuyado Sakamoto has an infinite supply of deep well water in their kitchen, and spring water in the outside faucets, so dousing foods with a continuous stream of water does not cause consternation. They flush their white rice under cold running water for at least three hours.

Also, the key to excellent white rice is to only polish it in small quantities, and to store it in the refrigerator after polishing, since it will quickly deteriorate. In the countryside, many people either grow their own rice, or buy it hulled but unpolished (true brown rice) from their local Japan Agriculture cooperative. We have our own rice-polishing machine, but there are coin-operated ones on the roadsides here and there, and the cooperatives will polish rice to order, taking off the bran to make white rice.

Foods and liquids in Japan were traditionally measured by *go* (180 ml/6 fl oz), and many still are today. This rice recipe is for three *go*.

MAKES 5 CUPS, ABOUT 900 G/2 LB

540 ml (18 fl oz) measure of Japanese white rice (about 450 g/1 lb)

Put the rice in a sieve set over a small heavy pot. Place under a tap and flush with water to the top of the sieve and pot. Lift up the sieve, drain the water in the pot, and scrub the rice in your palms to dislodge any bran. Flush and drain the rice (without scrubbing) another 5–10 times until the water runs clear, or you lose patience.

Slide the drained rice into the pot, add 540 ml (18 fl oz) cold water, cover with a lid, and leave to soak for 30 minutes. Bring to a boil over high heat without opening the lid. When you start to see bubbles escaping out the top of the pot (about 4 minutes), adjust the heat to low and cook for 10 minutes. Remove the pot from the heat without opening the lid and let the rice rest for 5 minutes. Wet a rice keeper (*ohitsu*) or flat wooden tub (*handai*, page 275) and dump the rice into it. Spread out with minimal handling to avoid breaking the delicate grains, and cover with damp muslin (cheesecloth) until ready to serve.

THE JAPANESE BREAKFAST

When I first arrived in Japan, two things confounded me: the faucet on top of the toilet tank, and the 1-inch-thick puffy white 'bread' served at coffee shops.

Was it a drinking fountain or a hand washer, I mused, when first confronted with the faucet-equipped toilet. I was thirsty, but went for the hand-washing option – though technically, the water that ends up flushing the toilet is as clean as from a kitchen tap. I am surprised more western toilets have not incorporated the faucet into their design, as it's ecological and kind of genius, if you think about it.

I never did get used to that cake-like bread – think consistency of Wonder Bread (or angel food cake), but really thick. In fact, finding decent bread in 1988 was darn near impossible. I had to settle for a soft raisin bread that had a few flecks of wheat germ, but was otherwise just plain old white bread. And I tried to stick with green tea in the mornings, though only lasted about four months before begging a friend to send me some Peet's coffee. Today, the sad reality is that Japanese are eating less and less rice, and 'bread' (if you can call it that) has surpassed rice as the morning meal.

When first married, I rashly attempted preparing three meals a day for my husband, as well as homemade snacks for the 10 am and 3 pm tea breaks for the carpenters finishing our house. That did not last long. I accepted that my husband and I ate differently in the morning and were not on the same wake-up schedule, and was okay with that. As our sons were born, the initial sleepless nights segued into figuring out how to feed our 4-year-old while dealing with a new baby, and then another, less than two years later.

As a child of the 1960s and '70s, cereal and instant breakfast had replaced the pre-divorce era of eggs-and-toast family breakfasts, but I still preferred toast or English muffins in the morning. I admit to feeding my sons cereal at certain periods, but eventually that came to an end, and mornings were a bit hit or miss: eat or not eat. Sometimes our oldest son ate homemade ice cream for breakfast and I did not have a problem with that. Since my husband and I both worked until 6 or 7 pm (albeit in home-based businesses), and our sons were homeschooled, we set our own schedule. Dinners tended to be late: around 8 pm or so, and for the most part, the kids slept in. But every day we sat down to a hot lunch and I still maintain that rhythm today, cooking lunch six days a week at my small English-immersion school.

One of the top Japanese women's magazines, *Misezu* (Mrs), approached me about a breakfast story they were doing a few years ago. They wanted to feature me cooking my favorite breakfast dishes. Unable to dissemble, I had to admit that I do not eat much beyond a piece of toast in the morning to accompany my coffee. But also added, so not to be churlish, that I do believe that the traditional Japanese breakfast is the best breakfast in the world. And the erosion of this quintessential Japanese meal is beyond heartbreaking.

The classic Japanese breakfast consists of a simple miso soup with perhaps a few pieces of vegetable or tofu floating in the bowl; a piece of grilled fish, whether that be air-dried, miso-marinated or salted; tofu in some incarnation, either fresh or deep-fried; egg in the form of a rolled omelette, a fried egg or a plain raw egg; a bowl of brown or white rice; and pickles. A meal such as this begins your day with a warm and satisfied belly, and a sense that you have eaten healthily and well; it infuses you with the feeling that you can do anything in the day going forward.

Unfortunately, you will have to stay at a Japanese inn to experience a traditional Japanese breakfast in any meaningful way, unless you prepare it yourself. I am most likely to serve this kind of meal for lunch at my school, rather than breakfast. Yet I do revel in the times I am able to be a guest at Sakamoto and wake up to their spare yet filling morning meal. Additional dishes beyond what Sakamoto typically serves are just gilding the lily.

Butter-drenched Dashi-maki Tamago: Crack 3 fresh eggs (at room temperature) into a small mixing bowl and whisk in 1 tablespoon Niboshi Dashi (page 202), 1 teaspoon coarse light brown Japanese sugar (*zarame*), and ¼ teaspoon each of *usukuchi shoyu* and sake. Drop 1½ tablespoons unsalted butter into a small bowl by the stove. Dollop about a quarter of the butter into a rectangular *tamagoyaki* pan set over medium–high heat, tipping the pan to cover the surface evenly with butter. Pour a quarter of the egg mixture into the pan to make a thin layer and allow to cook for a few seconds until half set. Nudge the egg with 2 cooking chopsticks into a roll, working from the end closest to you. Add another quarter of the butter, tip the pan to distribute, and pour in another quarter of the egg mixture, lifting the first roll up to allow the mixture underneath. Once half set, roll the egg towards you, coaxing it gently. Push the egg roll to the opposite edge of the pan and repeat two more times with the remaining butter and egg, to form a plump, buttery roll. Halve and serve hot on 2 small plates.

Ganmodoki (Fried Tofu Patties): Place 300 g (10½ oz) *momendofu* (page 279) or Japanese-style soft block tofu in a fine sieve set over a bowl and place a weight on top to press out moisture. Refrigerate overnight (or leave in a cold kitchen). Pour boiling water over 1 dried shiitake and soak for 30 minutes. Drain, discard the stem, and chop the cap into a medium dice. Smash the drained tofu in a Japanese grinding bowl (*suribachi*) with 1 teaspoon potato starch and 1 tablespoon grated mountain yam (*yama imo*). Fold in 1 tablespoon each of tiny dried shrimp (*koebi*) and black sesame seeds. Cut a 5 cm (2 in) piece of carrot and one of burdock into small feather-like pieces (*sasagiri*) and add to the tofu mixture with the diced shiitake. Fold in ½ teaspoon each of sake, coarse light brown Japanese sugar (*zarame*) and fine sea salt. Heat 1.5 cm (½ in) of neutral oil in a medium frying pan over medium–low heat. Pat the tofu mixture into 3 patties and fry for about 5 minutes on each side, until golden brown. Drain briefly on paper towels before serving burning hot with a drizzle of shoyu and a dab of grated ginger.

Seasonal Mushroom Miso Soup: Bring 600 ml (20½ fl oz) Niboshi Dashi (page 202) to a simmer over medium heat. Drop in a handful of seasonal mushrooms such as *shibatake* (scotch bonnet) or *nameko* (butterscotch mushrooms) – whole if small, or cut into one-bite pieces if large. Add 2 tablespoons chopped *negi* or scallions (spring onions). Bring to a simmer over medium heat to cook the mushrooms briefly – though if using *nameko*, stir them in at the last minute. Remove from the heat and place 2 tablespoons brown rice (*genmai*) miso into a soup ladle. Dip the ladle into the soup to catch up some broth, and stir the broth into the miso to emulsify. Dunk the ladle into the soup and quickly stir in the miso. Add 2 or 3 small pieces of wheat gluten (*fu*) into each of 4 small bowls. Ladle the hot soup over and serve immediately with a side bowl of Brown Rice (page 203).

'FAMILY MEAL'

I heard about Yuyado Sakamoto from my editor in Japan, Kim Schuefftan. Kim had much to say about the specialness of Sakamoto: the food, the place, the people, and given his credentials and 50-year residence in Japan (at that time), I listened. Kim is an ex–Kodansha International editor, who worked on and ghostwrote some of the seminal Japanese cookbooks from the 1970s and '80s, including the two most important works of the era that have yet to be supplanted today: *Japanese Cooking: A Simple Art* (the ingredients text) and *The Heart of Zen Cuisine* (all the text and recipes).

Kim is not one for superlatives, and chides me for my tendency towards them in my writing, but he often evoked Shinichiro and Mihoko Sakamoto's names with almost reverence. 'They might be the best cooks in Japan,' he enthused. Kim and I do not always see eye to eye on food, but I could not ignore the persistence of his conviction. He promised to arrange a trip to Sakamoto with me 'when the weather warmed'.

At that time, Kim was already in his seventies, and the snow-bound Noto winter is not for the faint of heart. A growing desire took hold of me, and I waited with impatience for spring to come. Spring came and went that year, but still no junket to Sakamoto, until Kim called in early summer with the auspicious news that he would be traveling to the Noto Peninsula with Kenji Miura, the photographer we shared. The point of their trip was to take photos and record interviews for a feature article on Noto, particularly Ohno Charcoal and Yuyado Sakamoto in the area around the town of Suzu, as well as Wajima lacquerware and the work of Kunikatsu Seto, one of the most gifted and important lacquerware artists of our day. Kim and Miura were staying as guests of the Sakamotos and would eat with the family. They also intended to make the transit via car, an 8-hour drive. Not a fan of long car rides, I opted for the plane. And I informed Kim (somewhat haughtily) that I was not going all the way to Sakamoto 'only to eat the family meal!' Little did I know.

That first night, I sat alone in the spacious tatami room where guests are served at a long low table. My server was Wabisuke, affectionately called Wabi, the Sakamotos' 9-year-old son. Shy, knowledgeable, adorable, Wabi captured my heart. At the time, my husband, Tadaaki, was still a free-range egg farmer with 3000 chickens, and Wabi an aspiring egg farmer. I wildly offered for Wabi to come stay with us later that summer, not taking into account that the deadline to turn in my very first manuscript (*Japanese Farm Food*) was September 1. Logistics and practicality prevented that visit from happening, and at this point, neither Wabi nor Tadaaki are interested in egg farming.

Wabi slipped quietly into the room, first carrying a tray of two dishes. Subsequent courses were presented one by one. Although I needed to wait for Miura to take his photos, I could savor each bite and each dish almost like a religious experience. This was a time when eating alone was essential to completely focus on the food, with no distractions. And Wabi's unobtrusive, gentle nature was the perfect 'entree' to the food. His minimalistic descriptions matched my desire to just hear the gist. Less about spoken words, this was about the chef talking to me through the food. And what was clear was that there were two people and two points of view in the kitchen – with Mihoko providing the base, and Shinichiro ('Shinchan' to all) providing the creative execution and finished dish.

The following night I was told we were eating '*en famille*', and I dared not demur. I had had my communion with Shinchan's food and did not want to be greedy. We sat in the narrow room for family eating and lounging, located between the kitchen and guest area. Nowhere convenient to put my feet, I just stuck them out under the table and apologized for the rudeness. Even after three decades in Japan, I find sitting on the floor becomes quickly excruciating if required to sit legs crossed ('daddy style') or, worse yet, on my knees (*seiza*) as in formal occasions.

Another local guest had been invited, so there were seven bodies crammed into a small space. I had heard that the soba at Sakamoto was legend, and we were in for a rare treat because Shinchan had made soba that night. Soba noodles take time and energy to make the dough and roll it out. And the exact timing of when to cook and serve must be decided. Except on special occasions, soba is never consumed by the family. And as such, Shinchan had only made a small amount, just for us guests to try.

Soba is ephemeral and *must* be eaten with great haste as soon as it hits the table. Kim had chosen that moment to fetch something from his room, so in a blink of an eye, he missed the soba noodles. It was heartbreaking, but unavoidable, because Shinchan adjured us to 'eat up' and we could not refuse. He also instructed us to eat the soba 'like sashimi': dab a little freshly grated wasabi on the noodles themselves, and dangle a few noodle ends in the smoky shoyu dipping sauce (tsuyu). I still feel a wrench of guilt at not speaking up on Kim's behalf. But to my defense, I was sure more was coming. Alas that was not the case.

I do not remember the dishes we ate that night, but there were many, all powerfully delicious, interesting and full of heart. The drink flowed, and the local guest lost his inhibition with the foreigners and became quite gregarious – the banter was lively. Shinchan, part cook, part philosopher, imparted more and more food wisdom to me that night, and I tried to keep up. And a highlight of the evening was Wabi performing an impromptu concert for us on his massive Korean drum. It was an unforgettable night and our friendship was forged.

The next morning, as I sat in my room overlooking the barren summer maple trees and the rapidly running brook swollen from the snow melting off of the mountains, I felt like I could just stay there all summer and write my book in that cocoon. Although an immensely alluring scenario, real life awaited me back in Saitama. And so I packed my bag and made my way downstairs.

I left wondering which meal of the three I had enjoyed made the biggest impression: the thoughtfully prepared and gorgeously presented breakfast and dinner served to the guests, or the eclectic casual fare eaten as a lively family group (I have since learned that restaurants call this '*makanai*' – 'family meal').

At this writing, seven and a half years and scores of meals have passed since my first visit, and to this day I still wonder. But maybe it is less a question of which meal is better, since the guests' meals and the family meals are equally well conceived. Perhaps it is a case of the concept and intent being different: exquisite yet spare, versus casual yet deeply flavored.

Mihoko's Suigyoza (Simmered Gyoza): Combine 150 g (5½ oz) lotus root, finely grated; 150 g (5½ oz) hand-minced pork butt (from the shoulder); 1 medium *negi* or 3 thick scallions (spring onions), finely chopped; 1 teaspoon each of fine sea salt and finely grated ginger; and ¼ teaspoon each of sake and freshly ground black pepper in a medium bowl. Knead until well incorporated. Place a gyoza skin in your non-dominant palm and, dipping your finger in water, wet half the circumference (the half furthest away from you). Drop a teaspoon of filling into the same half and fold the top over, pleating the edge as you press it closed. Cook in batches in a large pot of rapidly boiling water until the gyoza bob to the surface. Skim out with a slotted spoon and serve hot with shoyu, Roasted Red Chili Powder (page 203) and rice vinegar (people should mix a little of each in a small saucer for their own preferred balance of flavors).

関西

KANSAI

Osaka

WADAMAN SESAME

I met Takehiro Wada at the Winter Fancy Food Show in San Francisco, January 2016. The Wadaman sesame booth was next to Yamaki Jozo, our local soy sauce and miso company, whom I was there to support. In between cooking demos and chatting up potential buyers, I strolled over to Wadaman to taste some of their oils. While the gold and black sesame oils were lovely, the white sesame oil spoke to me immediately: elegant, bright, clear. This was like no other sesame oil I had ever experienced, and I was completely captivated.

Hundreds of thousands of people come through the Fancy Food Show, so my pestering questions to Wada were probably annoying. Who was this random blond woman asking about the source of his sesame? Most of his seeds are not grown in Japan, since there is virtually no viable commercial sesame production left in the country today. His gentle spoken JETRO (Japan External Trade Organization) handler tended to step in whenever I approached Wada, so I felt a bit of frustration at the inability to connect with Wada directly over those few days.

Once we were back in Japan, Wada kindly sent me a box of samples (seeds, pastes and oils), including some extra bottles of my new love: the white sesame oil. We began to chat periodically via telephone and email, and eventually a bond was formed. In May 2016, I had the opportunity to visit the Wadaman retail shop and factory, a 130-year-old family operation. Spending the day with Wada, who was slotted to become the 5th-generation president, sealed our budding friendship and collaboration. I became a vocal advocate for Wadaman sesame, and Wada came to understand my unwavering dedication to artisan Japan.

Wadaman's retail shop is located on a side street in Osaka, and the facade and inner design are a testament to a fine-honed aesthetic sense. But the factory visit was what cinched my devotion to the products. Although Wadaman processes a minute amount of organic Japanese gold sesame seeds, the bulk of their operation relies on seeds from contract farmers in other countries. The white seeds are sourced from Ethiopia, Bolivia and Guatemala; the black from Bolivia, Myanmar and Cambodia; and the gold from Turkey. While the majority of Wadaman's farmers grow their seeds conventionally, a small portion farm organically.

The seeds are packed in 50-kilogram burlap bags for shipping, and the first step in processing involves running the seeds down a conveyer belt to take off debris. Six cleaning steps later, the seeds are ready for roasting (a 3-step operation that involves low–high–low temperatures). I was particularly impressed by a last step, whereby the seeds are shot through an apparatus that detects color – discolored, cracked and wrong-colored seeds are pinged out with a laser-pointed blast of air. This attention to detail is emblematic of the quality of work at Wadaman. After roasting, 50% of the seeds will be sold whole, 15% will be ground and packed, 25% will be put through a 4- or 5-step millstone grinding process to emulsify them into unctuous pastes, and a precious 1% will be pressed to make oil. And 9% of the seeds will be incorporated into *furikake* sprinklings, dressings or other miscellaneous products.

All Wadaman sesame products are undeniably superior to similar ones on the market, but perhaps the oils are where one can truly taste and understand how exceptional Wadaman sesame is. Wadaman sesame oil is all first-press, which is the most pristine oil possible to extract. Equally impressive, they use 5 liters of seeds to produce 1 liter of oil (20% yield), whereas other midrange companies are usually using only 2.1 liters of seeds for 1 liter of oil (40–45% yield), and large sesame companies in Japan, such as Kadoya, employ the chemical solvent *n*-hexane in the extraction process to further increase yields.

Witnessing the roasting process in person led to an epiphany: the sesame roaster is just as important as the coffee roaster (a relatable analogy). In our area we have local organic sesame, and sometimes my husband grows it as well, but there is no question that my ability to roast our local seeds in a frying pan on the stove comes anywhere close to what a master sesame roaster accomplishes. Takehiro Wada's father, Etsuji, is the veteran roaster, and still roasts sesame every day from 8 am to 9 pm. Takehiro's wife, Mayuko, is currently learning the art from her father-in-law and eventually, after three to five years of daily training, will take over as roaster.

Takehiro himself was a newspaper correspondent for several years after university, before backpacking around India and Tibet for a year and a half. But he came back to his family company after having his own epiphany. In writing an article about the company, Takehiro came to realize the beauty and importance of his family's vocation. And with that rose a desire to be part of this craft and grow the business in a way that perhaps his father could not. Each person contributes to a family business in a different manner. Because of his experience overseas, Takehiro is able to bridge the gap between Japan and the international market, and slowly his family's exceptional products are becoming available across the globe.

According to the Wadaman website, 'Sesame seeds are high in nutrition and can add flavor and aroma to various kinds of dishes.' And as perhaps the best roasted sesame products in the world, Wadaman sesame adds exponentially more flavor and aroma than any other sesame, so well worth the higher tariff.

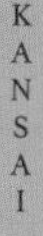

瀬戸内海

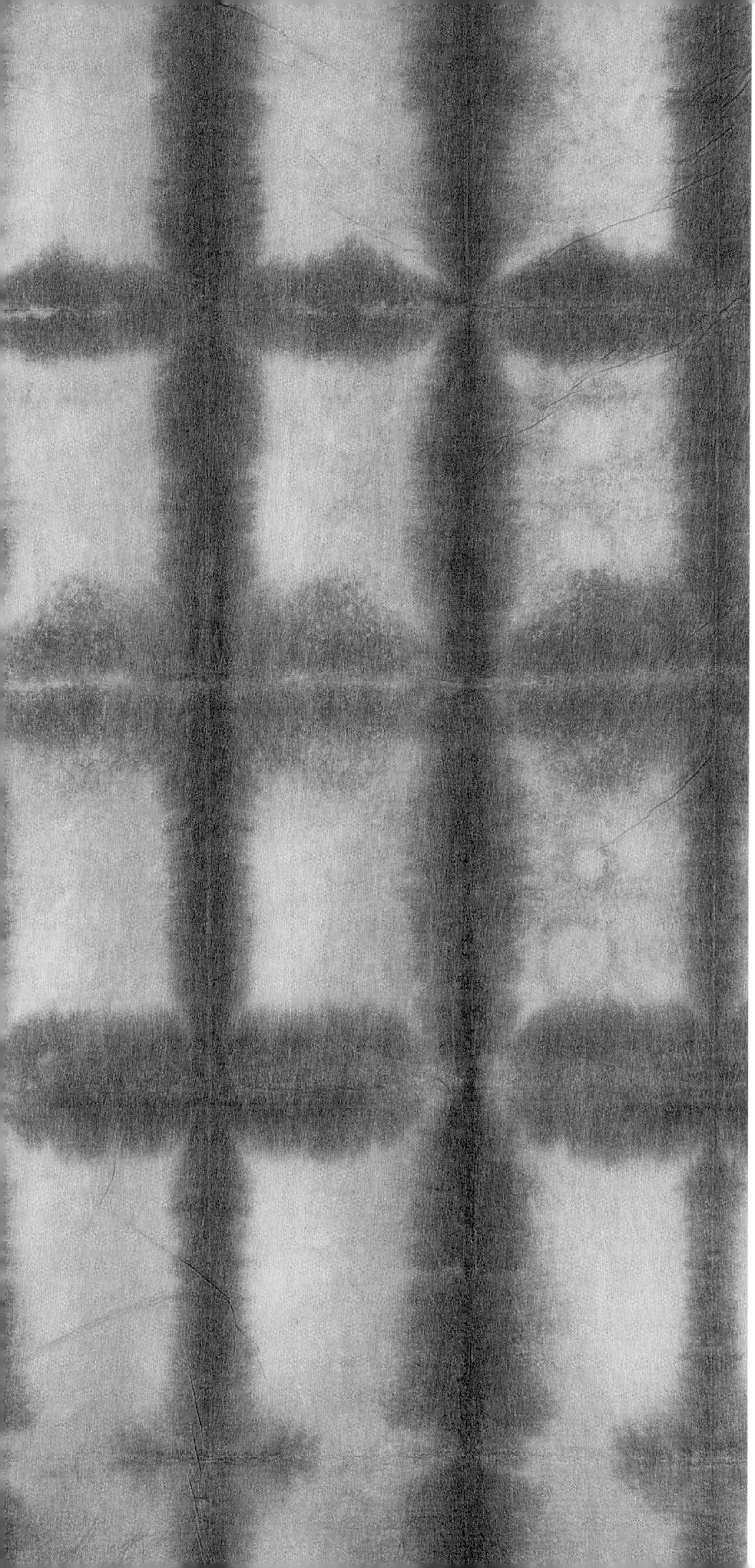

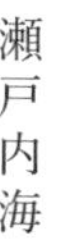

SETO INLAND SEA

Shodoshima

JAPAN'S OLIVE OIL ISLAND

When first married, I stocked the pantry with an affordable olive oil, in this case, a can of Spanish oil sourced through a friend. But as time meandered along and finances became more secure, I began to buy better grades, until I was using an organic olive oil procured at our local flea market. Somewhere along the line, I also purchased a bottle of high-end Italian olive oil at an international supermarket in Tokyo. One late spring day, I found myself alone at home, husband and children elsewhere. I harvested a couple of heads of the gorgeous red oak leaf lettuce I had planted from seed, mashed some early garlic in a mortar with a few pinches of Japanese sea salt, ground in some 'India Special Extra Bold' black pepper, and splashed in my homemade red-wine vinegar. What olive oil did I reach for? The high-end Italian.

Using such an oil on a solitary beautiful salad is not a hard grasp for any of us who care about what we are eating. Using a pricey oil for everything, including sautéed foods, is more of a stretch. The expense adds up. Nonetheless, I found that our simple field vegetables such as zucchini (courgette) were elevated multiple-fold when sautéed in the better oil (with Japanese sea salt). My American nieces were visiting at the time and I made them converts to zucchini. 'Try it!' I urged. And they did. More than once.

Olive oil is not the first thing that comes to mind when talking about Japanese ingredients. Nonetheless, Shodoshima, an island in the Seto Inland Sea of southern Japan, is known as 'olive island' and is home to thousands of olive trees. And Japanese olive oil production has a history of over 100 years.

While I did buy some of the Shodoshima olive oil at a food event many years ago, Japanese olive oil slipped off my radar as the years intervened. But recently I have found myself traveling to Shodoshima for a variety of reasons: one main one being to

explore the strikingly delicious local olive oils such as Olive no Mori produced by Shodoshima Healthy Land, and Takao Nouen no Olive Hatake by Takao Olive Farm. Admittedly dear, these oils have been garnering gold medals in prestigious competitions such as the Los Angeles County Fair (Olive no Mori) and the New York International Olive Oil Competition (Takao Nouen no Olive Hatake). What sets these oils apart is the small scale of their production, their location on Shodoshima, the care that goes into the trees themselves, and of course the blending of the oils after pressing.

Stroking Olive no Mori's 1000-year-old olive tree, which overlooks the Seto Inland Sea, I felt the power of the ages. Although transplanted from Spain, the tree symbolizes the deep historical roots that lie behind the ancient food culture of olive oil. We stand under the spreading branches of the majestic tree while Utsumi-san, the olive-tree expert, gently shakes the branches to dislodge the residual flowers that did not become tiny olive buds. This operation relieves the tree of trying to extricate them itself, much akin to deadheading rosebushes. The tree can thus focus its energy on growing vibrantly flavorful olives. Utsumi-san explains, 'Things that grow in the field become happy if you touch them.' I can attest to that, having grown things myself.

Before I visited Takao Olive Farm, I spoke with the owner at an olive oil dinner in Tokyo. A slight man, Toyohiro Takao has a gentle demeanor that comes through in his oil. I was taken with what he said about his trees: 'Each tree has a different personality, and when I walk among them I compliment them, ask them how they are feeling, bid them good morning.' Again, the personal touch here is key. Nonetheless, sold in precious 64 gram (2¼ oz) bottles for about 2000 yen (US$18), Takao Nouen no Olive Hatake is not for every day or for everybody.

As a writer of Japanese cookbooks, I have always recommended using rapeseed (canola) oil for most dishes, since it is the traditional oil used in Japan for centuries. But since visiting Shodoshima in 2015, I have broken down the barrier to olive oil and am now using it often when preparing dishes for Japanese food events. The fruity, sometimes spicy character of the oil lends itself to the kind of farm food I tend to serve. A good olive oil holds up to the strong flavors of soy sauce and fish sauce, and essentially enhances those two seasonings. And Italians find that barley (*mugi*) miso pairs particularly well with olive oil.

So what exactly constitutes a 'good' olive oil? To clarify, it goes without saying that extra-virgin olive oil is the oil of choice, produced by pressing whole olives without heat or chemicals. Otherwise, olive oil should be clear, bright ... drinkable.

Ristorante Furyu
Shodoshima

NOBUTO SHIBUYA

Nobuto Shibuya is irrevocably committed in his mission to bring good food to Shodoshima, an inviting tourist-destination island in the Seto Inland Sea. Four years after opening Ristorante Furyu in 2011, Shibuya-san opened Morikuni Bakery, a tiny bakery and cafe making Japanese and western breads with well-sourced flour. One year later, in 2016, a year of the Setouchi Triennale (an art and food festival in the inland sea), his gelateria made its debut. Like all of his eateries, Minori Gelato uses milk and other materials local to Shodoshima and its environs, rather than solely relying on ones imported from the main island of Honshu. Shibuya-san, a transplant from Chiba prefecture after the Tohoku Earthquake and Fukushima nuclear meltdown, has set an unwavering course towards fostering pride in the ingredients of his adopted island home.

Intrinsically Italian, the dishes at Furyu are shaped by the local fish and meat, Shibuya-san's homegrown vegetables, house-fermented fish sauce, and artisanal Shodoshima olive oil and salt. This is Italian cuisine with an island flair: light, bright flavors, and dishes that take advantage of the bounty of seasonal fruits and vegetables. And there is a thoughtful yet reasonable wine list. The desserts often include one or more of the island gelato flavors from his shop across the street: totally local, super delicious.

I first traveled to Shodoshima to write a story for *Misezu* (Mrs), one of the top women's magazines in Japan. Flattered to be asked, and excited to finally see Shodoshima, I agreed without hesitation to the one-night stay, involving a half day of transit on either end. It was a busy day and a half on the island, involving multiple venues, each one more delightful and distinctive than the last. Due to the packed schedule, our stop at Furyu had a short time limit, and the truncated bites could not even be called a meal. Dishes were whisked in for the tasting, then whisked out, leaving me wishing for everyone to leave me there to enjoy the food on my own. Not to be, we piled back into the van and drove to the next spot.

Unable to get the food at Furyu out of my mind, I was already wondering when I could return.

Unable to get the food at Furyu out of my mind, I was already wondering when I could return. And as luck would have it, the return visit happened within a few short weeks; and I have been back numerous times since. My editor and photographer and I were waiting at Ikeda, one of the six ferry terminals on Shodoshima, with the highly competent Sachie Karasawa of Shodoshima Healthy Land, maker of Olive no Mori oil. I glanced up at the ferry map and spied a direct ferry from Himeji to the Fukuda port on Shodoshima. Bingo! In two weeks, I was going to be at Himeji giving a presentation at a children's food event for the celebration of the 5-year renovation of Himeji Castle – almost 700 years old and registered in 1993 as one of the country's first UNESCO World Heritage sites. And my train tickets to and from my home had been paid for by the organizers. Sachie offered me a room at Healthy Land's guesthouse, and to chauffeur me around if I came. A plan was born.

Sachie and I revisited the same spots, as well as Toshiki Kaba's salt shack (page 230) on the tip of a small peninsula-like trajectory jutting off the island to the southeast, and the very charming small island of Teshima, a Benesse 'art island', younger sister to the famed Naoshima further to the west. But Furyu and Nobuto Shibuya's bright, seasonal, refreshing food, known as *modoki ryori*, remained one of the striking highlights of that trip. And I have never arranged a trip since then that did not take Furyu's off days into consideration.

Shibuya-san is mild and understated like his food, but the quiet passion is apparent in how he approaches his menus, and in what he has accomplished in the local community. He is humble, kind and unfailingly generous. On one recent trip to Shodoshima, Shibuya-san drove me back to my hotel, forty-five minutes away from the restaurant, since Sachie and her husband had left me after dinner so Shibuya-san and I could chat at leisure about the food and his projects. He has offered again, but this time I booked a hotel closer to the restaurant.

Shibuya-san sources pricey ingredients such as Toshiki Kaba's Goen salt and Takao Nouen's olive oil, yet also ferments his own Japanese sand lance (*ikanago*) fish sauce. He uses these ingredients honestly, with great precision and thought, building up the plate like a canvas of color from an immense palette of natural resources. He cooks with an exceptionally light hand and the ingredients sing individually as well as in union. Many of the bits and pieces that appear on the plate come from the land where the restaurant stands, and it is with great pride that he explains each dish and the provenance of each ingredient. This extreme adherence to seasonality is what draws me to any restaurant that I love, and this kind of eating experience is soothing, comforting and curative. Also, we do not eat food in a vacuum. There is no denying that the context of the restaurant and the selfless dedication of the chef enhance the overall experience. The fact that Shibuya-san gives back to his adopted community is not lost on me, and makes me appreciate him and his food even more.

Every three years, the Setouchi Triennale is a type of outreach for tourists, to help guide them while also promoting art and food in the area. Special art installations are erected for the Triennale year – some sponsored by Benesse, some not. There is also a strong focus on food, and with the increase in visitors, t-shirted guides (including English-speaking ones) meet the ferries, passing out pamphlets. Naoshima is the most well known for art and food, Shodoshima for soy sauce (page 242), hand-pulled somen noodles and olive oil, and Teshima for citrus.

The Seto Inland Sea covers a wide swathe of Japan, stretching from Himeji to Okayama to Hiroshima. There are 3000 islands in the sea, and islands can be notoriously bereft of good eateries. Shibuya-san has taken on the mantle to increase the food profile of Shodoshima by adding his gelateria and hip but tasty bread shop to his already well-received restaurant, Furyu. I wonder when Shibuya-san sleeps, but as a frequent visitor to the island, I am grateful for his efforts.

Tako Sarada

OCTOPUS AND GROUPER SALAD WITH FISH SAUCE–CITRUS VINAIGRETTE

This gorgeously spare seafood salad makes for a stunning presentation when served on a glass plate.

SERVES 4

100 ml (3½ fl oz) mild rice vinegar

2 tablespoons light brown Japanese cane sugar (*kibizato*, page 15)

¼ teaspoon fine sea salt

2 small sprigs of thyme

1 bay leaf

½ teaspoon yellow mustard seeds

½ teaspoon fennel seeds

¼ small, plump *mizu nasu* eggplant (aubergine), sliced 6 mm (¼ in) thick

¼ small prickly Japanese cucumber (*yotsuba kyuri*), cut into 6 mm (¼ in) rounds

2 small okra, trimmed and halved lengthwise

½ small red pepper (capsicum), seeded and cut lengthwise into 6 mm (¼ in) strips

4 small red whelks (*aka-nishigai* or *tsubugai*) or other whelks, weighing about 75 g (2¾ oz)

½ leg of a small octopus (*tako*), weighing about 75 g (2¾ oz)

¼ skinless, boneless fillet of grouper (*akou*), weighing about 75 g (2¾ oz)

1 skinless, boneless fillet of horse mackerel (*aji*), weighing about 75 g (2⅔ oz)

60 ml (2 fl oz/¼ cup) extra-virgin olive oil

juice of 2 *sudachi* (page 18) or ½ Meyer lemon (about 2 tablespoons)

1 teaspoon Japanese fish sauce, preferably sand lance (*ikanago gyosho*, page 13)

¼ teaspoon flaky sea salt

2 teaspoons finely chopped chives, for garnishing

Bring the vinegar, sugar, fine salt, thyme, bay leaf, mustard seeds and fennel seeds to a simmer in a small saucepan. Place the eggplant, cucumber, okra and red pepper in a small bowl and pour the hot vinegar solution over the vegetables. Weight with a small plate to keep the vegetables submerged and let cool to room temperature. Refrigerate to chill.

With a razor-sharp knife, halve the whelks crosswise. Cut the octopus leg, grouper and horse mackerel into 6 mm (¼ in) slices, as if for sashimi. Divide the fish and seafood evenly among 4 chilled plates. Add a few pieces of each of the drained pickled vegetables. In a small bowl, whisk the olive oil into the *sudachi* or lemon juice, fish sauce and salt until well emulsified, and drizzle on the salad. Sprinkle with the chives and serve immediately.

Hiyashi Sukuwasshu Su-pu

CHILLED BUTTERNUT SQUASH SOUP WITH GORGONZOLA MOUSSE

This lightly flavored squash soup acquires richness from the gorgonzola mousse.

SERVES 4

1 small onion, finely sliced

1 teaspoon butter

500 g (1 lb 2 oz) peeled and seeded butternut squash (pumpkin), cut in 4 cm (1½ in) cubes

pinch of flaky sea salt

100 g (3½ oz) gorgonzola cheese

200 ml (7 fl oz) milk

5 g (¼ oz) gelatin leaves, softened in cold water for 10 minutes

75 ml (2½ fl oz) cream

3 small egg whites, at room temperature (about 80 g/ 2¾ oz)

pinch of fine sea salt

1 teaspoon grappa

coarsely ground black pepper, for serving

Sauté the onion in the butter in a medium saucepan over low heat, to take the raw edge off. Add the squash and 750 ml (25½ fl oz/3 cups) water and bring to a boil over medium heat. Simmer briskly for about 15 minutes, until completely soft. Add the flaky salt and purée the squash with the cooking liquid. The consistency should be like thick cream, so add water if needed, or simmer down if it is too runny. Cool, then chill for at least 2 hours.

Mash the gorgonzola to a paste through a fine mesh sieve (*uragoshi*, page 275) into a medium mixing bowl. Heat the milk over medium–low heat in a small saucepan. Once warm, remove from the heat and stir in the drained gelatin until dissolved. Slowly stir the milk into the gorgonzola until emulsified. Chill in the fridge until cool to the touch.

Beat the cream in a small stainless bowl set inside a bowl of ice cubes, until thick and creamy but not at all stiff.

Beat the egg whites with the fine salt on high speed in a medium mixing bowl (without ice) until stiff peaks form.

Fold the thickened cream and grappa into the gorgonzola mixture. Gently fold in the beaten egg whites, taking care not to deflate. Store the mousse in the fridge until needed.

Ladle the soup into 4 chilled soup bowls and spoon about a heaping tablespoon of the gorgonzola mousse into the middle of each. Sprinkle the mousse with black pepper and serve.

高尾農園
オリーブ畑

Ika no Fettochi-ne, Piri-Piri Yaki Yasai

RED WHELK AND SQUID FETTUCCINE WITH SPICY SUMMER VEGETABLES

Shodoshima, located in the Seto Inland Sea, has a wealth of seafood and fish available at any given time. This fettuccine dish showcases the best of what the island has to offer. Japan's range of shellfish is astounding and here the whelks, called *tsubugai* in most of Japan, are a variety local to the area called *nishigai,* or more specifically, *aka-nishigai* (red whelks), and the squid (*ika*) is particularly tender.

Japanese squid is line caught so the guts do not get smashed. When guts are smashed, they permeate the snow white flesh, thus imparting a fishy taste. When in doubt, a quick douse with boiling water followed immediately by a plunge in ice water can help remove unpleasant smells. Repeat, if needed.

SERVES 4

1 very small squid (*ika*) weighing about 100 g (3½ oz), gutted and rinsed

4 small red whelks (*aka-nishigai* or *tsubugai*) or other whelks, weighing about 75 g (2¾ oz)

1 tablespoon extra-virgin olive oil

1 small zucchini (courgette), cut into 6 mm (¼ in) rounds

8 small oval cherry tomatoes, halved lengthwise

2 garlic cloves, finely chopped

1 small dried red chili (*chile japones*, page 278), finely chopped

150 g (5½ oz) fresh fettuccine

1 teaspoon Japanese fish sauce

1 teaspoon finely chopped parsley

Cut the squid body into thick bite-sized rings, and the tentacles into 3 cm (1¼ in) pieces. Quarter the whelks crosswise, place in a sieve and rinse with cold water. Shake off excess moisture.

Bring a large pot of well-salted water to a boil for the fettuccine. Heat the olive oil in a large frying pan over medium–high heat and sear the zucchini rounds quickly on both sides. Take the pan off the heat and transfer the zucchini to a dinner plate with a slotted spoon, taking care to leave as much oil as possible. Return the pan to the heat and sear the squid and whelk pieces on all sides for about 1–2 minutes, until cooked through and creamy colored. Spoon the pieces out to the plate with the zucchini. Adjust the pan to medium heat and slide in the tomato halves. Stir-fry for 2–3 minutes, until starting to collapse. Stir in the garlic and chili and cook for 30 seconds before removing from the heat.

Cook the fettuccine in the boiling water until al dente, scoop out with a large wire-mesh strainer, and dump into the frying pan along with the zucchini, squid and whelk. Sprinkle in the fish sauce and stir-fry for 1 minute over high heat before serving with a sprinkling of parsley.

Nibedai, Edamame, Ke-pa-, Komesu So-su

SNAPPER WITH EDAMAME, CAPER AND RICE VINEGAR SAUCE

In Japan, fish is most often cooked with the skin on, and the skin is a highly prized part of the fish. Here the skin is grilled crisp so it is appealingly crunchy against the moist flesh.

SERVES 4

4 small snapper (*nibedai*) fillets, skin on, weighing about 75 g (2¾ oz) each

½ teaspoon flaky sea salt

½ teaspoon freshly ground white pepper

1 tablespoon cake flour

3 tablespoons extra-virgin olive oil

2 small oval cherry tomatoes, halved lengthwise

4 rounds of a small zucchini (courgette), cut 5 mm (¼ in) thick

4 rounds of a thin Japanese eggplant (aubergine), cut 5 mm (¼ in) thick

4 rounds of a small potato, cut 5 mm (¼ in) thick

2 tablespoons rice vinegar

2 teaspoons small vinegar-packed capers

4 tablespoons cooked edamame beans

2 tablespoons unsalted butter

Sprinkle the fish on both sides with ¼ teaspoon of the salt and the white pepper. Let sit for 10 minutes. Blot the fillets dry with spongy paper towels. Dust on both sides with the flour. Shake off.

Heat 2 tablespoons of the olive oil in a medium frying pan over medium–high heat. Once hot but not smoking, sear the fish on the skin side for about 3 minutes, until well browned. Flip, cook 30 seconds more, and remove to a dinner plate with a spatula.

Heat the remaining 1 tablespoon of olive oil in a large frying pan over medium heat until starting to sizzle. Quickly lay in the tomato halves, cut-side down, along with the zucchini, eggplant and potato rounds. Sear the tomatoes for only 1 minute on each side and remove to a plate. Cook the other vegetables for 2–3 minutes on each side, until cooked through and golden brown. Remove from the heat and immediately arrange one piece of each vegetable in the middle of 4 plates to form the corners of a square. Do not wash the vegetable pan. Set the seared fish fillets on top of the vegetables, so you can still see some of the vegetables peeking out.

Return the pan to medium heat and swirl in the vinegar, capers, edamame, remaining ¼ teaspoon salt and the butter. Simmer for 30 seconds, then spoon over the fish and vegetables and serve.

Shiro Wain to Shinamon Nikomi Ichijiku, Banira Aisu

CINNAMON-POACHED FIG WITH VANILLA ICE CREAM

A beautiful medley of flavors, with the cinnamon and star anise playing well against the fig.

SERVES 4

Vanilla Ice Cream

500 ml (17 fl oz/2 cups) cream

250 ml (8½ fl oz/1 cup) whole (full-cream) milk

135 g (5 oz) granulated sugar

1 vanilla bean

6 medium egg yolks, at room temperature (about 100 g/3½ oz)

500 ml (17 fl oz/2 cups) mild white wine such as sauvignon blanc

150 g (5½ oz) light brown Japanese cane sugar (*kibizato*, page 15)

½ cinnamon stick

1 star anise

2 ripe figs, peeled

8 g (¼ oz) gelatin leaves, softened in cold water for 10 minutes

8–12 blueberries, for garnishing

4 sprigs of mint, for garnishing

To make the ice cream, pour the cream, milk and sugar into a heavy medium saucepan. Halve the vanilla bean lengthwise and scrape out the seeds with the back of the knife. Scrape the seeds into the pan along with the empty pod. Place over medium heat, stirring occasionally, until the sugar has dissolved and the mixture is hot. Mix a ladle or two of hot cream into the egg yolks in a small mixing bowl and stir to emulsify. Scrape the yolks into the saucepan and continue cooking over medium heat, stirring continuously, until the mixture has thickened and coats the back of the wooden spoon. Strain and let cool to room temperature. Chill, then churn in an ice cream maker.

Bring the wine, sugar, cinnamon and star anise to a simmer in a small saucepan to burn off a little alcohol and dissolve the sugar. Slide in the figs and cover with a drop lid (*otoshibuta*, page 275) or a piece of parchment (baking) paper. Adjust to a simmer and cook for 3–5 minutes – the figs should not be mushy. Remove the figs to a plate with a slotted spoon and leave to cool to room temperature.

Strain the simmering liquid into a clean saucepan and add any accumulating liquid from the plate with the figs. Drain the gelatin, and stir into the hot liquid (off heat) until completely dissolved. Pour into a small bowl to cool, and chill until set.

Halve the figs lengthwise. Place 1 fig half on each of 4 dessert plates. Dollop a soup spoon or so of the chilled and set syrup next to the fig. Form torpedo-shaped portions of vanilla ice cream using 2 spoons, and put 1 on each plate. Garnish each with 2 or 3 blueberries and 1 sprig of mint and serve immediately.

ISLAND SALT

Japan is an archipelago, so it seems unthinkable that there would not be hundreds, if not thousands, of artisanal salt makers along the almost 30,000 kilometers of coast. However, a government-mandated salt monopoly severely limited the production and sale of salt for more than nine decades, from 1905 to 1997. The government decreed salt making to be their sole domain, partly to develop the domestic salt industry, and partly to fund the Russo–Japanese War of 1904–05. And in 1971, the Act on Temporary Measures for the Modernization of the Salt Industry eliminated all remaining salt fields, thus ringing the final death toll on any last vestiges of Japanese artisanal salt production. So-called table salt (produced in Japan by a proprietary method of ion-exchange membrane electrodialysis) was the only salt available in Japan for most of the 20th century, until medical professionals began expressing grave concerns. This table salt, which was 99% sodium chloride, lacked the essential minerals present in naturally produced salt and was therefore causing health issues.

When I first came to Japan in 1988, there was a meager selection of uninteresting salts on the shelves, so I used *sel gris* and *fleur de sel* from Normandy, before moving onto Trapani *fiore di sale*. Eventually I started noticing promising-looking small packets of what seemed to be artisanal sea salt and began trying them. The salts came from all over Japan and initially were mostly fine salts. As time passed, crystal-type salts made their appearance, and I found multiple Japanese salts that excited me, thus supplanting the Trapani salt from Sicily.

Today there are many salt makers, both large and small, artisanal and not, as well as tourist destinations where you can experience the salt-making process yourself, such as *moshio-yaki* in Hiroshima. *Moshio-yaki*, an ancient technique dating back to the first half of the Kofun period (300–538 AD), is thought to be one of the oldest salt-making methods in Japan.

Early references to the exact nature of this *moshio-yaki* process are unclear, and slightly conflicting, but essentially involved dried *hondawara* seaweed and concentrated seawater. However, in 1982, remnants of stone and pottery used for salt making were discovered by Norihide Matsuura (now president of the Moshio Association in Hiroshima) at an archaeological site on the island of Shikoku. Matsuura began replicating the ancient *moshio-yaki* process in 1983, and in 1989 succeeded, by gently simmering down sun-dried *hondawara* seaweed and concentrated seawater in an earthenware pot before harvesting the salt. Now a number of salt makers, from islands in the Seto Inland Sea to Okinawa, are producing a modern version of *moshio*, whereby they boil down concentrated seawater in steel vats with a huge muslin bag of seaweed to extract varying grades of salt.

Most artisanal salt makers, however, prefer a gentler method of salt extraction, since it results in an appreciably milder salt on the tongue.

Basically, salt making involves three crucial steps: harvesting the seawater; concentrating the seawater (a process known as *enden*); and slowly heating the concentrated water to gradually extract the salt solids. The seawater can be deep water such as that pumped up by my pal Hajime Nakamichi of Wajima no Kaien salt, or water pumped from the side of a pristine island inlet, such as for Nami Hana Do's Goen salt on Shodoshima, or it could arrive in Japan as ballast on ships returning from Mexico or Australia (cheap!).

And the seawater concentration process can be as fascinating and visually stunning as the method used on Agunijima, where the seawater is dripped down hanging bamboo, or the greenhouse system rigged up by Toshiki Kaba of Nami Hana Do. According to Kaba, the *enden* process is crucial because it removes calcium deposits. Kaba pumps salt water into large holding tanks and leaves it for three to five days to allow the solids to sink to the bottom of the tank. The top portion of the seawater is pumped into fiberglass tanks located in a small greenhouse, where the

water is then piped up through a continuous shower system to allow it to evaporate naturally from the normal 3% salt concentration of seawater to 10%. During this round-the-clock process that lasts one to two weeks, calcium particles adhere to the corrugated plastic gutters, from which the water is cycled back into the shower system.

Kaba heats the concentrated water in a small shack below his house where he has built a 2.5 meter (8 foot) square brick base fitted with an iron trough of the same size. He builds a small but raging wood fire under the trough, and this heats the salt water enough to allow the salt solids to gradually form. As the seawater evaporates over a 24-hour period in the summer, or three days in winter, Kaba slowly adds additional warm seawater to the trough from a small holding basin above. He mixes the early- and late-formed crystals together in a barrel, packs the wet salt into muslin bags, then leaves it to drip out naturally (if air-dried, Kaba says the salt would become bitter).

Toshiki Kaba relocated to Shodoshima from Gifu prefecture in northwestern Japan with his wife, Kazumi, over a decade ago. He says that working in construction in Gifu, especially during the snowy winter, almost killed him. Newly married to Kazumi, he announced to her, 'Let's go to a warm place.' The criteria for their new home: an old house, the sea and tangerine trees (because that would mean a moderate climate). They found all three on Shodoshima and have lived on the island since.

Due to the virtual death of artisanal salt making, salt was no longer being produced on Shodoshima. Perceiving the abundance of seawater and the gap in the market, Kaba launched himself into salt making a few years into their life on the island. Initially, he set up operation by the water's edge at the foot of the cliff below the hillside where their house is perched. He built a fire and boiled the seawater down in a large metal pot. He brought the salt to Kazumi, who pronounced it 'not tasty'. Galvanized by Kazumi's negative reaction and the desire to make a salt that Kazumi would like, Kaba researched better methods to produce his salt. It took several years, but now Kaba's Goen salt is in such demand that he can barely keep up, despite producing 100 kilograms (222 pounds) per month.

It is heartwarming to see Kaba's salt being used in all of the restaurants where I eat on Shodoshima – that feeling of a cooperative community is palpable on the island.

And it was because of that community spirit of Shodoshima that I recently introduced the island to Netflix for the 'Salt' episode of Samin Nosrat's *Salt Fat Acid Heat*. We cooked at Yamaroku Shoyu (page 242), made miso with Kaba's wife, Kazumi, and checked out Kaba's salt-making set up. Regrettably, the Netflix crew had already visited a *moshio* operation on another island, so Kaba's intriguing salt process and lovely mineral-rich salt did not make the final episode of *Salt*.

Managatsuo, Shiozuke Yasai, Sudachi

BUTTERFISH ON SALT-MARINATED SUMMER VEGETABLES WITH SUDACHI

The butterfish skin is seared crispy, but the flesh is only half cooked, so using sashimi-grade fish is essential. Substitute yuzu or Meyer lemon if you are unable to source *sudachi*.

SERVES 4

2 small Japanese cucumbers, cut into small dice

2 small round Japanese eggplants (aubergines), cut into small dice

1 small red bell pepper (capsicum), cut into small dice

1 teaspoon flaky sea salt

1 small tomato, cut into small dice

1 small basil leaf, finely chopped, plus 4 small sprigs for garnishing

60 ml (2 fl oz/¼ cup) extra-virgin olive oil

2 tablespoons freshly squeezed *sudachi* (page 18) juice

8 × 4 cm (1½ in) pieces of butterfish fillet, skin on, weighing about 40 g (1½ oz) each

Toss the cucumber, eggplant and red pepper with ¼ teaspoon of the salt in a small mixing bowl and leave for 10 minutes to release liquid.

In another small mixing bowl, stir ¼ teaspoon of the salt into the tomato and chopped basil leaf. Squeeze the salted cucumber, eggplant and red pepper inside spongy paper towels and drop into the bowl with the tomato. Whisk half the olive oil into the *sudachi* juice in a small bowl until emulsified. Stir into the vegetable mixture.

Sprinkle both sides of the butterfish pieces with the remaining ½ teaspoon of salt from 30 cm (1 ft) above (*tateshio*), for even coverage. Let sit for 10 minutes. Blot off any liquids that have formed on the skin or flesh surfaces.

Heat the remaining olive oil in a large frying pan over medium–high heat and when hot but not smoking, sear the fillets for 1 minute, skin side down. Remove to a plate, but flip them as you transfer them so the skin side is up.

Spoon the vegetable mixture onto 4 plates and rest 2 butterfish fillets against each other in the middle of the vegetables on each plate. Garnish with the sprigs of basil. Serve as a first course.

Yaki Nasu Su-pu,
Kunsei Aji

CHILLED ROASTED EGGPLANT SOUP WITH SMOKED HORSE MACKEREL

Smoky charred eggplant (aubergine) finds its way into many Japanese recipes, even miso soup. Here the silky, rich eggplant texture is juxtaposed by the taut slices of barely smoked horse mackerel. Use the best four center slices of two of the fillets and reserve the rest for another dish or as a bite before dinner.

SERVES 4

4 small fillets of horse mackerel (*aji*), weighing about 80 g (2¾ oz) each

1¾ teaspoons flaky sea salt

6 small Japanese eggplants (aubergines), weighing about 400 g (14 oz) in total

2 tablespoons extra-virgin olive oil, plus extra for serving and rubbing the smoking grate

1 handful (heaping ½ cup) olive wood chips, soaked in water for 30 minutes

1 teaspoon finely chopped chives

freshly ground black pepper

Place the horse mackerel on a large plate and sprinkle with 1¼ teaspoons of the salt. Leave for 30 minutes to allow excess moisture to leach out naturally. Pat dry in spongy paper towels and set on a rack for 30 minutes to tighten the flesh a bit.

Prepare charcoal in a barbecue and char the eggplants whole over the hot charcoal until all of the skin has blackened. Cool in a bowl covered with a plate to help sweat off the skin. Once cool, peel and put in a blender with 250 ml (8½ fl oz/1 cup) water, the olive oil and remaining salt, and purée to a silky smooth, spoonable consistency. Chill.

Push the charcoal to one side of the barbecue, and sprinkle the soaked and drained wood chips over the hot charcoal. Set a drip pan next to the charcoal, place the cooking grate in the barbecue, and rub the grate area above the drip pan lightly with olive oil. Cover with the lid, open the vent holes halfway and allow the barbecue to fill with smoke. Working quickly so as not to lose the smoke, open the lid, place the horse mackerel fillets, skin side down, on the grate area above the drip pan. Replace the lid and smoke for 5 minutes. Remove from the smoker, allow to cool, then chill in the refrigerator.

Cut 2 of the smoked mackerel fillets at a diagonal into 12 mm (½ in) sashimi-style slices.

Ladle the soup into chilled bowls and carefully rest 2 of the most beautiful center slices of the fish in the middle of each. Sprinkle with a few chopped chives and dribble in a couple of drops of olive oil and a quick grind of pepper.

Awabi, Satsuma Imo, Awabi no Kimo no Rizotto

ABALONE WITH A SWEET POTATO AND ABALONE LIVER RISOTTO

The abalone texture is soft yet slightly chewy, and the sweet potato mitigates the gentle acrid quality of the abalone liver, thus giving balance to the dish.

SERVES 4

2 small abalone about 9 cm (3½ in) wide, plus 2 abalone livers, and 4 small abalone shells for serving

½ small yellow-fleshed sweet potato weighing about 75 g (2¾ oz), scrubbed

1 tablespoon dry white wine

1 tablespoon extra-virgin olive oil

1 medium onion weighing about 125 g (4½ oz), finely diced

200 ml (7 fl oz) measure of Japanese white rice (about 170 g/6 oz)

1 tablespoon unsalted butter

⅛ teaspoon flaky sea salt

⅛ teaspoon freshly ground black pepper

½ teaspoon finely chopped chives

Set the abalone meat (but not the liver) on a plate and place inside a bamboo steamer. Cover with the lid. Fill a large wok one-third full with water and bring to a boil. Nestle the steamer basket into the wok over the water, and steam the abalone for about 30 minutes, until soft in the center – check with a bamboo skewer. Remove the plate from the steamer. Once the abalone is cool, slice thinly.

Place the sweet potato in a medium saucepan and cover generously with cold water. Bring to a boil over high heat and cook for 15 minutes, until 80% softened. Drain, peel and cut into 1 cm (½ in) cubes.

Drop the abalone livers into a very small saucepan with the white wine. Bring to a simmer over medium heat and immediately remove from the heat. Allow to cool in the liquid. Once cool, remove the liver, dice, and return to the pan.

To make the risotto, bring 500 ml (17 fl oz/2 cups) water to a simmer over high heat, then adjust the temperature to low. Heat the olive oil in a small heavy pot and sauté the onion over low heat until starting to soften. Add the rice and adjust the heat to medium. Stirring constantly, cook until you see some white spots on the rice. Stir in 200 ml (7 fl oz) of the hot water. Keep stirring until the rice is about half done in the center (add extra splashes of hot water if needed, but reserve 100 ml/3½ fl oz for finishing). When the rice is half done, you can remove the risotto (and water) from the heat and finish it just before serving.

Add 100 ml (3½ fl oz) hot water to the risotto, as well as the cubes of sweet potato, the liver and its simmering liquid. Stir over low heat for about 5 minutes to incorporate. Add the butter, stirring until melted.

Set a decorative abalone shell in the middle of each of 4 salad plates. Spoon a dollop of risotto into the shells, allowing it to spill out onto the plates. Fan out 4 or 5 slices of abalone on top of the risotto and sprinkle with a pinch each of flaky salt, fresh pepper and chopped chives. Serve hot.

Ori-vu Bi-fu, Kapona-ta

PAN-SEARED OLIVE BEEF WITH CAPONATA

Cattle around Shodoshima eat the olive 'cake', the by-product solids that remain after extracting oil from olives. The beef that results is called 'olive beef', and is purported to have a hint of olive flavor to the meat. Personally, I have not been able to detect that, but nonetheless find the meat tasty and soft in texture. This dish is finished with salt mixed with dried black olive.

SERVES 4

Olive Salt

½ small, oil-packed, pitted black olive

3 tablespoons flaky sea salt

Caponata

1 small onion, sliced

1 small zucchini (courgette), cut into large dice

1 small red bell pepper (capsicum), cut into large dice

1 small Japanese eggplant (aubergine), cut into large dice

4 okra, blanched for 30 seconds in salted water, halved lengthwise

2 tablespoons extra-virgin olive oil

125 ml (4 fl oz/½ cup) tomato purée

1 tablespoon small capers

1 tablespoon sliced (flaked) almonds

1 tablespoon balsamic vinegar

a few pinches of light brown Japanese cane sugar (*kibizato*, page 15)

a few pinches of flaky sea salt

Steak and Sauce

320 g (11½ oz) rump steak (ideally 'olive beef'), at room temperature

½ teaspoon flaky sea salt

1 teaspoon mild honey

2 tablespoons extra-virgin olive oil

100 ml (3½ fl oz) marsala

1 teaspoon *moutarde a l'ancienne* (French mustard with seeds)

To make the olive salt, roast the olive in a small dry cast-iron frying pan over low heat until half dried. Chop finely and mix into the salt. Store at room temperature in a small glass jar.

To make the caponata, preheat the oven to 170°C (340°F). Strew the onion, zucchini, red pepper, eggplant and okra pieces on an oven sheet. Toss with the olive oil and cook for 10 minutes in the middle of the oven. Remove the okra to a small plate and stir the tomato purée, capers and almonds into the vegetables. Cook for 10 more minutes. Mix well and cook for another 5 minutes. Sprinkle in the balsamic vinegar, sugar and salt, and check the taste.

Reset the oven to 160°C (320°F). Sprinkle the beef all over with the salt, and rub with the honey. Heat the olive oil in a medium cast-iron frying pan over high heat. Once hot but not smoking, sear the steak for 3 minutes on one side, then flip and cook 2 minutes more on the other side. Roast the meat in the pan in the middle of the oven for 5–6 minutes. Remove from the oven and allow the steak to rest on a board, covered loosely with aluminum foil, for at least 10 minutes. Do not wash the pan. Slice the steak into 12 mm (½ in) thick pieces.

Immediately after the steak has been removed from the pan, add the marsala and cook down over high heat until reduced by half. Stir in the mustard, and keep warm. Add any accumulated juices from the meat board into the sauce before serving.

Swirl some marsala sauce into the center of 4 warm dinner plates and add a healthy spoonful of caponata onto the sauce. Fan out 3 slices of the beef on top of the caponata and artfully place 2 okra halves on each plate. Strew a little olive salt around the perimeter of the plates.

Ichijiku, Satsuma Aisu, Kure-mu Angure-zu

FRESH FIG WITH SWEET POTATO ICE CREAM AND CRÈME ANGLAISE

SERVES 4

There are several components to this dessert, which do take time to construct, but the pieces can be incorporated into other desserts or even eaten separately as a simple dessert. The perfectly ripe fig is a crucial element that pulls it all together magnificently.

Sweet Potato Ice Cream

200 g (7 oz) yellow-fleshed sweet potato, peeled and cut into 1 cm (½ in) dice

½ vanilla bean

500 ml (17 fl oz/2 cups) whole (full-cream) milk

100 ml (3½ fl oz) cream

150 g (5½ oz) granulated sugar

5 medium egg yolks, at room temperature (about 85 g/3 oz)

To make the ice cream, drop the sweet potato into a medium saucepan and just cover with cold water. Bring to a simmer over medium–low heat and cook gently for about 10 minutes, until soft. Drain, and purée until smooth in a food processor. Scrape into a medium mixing bowl.

Halve the vanilla bean lengthwise and scrape out the gooey seeds. Add the seeds and empty pod into a medium saucepan with the milk, cream and sugar. Bring to an almost simmer over medium heat. Ladle a small scoop of the warm milk into the egg yolks in a small bowl, and stir to emulsify and warm. Add back into the milk mixture and continue stirring over medium heat, until the mixture has thickened and coats the back of the wooden spoon. Strain into a medium bowl. Stir slowly into the puréed sweet potato to form a smooth custard. Cool to room temperature, chill, and churn in an ice cream maker.

Caramel

300 g (10½ oz) granulated sugar

Sponge

5 medium eggs, at room temperature

150 g (5½ oz) granulated sugar

150 g (5½ oz/1 cup) cake flour

50 g (1¾ oz) butter, melted

Chocolate Caramel Custard Sponge

60 g (2 oz) chocolate (55% cacao), chopped

60 g (2 oz) unsweetened cocoa powder

300 ml (10 fl oz) cream

2 tablespoons whole (full-cream) milk

120 ml (4 fl oz/½ cup) amaretto

8 medium eggs, at room temperature

200 g (7 oz) granulated sugar

Crème Anglaise (page 162)

2 small figs, peeled and quartered lengthwise

16 blueberries

4 grapes, halved crosswise

unsweetened cocoa powder, for dusting

4 sprigs of mint, for garnishing

To make the caramel, heat the sugar with 60 ml (2 fl oz/¼ cup) water over medium heat, without stirring, to dissolve the sugar crystals. Cook until the sugar becomes a deep golden brown and you can smell the caramelization. Pour immediately across the bottom of a 20 cm (8 in) square pan.

To make the sponge, preheat the oven to 180°C (350°F), and lightly butter and flour an 18 cm (7 in) round cake pan. Break the eggs into a stainless bowl set over, but not touching, barely simmering water. Beat on high speed until light and frothy and slowly add the sugar until the mixture is like thick whipped cream. Remove the bowl from the heat and sift the flour over the top. Fold the flour in very gently – this is the most important step. Carefully fold in the melted butter and scrape the mixture into the pan. Cook in the middle of the oven for 30–40 minutes, until a toothpick inserted into the center comes out dry. Cool. Measure 200 g (7 oz) of sponge and break it roughly into pieces.

To make the chocolate caramel custard sponge, preheat the oven to 160°C (320°F). Find an oven pan large enough to fit the caramel-coated pan, and fill it halfway up with water. Set it (without the caramel pan) in the middle of the oven. Melt the chocolate with the cocoa in a medium stainless bowl over hot water. Heat the cream and milk in a small saucepan, and stir into the melted chocolate until emulsified. Stir in the amaretto.

Separate the egg yolks and whites into 2 medium mixing bowls. Beat the yolks with 125 g (4½ oz) of the sugar until creamy. Beat the whites until soft peaks form, and slowly add in the remaining sugar, beating until a stiff meringue has formed.

Fold the yolk mixture into the chocolate mixture along with the broken pieces of sponge. Fold the meringue in gently, taking care not to deflate, and scrape into the caramel-lined pan. Set the pan in the hot water bath in the oven and bake for 50 minutes. Cool before cutting and serving.

Swirl 2 tablespoons of crème anglaise on each of 4 pretty dessert plates. Cut 2.5 × 5 cm (1 × 2 in) pieces of chocolate caramel custard sponge and set one in the middle of each plate. Nestle 2 fig quarters on either side of each piece, one face up, the other face down. Strew with 4 blueberries and 2 grape halves per plate, and spoon an oval of sweet potato ice cream on top of the sponge. Sift a little cocoa over the top, garnish with the mint and serve immediately.

KIOKE

Shodoshima is not only home to thousands of olive trees (page 216), but also houses half of the wooden soy sauce barrels in Japan. While olive oil production is relatively young, at about 115 years old, soy sauce production has been thriving on Shodoshima for over 400 years.

Post–World War II, soy sauce makers were encouraged to modernize the 1000-year-old tradition of fermenting soy sauce in wooden barrels (*kioke*) in favor of using stainless steel. As with many residents of Japan's small islands, Shodoshima soy sauce producers think independently from 'mainland' Japan, and they chose not to follow this mainstream shift. Yamaroku Shoyu is one of twenty soy sauce makers on Shodoshima who still ferment their soy sauce in wooden barrels.

'In the hot and muggy summer, the *shoyu moromi* (soy sauce mash) becomes active, making gurgling sounds as the fermentation accelerates. When I climb the ladder and walk the planks between the wooden soy sauce barrels, the *moromi* in each barrel becomes noticeably more active, as if it is talking to me, telling me it is happy to have my presence. We have a mutual love for each other.' Yasuo Yamamoto speaks of his *moromi* with the passion of a small business owner. The *moromi* is like a part of his family; in fact, it is the past and future of his family, and Yamamoto takes this stewardship seriously. So seriously that Yamamoto and two Shodoshima carpenters traveled to the last viable large wooden barrel maker (Fujii Wood Work in Sakai near Osaka) in 2012 in order to learn the craft of fashioning large wooden barrels: from preparing the cedar slats and bamboo pins, to weaving the bamboo hoops. The beneficial microorganisms that thrive in Yamaroku's 150-year-old *ogata kioke* (3600-liter wooden barrels) create an impossible-to-duplicate, one-of-a-kind shoyu. To lose this food culture is unimaginable.

There is a movement afloat to preserve ancient Japanese fermentation methods before they are lost forever. While we will not see them disappear in our generation, they very likely will in our children's or grandchildren's. Fermentation relies on a healthy environment where microbes thrive, and where the enzymes and yeasts can work in symbiosis. Therefore, *kioke* are the best vessels for fermentation since the wood itself is host to millions of microbes. Less than one hundred years ago, all Japanese fermented products, such as shoyu, miso, mirin, rice vinegar, sake and pickles, were made in *kioke*. Some maintain that authentic Japanese fermented foods cannot be created without one essential ingredient: the barrels. Yet traditional fermented food and drink produced in *kioke* has sunk to only 1% of the total market.

Normally, learning such a craft takes years, but in the case of Yamamoto and his cohorts, it took an initial three days, and then years of practice to get it right. They made their first *kioke* in September 2013, four more in January 2015, and an additional four in January 2016. This year (2019) they will make eight barrels, three of which will be sold to other artisanal makers.

Yoshino cedar is legendary as the best wood to use for buckets and barrels. A chance meeting with the head of the Yoshino Cedar Wood Products Association led to a mutually supportive relationship between the wood suppliers and Yamamoto's group. Now the Yoshino wood group saves the boards and slabs needed for future *kioke*, since the wood needs to dry for two to three years before using.

As for the bamboo, Yamamoto searched in Kyoto for the appropriate variety, but gave up due to transportation issues. He then asked a neighbor if there was any bamboo on Shodoshima of the requisite height and variety. 'What?' the neighbor shot back. 'Your grandfather and I planted bamboo for the bamboo hoops years ago. Didn't you know that?' Yamamoto has no more worries regarding sourcing bamboo for the braided hoops of his *kioke*.

In the 1920s there were tens of thousands of *kioke* makers in Japan, a number too large to attempt even to estimate. By the end of World War II, there were maybe one million barrels left in sake breweries alone, but within ten to fifteen years, the demand for *kioke* dwindled dangerously, and many coopers gave up their metier. With growing use and lower costs of stainless steel after the war, traditional wood vessels lost favor. From the 1970s to 1990s, there were still master coopers in Japan, but their population was aging. Today, Takeshi Ueshiba of Fujii Wood Work in Sakai is the last master craftsman of *kioke* in the country.

While *kioke* shoyu and miso production has managed to just barely survive, *kioke* sake production did not fare as well. Barrel-fermented sake had ceased completely until Sarah Marie Cummings took up the challenge to reintroduce this traditional fermenting method. Thanks to Cummings' efforts, today there are sixty to eighty *kioke* sake producers in Japan (though it is still only 0.1% of the market).

Cummings also created Oke Society, a non-profit organization to promote bucket and barrel production. According to Cummings: 'Superior products are made in these wooden vessels, and there is surprisingly little research to prove what makes these products so special. We hope to encourage and facilitate research and promote Japanese *oke*-brewed and -fermented products around the world ... With cooperation, I do believe that the *oke* cooper will prosper and I am confident that there will be more great *oke* makers in the future.'

(NB *Oke* means 'bucket' and *taru* means 'barrel', and the distinction speaks to the level of craftsmanship. An *oke* is meant for multiple uses and can be as small as a cup or as large as a giant shoyu barrel. A *taru* is essentially made for one use, as in a barrel of sake for wedding parties. *Kioke* is the word most often used when referring to large *oke* used for fermenting sake, shoyu and miso. For better visual understanding, *kioke* is translated as 'barrel' in English, because calling them 'buckets' would cause bewilderment.)

I have seen firsthand the excitement and pride in the eyes of some of the remaining makers of *kioke*-fermented products, and know that if we support them, they will flourish.

Grandma Yamamoto's Maze-gohan (Mixed Rice): Soak 6 small dried shiitake in 500 ml (17 fl oz/2 cups) water overnight to make shiitake dashi. Soak a 10 cm (4 in) piece of konbu in 500 ml (17 fl oz/2 cups) water overnight for konbu dashi. Soak 25 g (1 oz) small sun-dried fish (*iriko*) in 1 liter (34 fl oz/4 cups) water overnight for *iriko* dashi. The next day, strain the shiitake dashi, squeezing the mushrooms to express all moisture. Discard the stems and finely chop the caps. Discard the konbu (or use in another dish). Simmer the *iriko* in its soaking water for 5 minutes. Strain out and discard the *iriko*, reserve the dashi.

Cut 2 tofu pouches (*usuage*) and 300 g (10½ oz) chicken thighs into 1 cm (½ in) dice. Toss the chicken with 60 ml (2 fl oz/¼ cup) Yamaroku Kikubishio shoyu and let sit for 30 minutes to absorb flavor. Cut 2 medium carrots and 200 g (7 oz) *konnyaku* into a fine 5 mm (¼ in) dice. Shave off very small pieces from ½ medium burdock with a razor-sharp knife like sharpening a pencil (*sasagiri*).

Pour the shiitake dashi, konbu dashi and *iriko* dashi into a large, wide pot with ¼ cup small dried shrimp (*sakura ebi*) – the wide pot will speed up the reduction of the liquids. Drop in the carrot and bring to a simmer over medium–high heat. After 2 minutes, add the burdock and simmer another 1 minute. Add the *konnyaku* and simmer 2 more minutes before adding the *usuage*, shiitake and chicken (with its marinating liquid). Simmer briskly for 2 minutes before stirring in 150 ml (5 fl oz) Yamaroku Kikubishio shoyu and 50 ml (1¾ fl oz) Yamaroku Tsurubishio *saishikomi shoyu* (double-brewed shoyu). Simmer a few minutes more until the liquids have reduced and the ingredients are well seasoned. Remove from the heat.

Scrub and flush a 900 ml (30½ fl oz) measure of Japanese white rice (about 750 g/1 lb 11 oz) several times with cold water. Drain, and slide into a heavy medium pot with 900 ml (30½ fl oz) cold water. Cover and bring to a boil over high heat (about 7 minutes), adjust the heat to low and cook for 12 minutes. Never open the pot once you start cooking the rice. Remove from the heat and let sit for 5 minutes before turning out into a low-sided wooden tub (*handai*) or wooden salad bowl that has been wet with water. Scoop a spoonful of the simmered ingredients onto the rice with a slotted spoon, and gently cut into the rice with a rice paddle (*shamoji*). Continue cutting in spoonfuls of ingredients until the rice is just studded with color. You should still be able to see white pieces of rice. Any leftover simmered ingredients can be tossed into an egg stir-fry, and leftover *maze-gohan* can be use to make rice balls (*onigiri*).

TEISHOKU: THE JAPANESE TRAY MEAL

I had heard from Travis Lett that MTN, his cool izakaya on Abbot Kinney in Venice, California, was now serving *teishoku*. I could not resist the invitation to stop by and try this new addition to the menu.

Thanks to the expert kitchen at MTN, we had collaborated for a wildly successful preview of my *Japan: The Cookbook* in October 2017, a good nine months before the book debuted. I already knew what kind of brightly compelling, seasonal Japanese food Travis and his crew were creating, so a stopover in LA to enjoy more of it was an attractive proposition.

International entry into LAX is always a challenge, and this trip was no different. The rental car proved to be a dicey, fly-by-night operation called Ace Rent-a-Car: no regular shuttle van, a dodgy office located off the grid somewhere near the airport. Equipped with video phones to communicate with the agents (!) ... a nightmare, which included a US$30 Uber ride, and about an hour of wasted time. Late to arrive, I scored a rare parking place in front. My friend was waiting patiently, perched on a stool at a high table under the open-air ceiling portion of our MTN rendezvous.

After dropping (and cracking the screen of) my new iPhone X, the flurry finally calmed, and we ordered. 'Do you want the miso soup American-style or Japanese?' my server inquired. Once again flustered, I asked for clarification. Apparently, 'American-style' means miso soup before the meal. Never heard of this, so declined. For me, *teishoku* means some sort of tray-related meal. In other words, the meal could be ultra-casual or quite upscale, but the common denominator is that the meal is served on a tray. I awaited my *teishoku* with great anticipation. And I was hungry after the long flight, since I had eaten my homemade airplane sando in the JAL lounge in Tokyo, and nothing since.

The *teishoku* arrived: several small mounds of Japanese dishes together on a dinner plate with a fluff of beautiful greens dressed with a Wadaman sesame oil–based vinaigrette, a bowl of rice, and the miso soup. But no tray. I was devastated. The dishes were prepared with care and heart – the produce from local farms shined clear – but the dinner plate did not work. The vinaigrette slurped into the other dishes, and I felt visually overwhelmed to have everything on one plate, no matter how wonderful each bite was. Although the tray is not truly a defining element of *teishoku*, there is something about the tray, which unifies the separate dishes, so perhaps is essential. And often, the lacquer tray itself is a gorgeous piece of workmanship that elicits a powerful feeling of joy and appreciation from the diner, so in a way is the anchoring factor that ties the food and the small dishes together into a cohesive whole.

In Japan, there is a wide range of *teishoku*: dirt cheap to expensive. But more often than not, no matter the price, the dishes are often sad and overcooked, poorly seasoned ... nothing special. However, I've found three stellar examples of *teishoku* on and around the island of Shodoshima.

A short ferry ride from Shodoshima is Teshima, a small picturesque island that is home to several interesting Benesse art installations, lemon trees, homemade lemonade shops, as well as a couple of excellent *teishoku* restaurants: Shima Kitchen and Umi no Restaurant. Umi no Restaurant is an attractive warehouse-like structure with high ceilings and inside seating surrounded by glass. However, it does not get much better than eating on the canopied open-air terrace that extends over the water. And the *teishoku* is light, womanly, young food – perfectly suited for eating while looking out over the sea with a glass of champagne. The first time we went there we had already eaten lunch, so we whiled away a couple of hours working on our computers, sampling a few bites while waiting for the

ferry. I vowed to go back at the earliest opportunity, and have enjoyed various renditions of their olive beef *teishoku* on several leisurely occasions.

By contrast, the *teishoku* at Morikuni Shuzo, the lone sake brewery on Shodoshima, is the very definition of traditional fare. This is exactly the kind of old-fashioned food that is usually flat, tired and overdone. But at Morikuni, the grandmother of the owners oversees preparation of the *teishoku*, and she puts her heart into each and every dish. The general meal does not change, and I have eaten it several times over several years, but every time I marvel at each bite and wonder how the sparkle can remain. This clarity, and personal touch to the execution of the dishes served, is all thanks to the Morikuni grandmother.

Seated at the counter, I chat with her each time I go, and always convey my gratitude for what she has created. One would think it should be expected: good, honest country food, but it's really not. I see the glow in her eyes when we talk, and her pleasure for the compliments and recognition, often taken for granted, and I, too, am warm inside.

Shimayado Mari, a serene inn that also serves exquisite local dishes from excellent ingredients, is located at the far eastern tip of Shodoshima. At lunch we can enjoy *teishoku* of the highest level in one of Mari's exceptionally well-appointed traditional Japanese rooms. Mari is where special guests of the island are invited for a meal. The dishes are not brought all at once, but added to the tray slowly in a thoughtful progression. The presentation of each dish is stunning. There is much attention to detail and, although there is a sense of familiarity to the flow of the lunch, somehow this *teishoku* is quietly impressive, almost awe-inspiring in its elegant restraint. Alternatively, one can always opt for dinner, a movingly simple yet painstakingly created seven-course meal that involves a tray, though could never be called '*teishoku*'.

Like everywhere in the world, there is plenty of mediocrity in Japan, and *teishoku* almost encourages that mediocrity because of the anonymous nature of so many of these meals. Served on a tray, 'more' seems to hold importance over taste. Japanese cafeterias exist in companies, hospitals and public buildings of all kinds, and each serves a style of ubiquitous tray food, which is more there to fill the stomach than anything else, and is almost never tasty. But the good ones, few and far between, make you sit up and take notice, because they show attention to detail and ingredient in each dish. They show love.

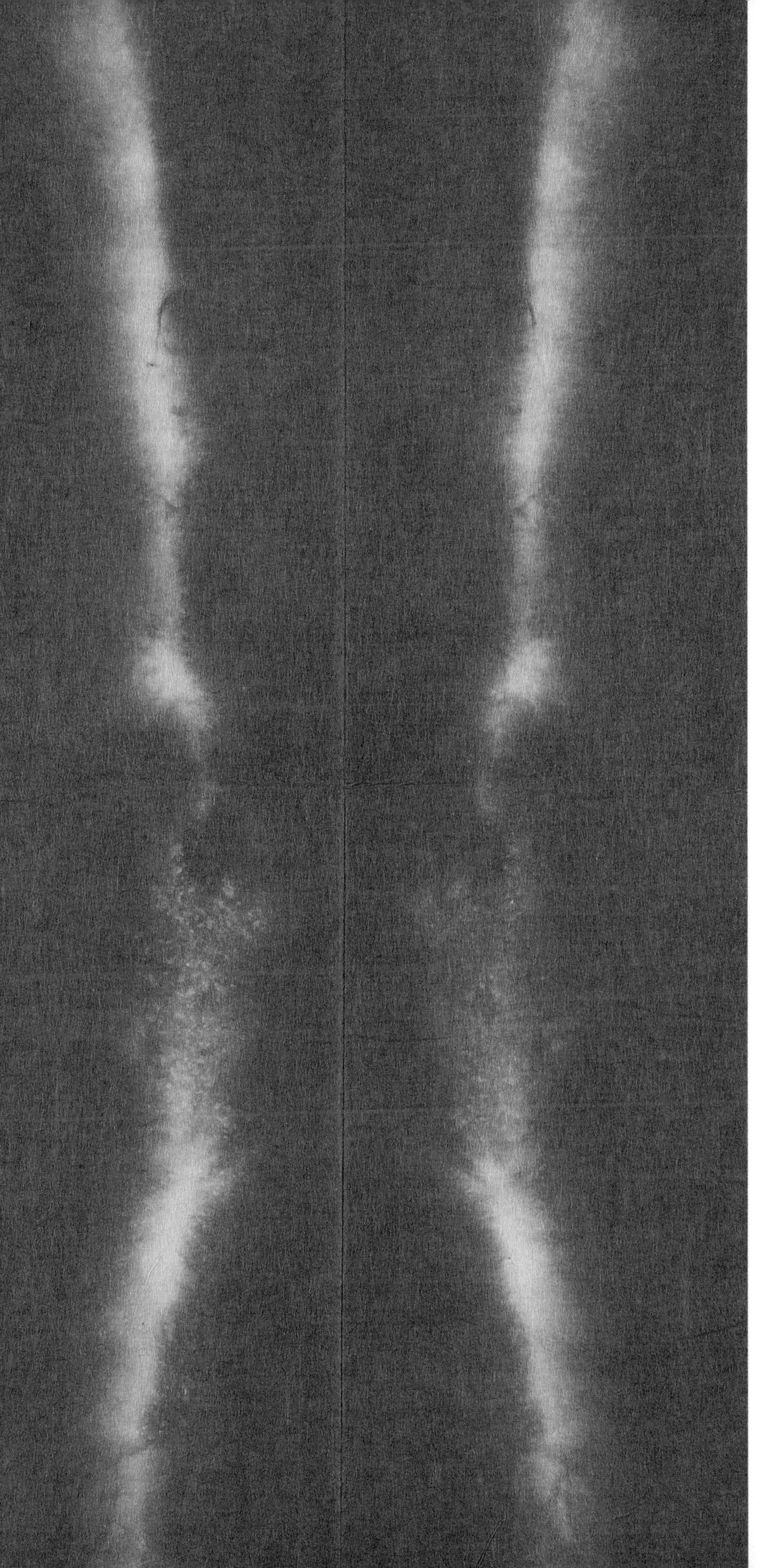

九州

KYUSHU

Kagoshima Prefecture
Kumamoto Prefecture
Oita Prefecture

Cainoya
Kagoshima-shi, Kogoshima Prefecture

TAKEYOSHI SHIOZAWA

Intense, driven, pensive, passionate … these are the adjectives that come to mind when describing Takeyoshi Shiozawa. When I eat at his restaurant, I often say, 'this is the best meal I have ever eaten,' and I mean it every time. I feel that the combination of Shiozawa's ingredient-driven dishes, enhanced by molecular techniques, coupled with one of the most outstanding wine pairings I have encountered, is unparalleled.

Less than ten minutes by taxi from Kagoshima-chuo Station, Cainoya is worth the train (or plane) ride from Tokyo to get there. Chef-owner Shiozawa has a deeply intuitive yet somehow philosophical approach to his breathtakingly innovative Italian cuisine. He employs modern cooking systems, but also incorporates classical Japanese techniques into his exquisite food. The chef works on his own vegetable fields before service and on the restaurant's off days, growing organic herbs and vegetables that he incorporates into his dishes. And he sources other important ingredients directly from his locale. The wine pairings selected by wife Tomoko are inspired, and complement each dish beautifully. Cainoya is a destination restaurant that will not disappoint.

As philosopher, farmer, and a dedicated advocate for Japanese food as the basis for the new Italian and French cooking that young chefs are doing around Japan, Shiozawa is just as intense as his recipes. Succinct, nothing left to chance, Shiozawa is a fan of modern equipment such as the Gastrovac sous vide, the blast chiller and the Rational oven. He designs his recipes with these machines in mind, so the food is tight and perfect, as only that precision can lend.

In conversation, Shiozawa's brow furrows, and he is extremely serious when the subject is food. He is a champion of local producers such as the Cinta Senese pork producer in Kagoshima prefecture who feeds his pigs seaweed. I was not able to visit that pig farmer before finishing this book, but certainly will in the future. And I am already thinking of when I can next book a flight to Kagoshima, hop a taxi to Cainoya, and slide into my special spot at the counter to be fed like I have never been fed before.

My first visit to Cainoya was with Sharon Jones, a close friend from Berkeley who is on the board of Chez Panisse. She was visiting Japan during the time I was gathering material and photographing for *Preserving the Japanese Way*, and accompanied me on various trips around the country. We arrived in Kagoshima a day early to eat at Cainoya. Yasushi Ozaki, Japanese editor of sushi master Jiro Ono (Sukiyabashi Jiro) and of the Japanese translation of Alice Waters' *The Art of Simple Food*, had set the dinner up for us in thanks for favors we had both done. The dinner was impressive, if not unforgettable, but also expensive. We paid for the wine.

The next day, met by my photographer Kenji Miura, and by Saori Abe, my Fuji TV director at the time, we traveled by local train down to Yamagawa near the tip of a peninsula jutting off the southern end of Kagoshima prefecture. Before visiting the katsuobushi producer Sakai Shoten, we had lunch where we were to stay the night. The fish served at this little fish restaurant overlooking the bay was a) not local and b) previously frozen. Nothing was good about the so-called 'local meal', so without skipping a beat, I called Shiozawa to ask if we could eat a more casual meal than the one we had at Cainoya the night before, and dine at the counter I had noticed. He agreed. And with that, our plans for that night changed. All this took place before our visit to Sakai Shoten's life-changing katsuobushi operation. But that story has already been written and is in the *Preserving* book.

By hook or by crook, I have been back a number of times to Cainoya – often coupled with a visit to Sakai Shoten, and sometimes paid for as part of my negotiated fee for a consultation gig or speaking engagement. A long, leisurely lunch accompanied by wine is my meal of choice at the restaurant, and my anticipation of each of these meals almost makes me giddy. And in the aftermath of the meal, a golden aura surrounds me like a cocoon, floating back with me as I return to the hotel, once again with the warmth and satisfaction of having my whole being fed.

And in the aftermath of the meal, a golden aura surrounds me like a cocoon,floating back with me as I return to the hotel.

Akitaro, Ginan

MARLIN CONFIT WITH GINGKO NUTS

It is essential to cook fatty meat and fish gently and thoughtfully, always keeping in mind how to render fat yet maintain texture. The hauntingly bitter gingko nuts provide a nice foil to the rich fish. The dish will take several days to execute, but the gorgeous result will be worth it.

Trehalose is a type of sugar that Takeyoshi Shiozawa uses to soften the salinity of his salt. The ratio is 10:3 salt to trehalose.

NB Outside of Japan, katsuobushi, which is made from skipjack tuna, is most often called by the misnomer 'bonito'.

SERVES 4

Trehalose Salt

30 g (1 oz) trehalose powder

100 g (3½ oz) fine sea salt

300 g (10½ oz) well-marbled blue marlin, cut crosswise into 4 rectangular pieces, plus the center bones of 1 blue marlin

6 × 10 cm (4 in) squares of konbu, weighing about 60 g (2 oz) in total

1¼ teaspoons good-quality katsuobushi dashi powder (non-MSG variety)

8 unshelled raw gingko nuts

3 large slices of dried porcini mushrooms

⅛ teaspoon *ayu* fish sauce

250 ml (8½ fl oz/1 cup) extra-virgin olive oil

micro herbs, for garnishing

To make the trehalose salt, stir the trehalose powder into the salt. Store in a clean glass jar. Keeps indefinitely.

Place the marlin fillets into one vacuum seal or resealable bag with ¼ teaspoon of the trehalose salt, seal and refrigerate overnight to wet-age. Soak the konbu in 1 liter (34 fl oz/ 4 cups) water in a medium saucepan overnight.

Preheat the oven to 150°C (300°F). Spread the marlin bones out on an oven pan and bake slowly for 1 hour. Scrape the cooked bones into a medium stockpot with 1 liter (34 fl oz/4 cups) cold water and bring to a simmer over medium–low heat and cook for 30 minutes. Do not let the liquid simmer wildly or the broth will become cloudy. Strain, and stir in 1 teaspoon of the dashi powder and ¼ teaspoon of trehalose salt.

Heat the konbu in the soaking liquid and simmer gently for 45 minutes at 85°C (185°F). The liquid should reduce by half. Strain and add the konbu dashi to the bone stock. Check the taste, and add extra dashi powder or trehalose salt if needed. Cool the stock in a blast chiller or in an ice bath.

Shell the gingko nuts and grill the shells lightly – they will add a smoked flavor to the broth. Drop the grilled shells and porcini into 250 ml (8½ fl oz/1 cup) water, along with the fish sauce, remaining ¼ teaspoon of dashi powder and a pinch of trehalose salt. Bring to a simmer, then remove from the heat and cool in the blast chiller or an ice bath.

Peel the gingko nuts, drop them into a vacuum seal or resealable freezer bag with the gingko and porcini broth, seal and refrigerate overnight.

Place 1 piece each of the marlin fillets into a vacuum bag or resealable freezer bag and divide the cooled marlin bone and konbu stock between the bags. Seal and cook sous vide (page 272) at 50°C (120°F) for 20 minutes, or in a Gastrovac for 2 cycles of 10 minutes. Leave overnight to cool in the refrigerator.

Heat the olive oil in a small heavy frying pan over the very lowest heat possible, to 35–40°C (95–105°F). Remove the marlin pieces from the bags and slip into the oil. Cook ever so gently for 45 minutes, without turning, to make marlin confit. Cool to room temperature in the blast chiller or with an ice bath.

Working with 2 pieces of marlin at a time, sear the fish on all sides in a dry frying pan over high heat. Place the pieces on 2 stunning rectangular plates while you sear the remaining marlin, and place on 2 more plates. In a small dry frying pan, sear the drained gingko nuts over high heat. Nestle 2 nuts beside each piece of marlin, garnish with a pinch of micro herbs and serve.

Sanma, Poruchi-ni

LAYERED PACIFIC SAURY AND PORCINI

Find a suitably gorgeous yet spare plate to show off this terrine. When sliced, the cross-section is stunning.

Ionized alkaline water with electrolytes is commonly used in coffee brewing and is available on Amazon. Substitute regular bottled water if needed.

SERVES 4, WITH LEFTOVERS

Bagna Cauda

150 g (5½ oz) garlic cloves, peeled

125 ml (4 fl oz/½ cup) whole (full-cream) milk

225 ml (7½ fl oz) extra-virgin olive oil

130 g (4½ oz) oil-packed anchovies

120 g (4½ oz) unsalted butter

Pacific Saury Terrine

8 whole Pacific saury (*sanma*), weighing about 1 kg (2 lb 3 oz) in total

90 ml (3 fl oz) extra-virgin olive oil, plus a few spritzes

4 small garlic cloves, finely chopped

1 tablespoon fresh rosemary needles

60 ml (2 fl oz/¼ cup) brown rice vinegar

125 ml (4 fl oz/½ cup) dry white wine, such as pinot grigio or sauvignon blanc

½ teaspoon Trehalose Salt (page 251), plus a few pinches

To make the bagna cauda, drop the garlic cloves into a small heavy saucepan. Add the milk and 125 ml (4 fl oz/½ cup) water (the liquid should cover the garlic). Bring to a simmer over medium–low heat, adjust the heat to a bare simmer and cook for about 10 minutes, until you no longer smell the raw hotness of the garlic. Drain the garlic, discarding the milk, and wash and dry the pan. Blot the garlic dry on spongy paper towels and drop back into the pan. Add the olive oil, anchovies and butter. Simmer for 2 hours on the lowest heat possible. Purée in a food processor until well emulsified. After serving, store the remaining portion in the refrigerator.

Gut and rinse the Pacific saury and soak in slightly ionized alkaline water for 10 minutes. Pluck the fish out of the water and fillet (without scaling), saving the bones, heads and livers. Quarter the center bones crosswise, and slice the heads down the middle to halve.

Heat the olive oil in a large heavy frying pan over medium–low heat. Scrape in the garlic, rosemary, fish bones and head pieces (but not livers), and cook, stirring, for about 10 minutes, until the fish liquids have cooked away and the bones start to sizzle. Add the brown rice vinegar and cook, stirring, until that liquid has cooked away as well. Stir in 600 ml (20½ fl oz) water, and cook over medium heat at a brisk simmer until the liquid has reduced to about 60 ml (2 fl oz/¼ cup). Strain the fish extract.

Warm 4 tablespoons of the bagna cauda in a small heavy saucepan over low heat, and slip in the fish livers. Sauté, stirring, over medium heat for 2 or 3 minutes, before adding the wine and fish extract. Simmer for 3 minutes more to reduce slightly. Emulsify in a food processor or blender until smooth.

Remove the skin from the fish fillets and lay out, belly side down, on a rectangular stainless pan. Sprinkle both sides with the trehalose salt. Brush the liver sauce evenly across the 'skin' side. Sprinkle with a few extra pinches of trehalose salt and spritz lightly with olive oil. Cook in a Rational oven on the fish setting, or roast in a preheated 190°C (375°F) oven for 10 minutes.

Line a terrine or loaf pan about the same length as the fillets with plastic wrap and, while still warm, lay the 3 largest fillets across the bottom, belly side down. Continue layering the fillets evenly so that there are 3 side-by-side stacks, forming solid layers without gaps. Press a large piece of plastic wrap directly across the surface and place another pan of the same size on top of the fish layers. Add small ramekins (or similar) into the empty pan to form a gentle but even weight to help compact the fish fillets into a solid mass. Chill in the blast chiller or an ice bath and store in the fridge overnight.

The next day, remove the fish terrine from the pan and halve crosswise. Place each in a separate vacuum seal or resealable freezer bag, seal, and chill overnight to further meld together.

Eggplant (Aubergine) Sauce

neutral oil such as canola, safflower or peanut, for deep-frying

2 small Japanese eggplants (aubergines), weighing about 200 g (7 oz) in total

Porcini

50 g (1¾ oz) dried sliced porcini mushrooms

¼ teaspoon Trehalose Salt (page 251)

100 g (3½ oz) frozen whole porcini mushrooms

freshly ground black pepper, for serving

To make the eggplant sauce, heat 7.5 cm (3 in) of neutral oil in a small heavy saucepan over medium heat. Trim the top off and peel one of the eggplants. Cut crosswise into 4 cm (1½ in) pieces. Once the oil is hot but not smoking, deep-fry the eggplant pieces for 2–3 minutes, until meltingly soft and golden brown. Drain on a thick layer of paper towels until cool.

Place a grate on top of a stovetop flame and grill the other eggplant, unpeeled, until blackened on all sides and completely soft. Cool to room temperature, peel and drop into a food processor with the fried eggplant and 2 tablespoons of the bagna cauda. Process until smooth and well emulsified.

Drop the dried porcini into a vacuum bag or resealable freezer bag with 125 ml (4 fl oz/ ½ cup) water and the trehalose salt. Heat to 50°C (120°F) in the Gastrovac or other sous vide (page 272) and cook for 45 minutes. Cool in the blast chiller or an ice bath.

Steam the frozen whole porcini at 50°C (120°F) until half thawed. Cool in the blast chiller or an ice bath, then slice thinly.

Strain the dried porcini liquid (discarding the mushrooms) into a new vacuum bag or resealable freezer bag with the sliced thawed porcini. Seal and cook in the Gastrovac or other sous vide (page 272) at 50°C (120°F) for 15 minutes.

Cut one of the sealed half-terrines into 1 cm (½ in) thick slices and choose 4 slices for serving. Pack the remaining slices separately in vacuum seal or resealable freezer bags to keep fresh. Store in the fridge or freezer.

Drain the porcini slices and sear on a dry heavy frying pan. Lay the porcini side by side to form a bed in the center of 4 salad plates and set a slice of terrine on top. Place a small spoon of the eggplant sauce on the side, sprinkle with the black pepper and serve.

Satsuma Imo no Fokatcha to Cainoya no Pan

SWEET POTATO FOCACCIA AND CAINOYA BREAD

Cainoya cuts this bread into individual portions and stores it in the freezer to be ready to heat up in the oven when needed. This highly recommended technique works exceptionally well.

MAKES 2 LARGE BREADS

Focaccia

800 g (1 lb 12 oz) yellow-fleshed sweet potatoes

1.2 kg (2 lb 10 oz/8 cups) 00 flour

200 ml (7 fl oz) whole (full-cream) milk

100 g (3½ oz) unsalted butter, melted

100 ml (3½ fl oz) extra-virgin olive oil, plus more for the pan

45 g (1½ oz/3 tablespoons) flaky sea salt

45 g (1½ oz/3 tablespoons) granulated sugar

8 g (¼ oz/2½ teaspoons) dried yeast

Cainoya Bread

900 g (2 lb/6 cups) 00 flour

220 g (8 oz) semolina

300 g (10½ oz) rice flour

30 g (1 oz/3 tablespoons) spelt flour

30 g (1 oz/2 tablespoons) Trehalose Salt (page 251)

30 g (1 oz/2 tablespoons) flaky sea salt

1.2 liters (41 fl oz) hard water (*kousui*) or water

4 g (¼ oz/1¼ teaspoons) dried yeast

8 g (¼ oz/½ teaspoon) *mizuame* or corn syrup

extra-virgin olive oil, for greasing the pan and brushing both doughs

extra-virgin olive oil, for serving

To make the focaccia, roast the sweet potatoes in their skins in a Rational oven, or in a preheated 250°C (480°F) oven, for 30 minutes, and peel when cool enough to handle. Simmer the peels in a medium saucepan with 1 liter (34 fl oz/4 cups) water for 30 minutes to make sweet potato water (you should have 800 ml/27 fl oz). Leave to cool, then strain.

Pass the sweet potatoes through a fine sieve (*uragoshi*, page 275), and mix in the flour until crumbly and completely incorporated into the sweet potato.

Mix the sweet potato water with the milk, butter, olive oil, salt, sugar and yeast on low speed in a stand mixer fitted with a flat kneading blade. Drop in a large handful of the sweet potato–flour mixture and increase the speed to high. Turn off the machine, scrape down the sides and add another handful of sweet potato mixture. Mix in at high speed. Keep turning off the machine, scraping down the sides, and mixing in more sweet potato flour on high speed until all of the mixture has been incorporated, and a smooth elastic dough has formed.

Spread into a large rectangular pan and 'ferment' overnight in a blast chiller on fermentation mode, or cover with plastic wrap and leave overnight in a warm place.

The next day, generously grease another large rectangular pan with olive oil, and spread the dough into the pan in a 3 cm (1¼ in) thick layer. Brush the surface of the dough with more olive oil and bake in the Rational oven on 'bike' mode for 22 minutes. (Alternatively, cook in the middle of a preheated 220°C/430°F oven for 20 minutes, until nicely golden brown.) At Cainoya, the bread is cooled in the blast chiller, cut into 4 cm (1½ in) squares, and frozen in the blast chiller in resealable freezer bags. Alternatively, cool to room temperature before serving, and store leftovers in the freezer.

To make Cainoya bread, whisk the 00 flour, semolina, rice flour, spelt flour and salts together in a large bowl. Mix the hard water, yeast and syrup together on low speed in the bowl of a stand mixer fitted with a flat kneading blade. Add in some of the flour mixture and increase the speed to high. Continue adding the flour in increments to form a stiff dough.

Ferment, form and bake, chill and freeze the bread following the same directions for the focaccia.

Remove a frozen piece of focaccia or Cainoya bread from the freezer and reheat quickly in the Rational, as is, or bake thawed pieces on a pan in a preheated 180°C (350°F) oven for 3 minutes. Serve the focaccia and bread hot with a small pool of extra-virgin olive oil alongside.

Viishisowa-zu

COLD POTATO SOUP WITH BUTTER GELATO AND BLACK PEPPER FOAM

SERVES 10

This whimsical combination of cold potato soup, butter gelato and black pepper foam is both gorgeous and flavorful, especially when prepared from freshly dug potatoes. This recipe has many steps and is worth making when you have a dinner party or want leftovers for the week. You will only need half the gelato and black pepper foam, so use them creatively in other dishes.

Takeshi Shiozawa washes his potatoes at the field, and then once back in the kitchen, soaks them in ionized alkaline water to sterilize before scrubbing.

Butter Gelato

200 g (7 oz) granulated sugar

30 g (1 oz) glucose powder

60 g (2 oz) skim milk powder

885 ml (30 fl oz) whole (full-cream) milk

300 g (10½ oz) unsalted butter, cut into small cubes

30 g (1 oz) *mizuame* or corn syrup

30 g (1 oz) Parmigiano Reggiano, cubed and processed to crumbs

15 g (½ oz) xanthan gum

Chicken Broth

bones of 1 small chicken

1 medium onion, sliced

1 celery stalk, sliced

1 carrot, scrubbed and sliced

5 cherry tomatoes

1 garlic clove, halved lengthwise

1 parsley stem

1 bay leaf

½ teaspoon flaky salt

¼ teaspoon freshly ground black pepper

Black Pepper Foam

300 ml (10 fl oz) whole (full-cream) milk

7 g (¼ oz/1 tablespoon) finely ground black pepper

4 g (¼ oz/½ tablespoon) soy lecithin powder

Potato Vichyssoise

1 kg (2 lb 3 oz) potatoes, scrubbed

2 tablespoons extra-virgin olive oil

1 garlic clove, halved lengthwise

1 medium onion, cut into rough triangular shapes (*rangiri*, page 276)

1 celery stalk, roughly cut on the alternating diagonal (*rangiri*, page 276)

1 teaspoon flaky sea salt

½ teaspoon freshly ground black pepper

1 liter (34 fl oz/4 cups) whole (full-cream) milk

To make the butter gelato, whisk the sugar, glucose and milk powder together in a heavy medium pot. Add the milk in slowly to incorporate smoothly into the dry ingredients. Stir in the butter, *mizuame* and Parmigiano, and begin to heat over medium–low until the sugars, butter and cheese have melted smoothly. Sprinkle the xanthan gum across the surface and stir in well to incorporate. Strain into a container and leave to cool. Cover, chill overnight and churn in an ice cream maker the following day.

To make the chicken broth, place the chicken bones in a large stockpot with the onion, celery, carrot, tomatoes, garlic, parsley stem, bay leaf and ¼ teaspoon of the salt. Add 4 liters (135 fl oz/16 cups) water and bring to a boil over high heat. Adjust to a simmer and cook gently for 2 hours. Skim off the scum as it forms. Strain, and add the remaining salt and the pepper to the broth.

To make the black pepper foam, bring the milk and black pepper to a simmer in a small saucepan. Pour into a stainless medium mixing bowl and cool to room temperature, then cover and chill until you are ready to serve.

To make the vichyssoise, bake half the potatoes in their skins in a Rational oven or in a preheated 250°C (480°F) oven for 30 minutes. Steam the remaining potatoes in their skins in the Rational oven or in a steamer for 30 minutes. Cool in a blast chiller, or let cool at room temperature, and peel the potatoes. By cooking them in their skins, the potatoes will strongly retain their natural flavor.

Stir the olive oil, garlic, onion and celery together in a large saucepan and sauté in the Rational oven or on the stove over medium–low heat. Add in the peeled potatoes, salt and pepper. Stir 350 ml (12 fl oz) of the chicken broth into the milk in a separate saucepan and gently warm. Add 500 ml (17 fl oz/2 cups) of milky broth to the pan of vegetables and simmer for 15 minutes. Purée immediately and pass through a sieve. Stir the remaining milky broth into the potato purée and bring up to 85°C (185°F) in the Rational oven, or on the stove over medium heat stirring continuously, until hot to the touch. Cool in the blast chiller, or cool to room temperature and chill in the refrigerator.

Sprinkle the soy lecithin over the chilled bowl of black pepper milk and, using a hand-held beater, beat up an airy foam. Spoon out what you need for garnishing the soup. Beat again to create more foam.

Ladle out about 60 ml (2 fl oz/¼ cup) cold vichyssoise per person in beautiful shallow bowls. Garnish with ovals of butter gelato and clouds of black pepper foam.

Karubona-ra

DECONSTRUCTED CARBONARA

When I first had this at Cainoya, I was struck by the ingenious method of this sort of untraditional mix-your-own creamy carbonara. Carbonara is one of my son's favorite dishes and we often discuss the best method for making it, since there are always pitfalls regarding the egg becoming granular, or the sauce coating the pasta being either too unctuous or not quite emulsified. With Takeyoshi Shiozawa's method, you avoid all of those shoals. Also the presentation is stunning, and the perfect size for a rich pasta course.

SERVES 4

2 thick slices of streaky bacon weighing about 60 g (2 oz), chopped

250 ml (8½ fl oz/1 cup) white wine

400 ml (13½ fl oz) cream (45% fat)

400 g (14 oz) Parmigiano Reggiano, grated

400 g (14 oz) pecorino, grated

¼ teaspoon shoyu

¾ teaspoon freshly ground black pepper

250 g (9 oz) fresh linguini, cooked al dente

4 medium egg yolks, at room temperature (and 4 half shells for serving)

truffle oil

1 teaspoon finely chopped Italian (flat leaf) parsley, plus 4 small sprigs for garnishing

Heat a heavy medium frying pan over medium–low heat and add the bacon. Stir-fry until the pieces begin to brown and the fat is rendering well. Cover and cook over low heat until the fat has completely rendered out and the bacon is crisp. Uncover, adjust the heat to medium and pour in the wine. Stir with a flat wooden spoon for 2 minutes, scraping the brown bits off the bottom of the pan. Add the cream, 200 ml (7 fl oz) water, the cheeses, shoyu, and ½ teaspoon of the pepper and simmer for 4 minutes more to thicken.

Toss the cooked pasta in the cream sauce and divide among 4 shallow bowls. Nestle the half eggshells in the center of each bowl of pasta and spoon a yolk into each shell. Stir 2 or 3 drops of truffle oil into each yolk using a pair of chopsticks. Sprinkle the bowls with the remaining ¼ teaspoon of black pepper and the parsley. Garnish with the sprigs of parsley and serve hot.

Ayu no Yaki Rizotto

SWEET FISH RISOTTO SQUARES WITH BROTH

This clever preparation is just as delicious as it is spectacular. In Japan, small fish are not scaled before cooking. These sweet river fish (*ayu*) are prized for their mild meat and acrid guts, and are eaten in their entirety to fully enjoy that juxtaposition. The method of precooking the risotto allows the dish to be made in stages and put together at the last minute. Serve this dish to elegant friends.

SERVES 4

10 cm (4 in) square of konbu

6 small sweet river fish (*ayu*), weighing about 500 g (1 lb 2 oz) in total

½ teaspoon Trehalose Salt (page 251)

360 ml (12 fl oz) measure of Japanese white rice (about 300 g/10½ oz)

2 tablespoons plus 1 teaspoon *ayu* fish sauce

200 g (7 oz) Parmigiano Reggiano, grated

vegetable oil spray

300 ml (10 fl oz) Katsuobushi Dashi (page 202)

1 heaping tablespoon deep-fried tempura bits tossed with green nori powder (*aonori no age tama*), or a few pinches of green nori powder (*aonori*)

12 cooked edamame beans

12 sprigs of micro herbs

freshly grated wasabi, for serving (optional)

Soak the konbu in 350 ml (12 fl oz) cold water overnight. Spread the fish out in a small pan and sprinkle on both sides with the salt. Refrigerate overnight, uncovered.

The following day, grill the fish over high heat, then cool in a blast chiller or in a bowl set over an ice bath. Pinch off the heads and discard, and remove the flesh from the bones. Tear the flesh, and also the bitter yet essential guts, into small pieces with your fingers.

Wash the rice according to the directions for Japanese Rice (page 205), then drain and scrape into a small heavy pot.

Remove the konbu from the soaking water (use for a second dashi or another dish). Measure out 330 ml (11 fl oz) of the konbu water and add to the pot of rice with 2 tablespoons of the fish sauce and the grilled fish. Cook according to the directions for Japanese Rice, but only for 8 minutes, after coming to a boil. As soon as the rice is cooked, immediately stir in the Parmigiano until well incorporated. Cool in the blast chiller or over an ice bath.

Place 4 square molds (6 cm/2½ in) in a small pan, and spray the insides of the molds and the tray beneath with vegetable oil. Press the rice mixture into the molds, patting down and smoothing the surface. Spray a small amount of oil on top of the rice as well. Unmold the rice squares and grill in a dry heavy frying pan over medium–high heat, similar to how you would grill rice balls (*yaki onigiri*). Allow the surface to sear so the rice is crackling but the inside remains soft.

Heat the dashi with the remaining 1 teaspoon of fish sauce. Place each risotto square in a shallow bowl. Garnish each with a scant teaspoon of *aonori no age tama* (or a pinch of *aonori*), 3 edamame beans and 3 sprigs of micro herbs. Dab with a little wasabi, if using. Pour the dashi into a small teapot and bring to the table. Pour about 50 ml (1¾ fl oz) of dashi over the risotto squares and eat immediately.

Sadorubakku
Aian Sute-ki

SADDLEBACK PORK WITH POTATO PURÉE

The succulent Cinta Senese pork served at Cainoya is raised locally in Kagoshima prefecture at Fukudome Sho Bokujo. These sienna saddleback pigs live naturally and the air around the ranch is sweet smelling – an unusual testament to their clean environment.

Cainoya only serves a dab of potato purée on each dish; feel free to be more generous, and use leftovers for another meal.

SERVES 4

20 cm (8 in) piece of saddleback pork shoulder, with a layer of fat running the length, about 400 g (14 oz)

½ teaspoon Trehalose Salt (page 251)

1 large cabbage leaf

¼ teaspoon flaky sea salt

¼ teaspoon freshly ground black pepper

1 teaspoon Italian herb salt

4 × 7.5 cm (3 in) sprigs of rosemary

Potato Purée

500 g (1 lb 2 oz) medium potatoes, scrubbed

200 ml (7 fl oz) whole (full-cream) milk

30 g (1 oz) parmesan cheese, finely grated

30 g (1 oz) unsalted butter

pinch of flaky sea salt

Place the pork in a blast chiller on 'meat mode', or in a home freezer, until half frozen. Slice the meat crosswise into 4 steaks 5 cm (2 in) thick. Even up the pieces to uniform shapes, and make shallow cuts in the outside fat to encourage rendering. Pack each piece of pork in a vacuum bag or resealable freezer bag and divide the trehalose salt evenly between the bags. Rub in the salt to distribute. Seal and leave overnight at the temperature of a cool wine cellar (about 15°C/60°F), to wet-age the meat for 8–12 hours. Return to the blast chiller or freezer until frozen.

Thaw the vacuum-packed pork at 45°C (115°F) for 1 hour, either by steaming or sous vide (page 272). Then, cook in a Rational oven on the multi-fresh setting, or sous vide (page 272), for 1 hour at 60°C (140°F). Place the bags of pork in the blast chiller or in an ice bath to cool but not chill.

Steam the cabbage leaf for 5 minutes, until very soft. Cool to room temperature, and cut into strips 6 mm (¼ in) wide and 4 cm (1½ in) long.

To make the potato purée, place the whole potatoes in a heavy medium saucepan and cover generously with cold water. Bring to a boil over high heat and simmer for 30 minutes, until soft to the core. Drain, cool and peel. Cut into a large dice and return to the pan. Heat the milk in a separate small saucepan, and mash into the potatoes with the parmesan, butter and salt. Keep warm until needed.

Form a small bed of cabbage on 4 attractive plates. Remove the chilled pork from the bags and sprinkle with the salt and pepper. Heat a medium cast-iron frying pan over low heat and place the pork pieces in the pan, standing them up on their fatty edge. Render out the fat slowly, then pour off the fat and discard. Adjust the heat to high and cook the fatty edge until brown and crispy. Cook the other surfaces of the pork until well sealed. Remove from the heat.

Sprinkle half of the herb salt on a plate. Press the fat side of each piece of pork into the salt, and place on top of each bed of cabbage. Sprinkle the remaining herb salt next to the fat side of the meat. Form 4 American football–shaped ovals of potato purée and drop them near the meat. Garnish with the rosemary and serve.

Momo, Jera-to, Re-mon

POACHED PEACHES WITH CIDER VINEGAR ICE CREAM

Poached fruit, tuiles and ice cream make a beautiful dessert with Japanese sensibilities. The peaches are poached in a generous amount of lemongrass-vanilla syrup – serve the leftover syrup over vanilla ice cream or simple custards.

SERVES 4

Tuiles

90 ml (3 fl oz) freshly squeezed orange juice

90 g (3 oz) unsalted butter, melted

90 g (3 oz) all-purpose (plain) flour

300 g (10½ oz) confectioners' (icing) sugar, sifted

Lemongrass-Vanilla Syrup

500 g (1 lb 2 oz) granulated sugar

½ lemon

½ vanilla bean

1 lemongrass stalk, cut into 10 cm (4 in) lengths

¼ teaspoon vanilla oil

pinch of freshly ground black pepper

2 yellow peaches

homemade butter cookies, crumbled

Vanilla Ice Cream (page 228), made with the addition of 60 ml (2 fl oz/ ¼ cup) apple-cider vinegar

micro herbs and edible flowers, for garnishing

To make the tuiles, preheat the oven to 180°C (350°F). Whisk the orange juice and butter into the flour and sugar in a medium bowl. Line baking sheets with silicone mats or parchment (baking) paper, and spoon ½-tablespoon pools of batter at regular intervals on the sheets. Bake in the center of the oven for 10 minutes, until lacy and golden brown. Working quickly, dislodge the hot tuiles with a fine spatula and drape them over a couple of rolling pins or pieces of dowel to cool into a curved shape reminiscent of roof tiles.

To make the lemongrass-vanilla syrup, add the sugar and 500 ml (17 fl oz/2 cups) water to a medium saucepan. Squeeze the juice of the ½ lemon into the pan, and drop in the squeezed portion as well. Halve the vanilla bean lengthwise and scrape the seeds into the pan, with the empty pod. Drop in the lemongrass, vanilla oil and pepper and bring to a boil over high heat. Remove from the heat, cool to room temperature, and strain.

Cut around the peaches crosswise to open them up. Leave the pits inside and match the peach halves back together, reforming the whole peaches. Place each peach in a vacuum bag or resealable freezer bag. Divide the lemongrass-vanilla syrup between the bags and seal. Cook in a Gastrovac or other sous vide (page 272) at 75°C (165°F) for 15 minutes. Take the peaches out of the bags, carefully cut out the pits and discard. Strain and refrigerate the syrup for other dishes.

Make a flat base of crumbled cookies on 4 plates to help the peach not slip and nestle a peach half into the crumble. Add a small scoop of ice cream into the cavity of each peach and top with a tuile and a scattering of micro herbs and flowers. Serve immediately because the ice cream will melt quickly.

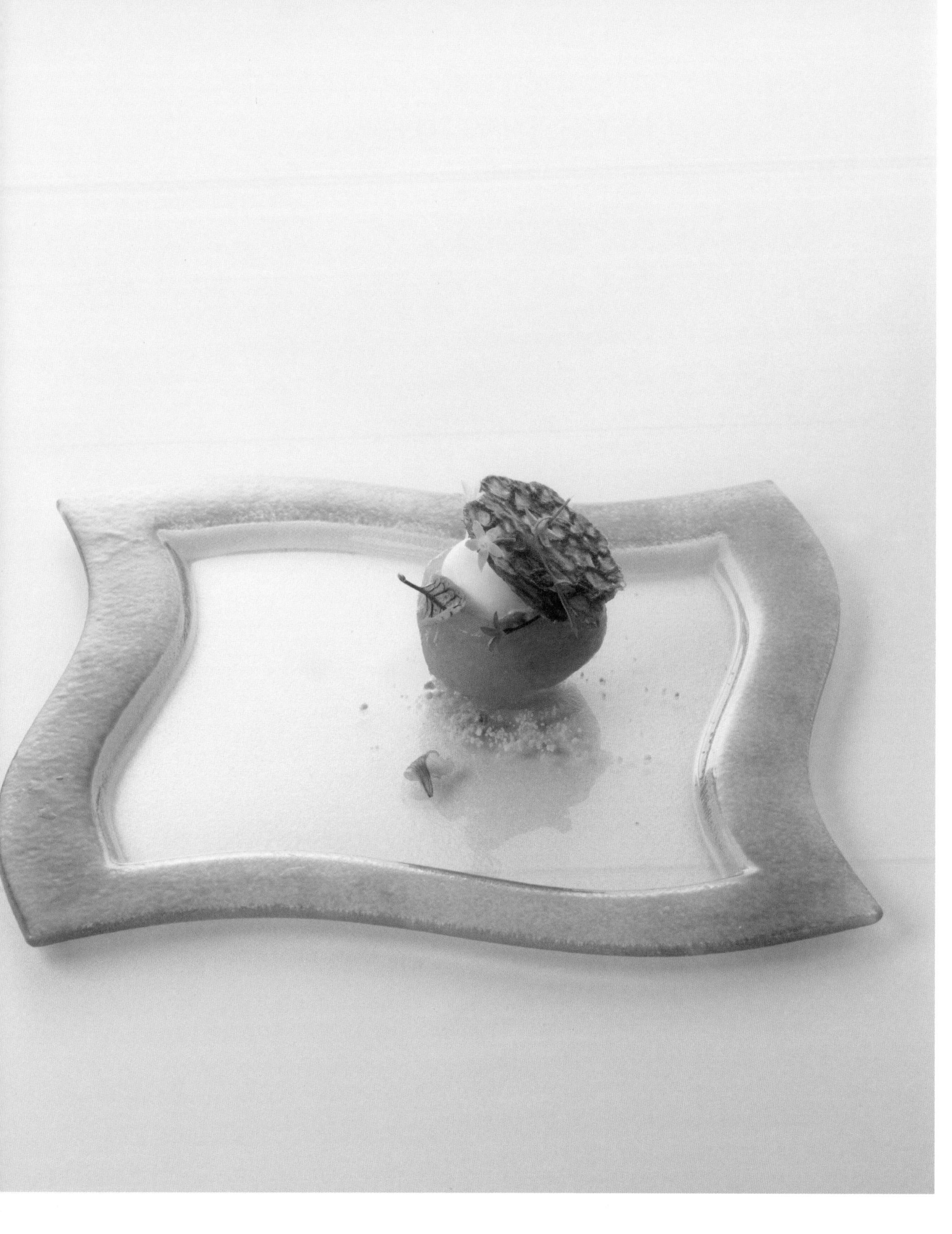

Finanshe, Chokore-to, Kabocha Su-pu

FINANCIERS WITH CHOCOLATE MOUSSE IN COLD KABOCHA SOUP

At the end of a meal, even after a gorgeous fruit dessert, there is something about chocolate that makes the evening so much more satisfying.

SERVES 8

Kabocha Soup

½ medium kabocha (pumpkin), weighing about 400 g (14 oz), unpeeled and not seeded

500 ml (17 fl oz/2 cups) whole (full-cream) milk

125 ml (4 fl oz/½ cup) cream

50 g (1¾ oz) granulated sugar

1 tablespoon dark rum (not as dark as Myers's)

1 tablespoon unsalted butter

Chocolate Mousse

300 g (10½ oz) chocolate (55% cacao), chopped

300 ml (10 fl oz) cream, well chilled

80 g (2¾ oz) granulated sugar

4 small eggs at room temperature, separated

Financiers

180 g (6½ oz) unsalted butter

150 g (5½ oz) confectioners' (icing) sugar, sifted

150 g (5½ oz/1½ cups) almond powder (ground almonds)

30 g (1 oz) unbleached cake flour

7 small egg whites, at room temperature (about 195 g/7 oz)

40 g (1½ oz) mild honey

100 g (3½ oz) fresh blueberries (optional)

To make the kabocha soup, place the half piece of kabocha in a bamboo steamer without removing the seeds. Fill a large wok one-third with water and bring to a boil over high heat. Set the steamer basket over the water and cook for 30 minutes, until the flesh is completely soft. Scoop out the seeds and discard. Scrape the flesh from the skin and discard the skin.

Cut the flesh into rough cubes and drop into a medium saucepan with the milk, cream, sugar, rum and butter. Heat to 80°C (175°F), an almost simmer, stirring over medium heat to melt the sugar, and cook off a little of the rum alcohol. Purée in a blender or food processor until smooth, and pass through a fine sieve (*uragoshi*, page 275). Cool to room temperature and chill well.

To make the chocolate mousse, place the chocolate in a medium bowl set over simmering water and melt, stirring occasionally. Warm 100 ml (3½ fl oz) of the cream and half of the sugar in another small bowl set over simmering water until the sugar has dissolved.

Once the chocolate is completely melted and warm to the touch, remove the bowl from the simmering water and stir in the egg yolks one by one. Add the warmed cream as well and stir until well incorporated. Cool to room temperature.

Beat the egg whites in a small mixing bowl on high speed until soft peaks form. Slowly sprinkle in 20 g (¾ oz) of the sugar, beating continuously until a stiff meringue forms. Fold carefully into the chocolate mixture with a large rubber spatula, taking care not to deflate the whites.

Beat the remaining 200 ml (7 fl oz) cream with the remaining 20 g (¾ oz) sugar until thick ribbons appear on the surface. Fold gently into the lightened chocolate mixture. Chill in the refrigerator until needed.

To make the financiers, preheat the oven to 180°C (350°F). Heat the butter in a small saucepan over medium heat until lightly browned. Whisk the confectioners' sugar, almond powder and flour together in a small mixing bowl. Scrape in the brown butter and stir to combine. Beat the egg whites in a medium mixing bowl until soft peaks form, and drizzle in the honey while continuously beating until they become a stiff meringue. Add the butter mixture into the bowl of beaten egg whites at one edge of the meringue. Fold in gently to avoid deflating. Spoon into an ungreased financier pan or mini cupcake pan. Drop a few blueberries into each financier, if using. Bake in the middle of the oven until golden brown, about 15–20 minutes, depending on the size of the molds. Leave to cool.

Add a ladleful of the kabocha soup into chilled shallow soup bowls, and place in a heaping rounded spoonful of chocolate mousse. Set 1 financier in the bowl as well and serve.

KUMAMOTO OYSTERS

Eating oysters in Japan goes back to ancient times. Up to the 1930s they were raised commercially and, after shucking, were packed in kelp-lined crates for shipping.

After World War II, Japan needed to build herself up economically, so local cottage industries had to compromise centuries-old practices in order to increase production in the new modern world. Recognizing that it would take several Kumamoto oysters to make up the volume of one Miyagi or Hiroshima oyster, the Kumamoto oystermen gave up cultivation of these smaller oysters and shifted all their energy into the production of nori (laver seaweed, the other local industry). Though Kumamoto oysters could still be harvested, commercial production came to a halt by the late 1950s.

Coinciding with the abandonment of Kumamoto cultivation was their rising popularity in the United States. In 1947, the Allied Government mandated that the Japanese send oysters to the US. They sent a combination of Miyagi and Hiroshima oysters, but filled out the order with Kumamotos. The Japanese picked the best specimens of each to send as a matter of national pride. The Kumos did not gain traction right away, but fairly soon began catching the interest of oyster aficionados. The US imported Kumo seeds from Japan through the 1950s, but due to the halt in Japanese production, they started growing the Kumos themselves on the West Coast. Lack of vigilance in protecting their brood stock, however, led to a panic in the mid-to-late 1980s, when suddenly the US oyster cultivators discovered there were virtually no true Kumos left.

A search led oystermen to Kumamoto, and eventually to an oyster field in Oakland Bay in Washington state (Taylor Shellfish), and to another in California (Hog Island Oyster Co.). Kumamoto oysters were kept in quarantine for three years. Given the low survival rate of oyster seed, Taylor Shellfish took the only 150 true Kumamoto oysters found in Oakland Bay and crossed these Washington Kumamotos with Japanese Kumamotos of the same DNA, thus giving the Taylor Shellfish brood stock added survival strength. This began a long period of cooperation between the American and Japanese oyster producers.

Fast forward to today: the Kumamoto prefectural government, recognizing the irony that the most popular oyster in the US was no longer cultivated in its birthplace, decided to re-establish the production of native Kumamotos. But in contrast to the vast expanse of Washington or California oyster beds, Kumamoto oyster production still barely makes a ripple in Japan. Heiji Nakano, the bespectacled scientist behind the farming project, shepherded us through the process.

Our first stop is the office of the Kagami-machi Fishermen's Cooperative. I eagerly sit down with two retired oystermen who have come at my request: Shigeru Iwase and Chikashi Sakamoto. Chatting with them about the past, I get the fanciful (and impossible) impression that their brown eyes are somehow blue, reflecting the sea. Both men were in their mid-teens when they started in the Kumamoto oyster business, though it has now been more than sixty years since production ceased.

Though their memories of oystering are hazy, how they ate those oysters is not. As we sat across a low table, the oystermen inched forward to the edge of their sofa and spoke. Their hands-down favorite way to eat oysters was with a mixture of sour orange (*daidai*) and soy sauce – country ponzu. Most likely the oysters were slightly blanched by pouring hot water over them. They also enjoyed oysters boiled in their shells in a large iron pot, opened and eaten with *sumiso* (rice vinegar and miso, page 128). Sometimes they were grilled over coals weighted down with a large pot to form 'oyster crackers'; other times, they were chopped up with salt and left to ferment a bit for *kaki no shiokara*, a delicacy that goes particularly well with sake. Or the oysters were simply steamed along with the nightly rice, flavored with a little soy sauce. One thing was clear: the old taste was better than the new, they agreed. But don't we all say that?

Iwase and Sakamoto both spoke with enormous respect for the great oyster pioneer Fusao Ota, a legendary scientist who died in his nineties a few years ago. He was a learned man who studied English in the early 1900s and spent his entire adult life documenting Kumo and nori production. His immaculate records allowed Heiji Nakano and his team to restart this obsolete local industry.

Each oyster 'mama' is vetted before harvesting any eggs, thus ensuring the Kumamoto oysters continue to have original DNA. The production is precious, as Japan's Kumos are available only for two short weeks, from mid- to late-March.

From the cooperative house, we bounced across the inland sea to a minute island where the water is pristine due to its remoteness, and to the fact that the inhabitants have never used chemicals. The 'farm' is a floating expanse of wooden crossbeams from which oyster bags are suspended.

Akio Yamazaki, a skillful pearl oysterman, is now growing Kumos. He steps with ease from beam to beam and clearly loves his job, taking pride in the unusual success rate of his farm. Yamazaki takes each bag out into the sun on a rotating basis, checking each oyster in the process, chipping off excess growth or separating ones that have cleaved to each other. Deeply tanned from the island sun, he looks up with a slow gentle smile and hands out a few oysters for us to inspect, 'Each requires care, but it's worth the effort.' We sample his handiwork and agree. Our first taste of Kumamoto oyster leaves a soft, briny impression. As we leave, Yamazaki gives me a small bag with six oysters, which we later pry open at the hotel and wash down with a cold beer. Heaven.

YUZU KOSHO

Yuzu kosho is a salty, citrusy, spicy condiment, most likely originally developed and commercialized by the Kawazu family in Oita prefecture. Whether or not the condiment was already being made in local homes, as anecdotal evidence suggests and was true for *kanzuri*, a chili and koji condiment revived and commercialized by a food company in Niigata prefecture, yuzu kosho has only been bottled and sold for the last few decades.

Portuguese missionaries introduced chili peppers to Japan in the mid-16th century. And in turn, Japanese brought them to Korea around that same time, thus altering the method for making kimchi, South Korea's national dish, which historically had been prepared by salt-pickling fish and vegetables without chili. Many people do not associate chili peppers with Japanese cuisine, but they are used to infuse a hint of spice into many dishes.

The characters for *togarashi* (chili) signify 'foreign mustard', and chilies are sometimes called *yogosho* ('western pepper'). In Kyushu, where chilies are widely grown and used commonly in daily cuisine, chilies are known as *kosho*, the Japanese word for black pepper, hence the condiment name: *yuzu kosho,* or colloquially, *yuzugosho*.

Yuzu kosho is becoming well known beyond Japan, perhaps because of the worldwide craze for ramen. And while yuzu kosho is extremely well suited for salt ramen, I like it thinned with olive oil and used as a drizzle for kelp-wicked sashimi, or mixed sparingly into vinegar for a spicy mignonette alternative on oysters. But stirred into mayonnaise, to slather in a thick sandwich or as a dipper for oven-baked French fries, might be the best use yet. Now experiencing a sustained national boom these last ten years, the local Kyushu condiment is made all over Japan. To varying degrees of success.

I included a recipe for yuzu kosho (one green, the other red) in each of my first two cookbooks, but no longer make it myself. Why?

In 2016, I began a consulting project to introduce top Japanese artisanal products to Australia. One of the products I selected was yuzu kosho, so I set about looking for the best one produced in Japan. To that end, I sent an email to Miyoho Asari, the legendary Oita prefecture koji maker, who discovered, developed and shared *shio koji* with the world. Asari-san's reply listed four producers (one of which was the Kawazu family). Upon perusal of the four websites, Kushino Nouen was the clear frontrunner. I tend to select by instinct and from the feel I get from the people and how they present themselves, and have not been wrong yet. Kushino Nouen yuzu kosho has proved to be the best made in Japan, confirmed by many other food people with whom I am in contact. And thus started my relationship with Kushino Nouen and Miwa Kawano, office manager and daughter of the Kushino family.

We visited Kushino Nouen in July 2018. The business is located in the tiny 4500-person town of Innai (now incorporated with slightly larger Ajimu-machi into the city of Usa), in Oita prefecture on the island of Kyushu. The Limited Express Sonic 11, a gorgeous retro-look train with glossy wooden flooring and moquette seats, took us from Kokura to Yanagigaura, where we were picked up by the surprisingly young but extremely capable Miwa Kawano. Miwa turned us over to her father, Masaharu Kushino, who took us through each step of the production process – all within a short walk of their home and office.

Kushino Nouen's yuzu kosho is made with green or red chilies, yellow yuzu peels from ripe fruit, and Japanese sea salt. The chilies are grown on their farm or by friends, and the fruit is grown on their own trees. This means that both the yuzu and chilies are harvested at optimal conditions, and Kushino Nouen is able to use non-pesticide-treated materials. The salt is chosen specifically to be best suited for interacting with the yuzu and chilies. Other companies use yuzu and chilies that are overripe and oversized in order to increase production and profit, but ultimately this affects the taste, making the yuzu kosho they produce inferior.

At Kushino Nouen, the chilies are sorted, sliced into strips, packed in salt, and left to macerate for a couple of months. The accumulated liquids are drained off and the chilies are put through a mixer to process into a rough paste, then packed back into crocks and left to ferment for one year.

The yuzu is harvested from mid-September to mid-October. The fruit is peeled, salted, packed in crocks and left to ferment for several months. The last step before bottling is to mix the salt-fermented yuzu peel and chili together using a mixing apparatus fitted with a massive stone bowl, crucial to avoid the introduction of heat. The final proportions in Kushino Nouen's yuzu kosho is 3 parts yuzu to 3 parts chili to 2 parts salt.

Yuzu, originating in the Yangtze River basin of China, found its way into Japan through the Korean Peninsula somewhere between late 500 and mid-700 AD during Japan's Asuka and Nara periods. Along with *sansho*, it is considered one of the oldest culinary flavors in Japan.

In 1974, the butterfly population around Kushino Nouen became threatened, so the local Japan Agriculture office offered incentives to farmers to plant yuzu trees. Masaharu Kushino took advantage of this opportunity and finally, in 1991, had trees mature enough to enable him to produce yuzu kosho. In 1994, Kushino Nouen's products were introduced at a food event at Seibu Department Store in Tokyo, and by 2008, yuzu kosho had taken Japan by storm, with no signs of it letting up thanks to key producers such as Kushino Nouen, who are making yuzu kosho responsibly and ethically, using local materials without additives or preservatives.

While writing *Preserving the Japanese Way* in 2014, I dubbed yuzu kosho 'the new Sriracha' – it still has not gotten there, perhaps because the ingredients are more precious, and the condiment itself is appreciably more expensive. While there are certainly other chili products in Japan, such as *kanzuri* from Niigata, for me they lack nuance and universality. Truly, yuzu kosho might be the only spicy condiment you need.

BACON SANDWICH WITH RED YUZU KOSHO MAYONNAISE AND COLESLAW VINAIGRETTE:
Marinate a 250 g (9 oz) block of bacon with 3 tablespoons each of Mikawa mirin and Yamaki shoyu and 1 tablespoon grated ginger for 1–2 hours. Massage ½ teaspoon flaky salt into 275 g (9½ oz) finely sliced cabbage, and ¼ teaspoon flaky salt into 125 g (4½ oz) julienned carrot. Leave to macerate for 10 minutes. Squeeze gently to express moisture and toss with 4 tablespoons chopped scallion (spring onion), a large handful of roughly chopped cilantro (coriander), and 2 tablespoons Wadaman gold sesame seeds. Whisk 60 ml (2 fl oz/¼ cup) Wadaman gold sesame oil into 1 tablespoon Iio Jozo rice vinegar until well emulsified, and toss with the cabbage mixture. Stir ¾ teaspoon Kushino Nouen red yuzu kosho into 6 tablespoons homemade mayonnaise, and spread on 8 slices wholegrain wheat bread, making sure to cover all the way to the corners. Tear 8 large pieces of red lettuce in half and lay 2 halves on each piece of bread. Mound a healthy 1 cm (½ in) layer of the slaw on half the pieces of bread. Cut the bacon into 16 slices, blot dry with spongy paper towels, and sear in a grill pan over medium–high heat until browned and caramelized on both sides. Lay 4 slices of bacon on each piece of bread without slaw, and sprinkle the meat with 1 tablespoon Wadaman gold sesame seeds. Close the sandwiches, cut in half and serve.

This is the only recipe in this book that is mine, but I thought it fitting to end with this delicious sando inspired by my obsession with the banh mi sandwich I buy from Gjelina Take Away in Venice, California, for my airplane trips home to Japan. Also fittingly, this was photographed by filmmaker Anna Schwaber who was traveling with Max Dornbush, purveyor of all things delicious for the Gjelina group, when they both came to hang out with me in Saitama. And now we have come full circle.

SUBSTITUTES, AND THEN SOME

The recipes in this book stay true to each chef's ingredients and methods. Rather than me reinterpreting and offering substitutes for the whole world, here are the recipes' authentic versions, so that you, the readers of the world, can find similar ingredients that are locally available – or eliminate some ingredients. Approach the recipes as they are meant to be: exciting, creative takes on food from seven very special, very different chefs. Have fun and play with the recipes, but pay attention to the base methods and the philosophy and heart behind the food. And when necessary, or when your cooking instinct takes control, substitute, substitute, substitute.

A WORD ABOUT SOUS VIDE

Sous vide is a gentle process of cooking foods in sealed plastic bags in a hot water bath at a low constant temperature, and can be done at home using different methods. The most low-tech, which involves no investment, is to put the food in heavy-duty resealable freezer bags. Do not seal, but clip one side of each bag so that it drapes over the outside of a pan of barely simmering water. If you have issues with the bags not wanting to stay submerged, slip some glass marbles into them.

Fill an appropriate-sized pan for the volume you are cooking with hot water, taking care to calculate water displacement from the bags of food. Insert a thermometer into the water and clip it to the side of the pan. Heat over medium–low until the desired temperature is achieved. It might be difficult to maintain the preferred sous vide temperature without fluctuation – so you will have to stay near to monitor the temperature and adjust the position of the pot on the heat. Using a flame tamer can help with keeping the temperature low; also, you can slide the pan partially off the heat source periodically if the water temperature should rise higher than you would like.

A bit higher tech, with a minimal investment, is to purchase a vacuum sealer – you might find that the sealer becomes your most used piece of equipment in the kitchen. But sous vide circulators for the home can now be had for about US$100, and are easily stashed out of sight in a drawer when not using.

WHERE TO BUY

Health Food Stores, Upscale Grocery Stores, Japanese Supermarkets: Since most Japanese or pan-Asian grocery stores tend to carry a high percentage of large company products, I recommend health food or high-end grocery stores. That said, a few Japanese groceries around the world make efforts to increase shelf space for small producers or organic products. Online is my preferred way to shop, unless I am visiting a specialty shop for dry goods or kitchen tools and hardware (page 170).

Not Recommended: Websites that list products without provenance or package photos. While not fond of the repackaging of Japanese products that became standard from the 1970s, I do recognize the practice led to wider distribution and understanding of Japanese products. However, in this current world climate, artisans are respected if not revered for the selfless work they do. Thus, minimal label design modifications and clear information regarding which company made the product, including details of processing and ingredient sourcing, is essential.

Organics: Most organic Japanese soy condiments repackaged for export by Muso and Mitoku (the two main Japanese organic companies) are produced using Chinese soybeans. Chinese organics are cheaper than Japanese conventional, and Japanese soybeans are grown for culinary use such as shoyu, miso, tofu and natto rather than for oil production, which is the fate of most soybeans grown in China, the US and Canada. This caveat does not imply a disapproval of these companies' products or a non-recommendation, nor does the use of Chinese organics apply to all of their products. Transparency is essential.

Japan

Amazon Japan: I am not a fan of the megastore concept, but let's face it, Amazon Prime is quite convenient. Since I live in the countryside, Amazon Japan has been a lifeline when sourcing unusual ingredients. amazon.co.jp

***Kanbutsu-ya* (dry good store):** Well-curated Japanese shops selling all manner of Japanese sea products and other dry goods (page 170). Also a great resource for information on how to use these ingredients.

***Kanamono-ya* (hardware store):** An honest and reliable source for traditional Japanese kitchen equipment and cooking utensils (page 170).

Australia

Fino Foods: Top-quality purveyor of European, Australian and New Zealand products for retail and the restaurant industry, Fino now has an 'Artisan Japan' line, which I curated and recommended. No current online shop. finofoods.com.au

Chef's Armoury: With stores in Sydney and Melbourne, Chef's Armoury also has a respectable online shop featuring a high percentage of organic Japanese products as well as Oigen ironware (page 48) and some fancy Japanese knives. I doubt most home cooks need a A$340 Japanese kitchen knife, but if you do, go for the majestic Kaiden Kodo 180 Santoku. But then, I don't need flamboyant swirls or embellishments on my knife blades. An honest finish reflects a clear heart. chefsarmoury.com

The Good Grub Hub: Has Moroi Jozo fish sauce (page 26) and a few other fairly good quality Japanese products, mixed in with quite a few seemingly artisanal condiments that I would not recommend. goodgrubhub.com

Spiral Foods: A reliable source for Japanese artisanal condiments, keeping in mind the caveat mentioned in the discussion of organics regarding the use of Chinese organics. spiralfoods.com.au

United States

The Japanese Pantry: A highly recommended source for Japanese artisanal products, especially Wadaman (page 212) sesame products (best in the world), green *sansho* powder and *shichimi togarashi* (seven spice). Yamaki shoyu (bottled in Japan) is available along with several other soy sauces. Top-quality konbu (from venerable Konbu Doi) and Iio Jozo vinegars (best in Japan) are also standout products. Avoid the mass-produced liquid *shio koji* product – just make your own from superior rice koji and sea salt and liquefy it in a blender. thejapanesepantry.com

Mikuni Wild Harvest: Initially founded by a truffle hunter, Mikuni Wild Harvest has a limited amount of Japanese products available in their online shop, but also supplies to Whole Foods and other upscale groceries. In the 'Boutique, Artisan and Exotic' section of their site, you can find the Yamaki misos and shoyu repackaged by Gold Mine Natural Food Co., as well as organic tamari (Chinese soybeans), Takuko white shoyu, the Haku line of bourbon barrel–aged shoyus and fish sauce, as well as Mikuni's proprietary Yamaki Orchard ponzu and other Japanese citrus products. mikuniwildharvest.com

Mitoku: A reliable source for Japanese artisanal condiments, keeping in mind the caveat mentioned on page 272 regarding the use of Chinese organics. Of note, Mitoku sells the very excellent Mikawa mirin and a good-quality brown rice koji for making your own miso. mitoku.com

Gold Mine Natural Food Co.: Now owned by Japan Gold USA (Muso); carries the Ohsawa brand of repackaged Japanese products. Some products contain Chinese organics, though Gold Mine does also repackage Yamaki Jozo shoyu and miso – Yamaki Jozo is located in Kamikawa-machi, the township where I live in Japan. The Yamaki soy sauce is sold under Ohsawa's Nama Shoyu label and, in general, suffers no issues of degradation. The Gold Mine Yamaki misos that I have sampled show marked signs of oxidation, which points to mishandling in the repackaging and storing process. Oxidation causes miso to become several shades darker than it should be and also intensifies its flavor, though does not mean it has gone bad. goldminenaturalfoods.com. Wholesale: japangoldusa.com; muso-intl.com

Eden Foods: Another reliable source for Japanese artisanal condiments, keeping in mind the caveat mentioned on page 272 regarding the use of Chinese organics. Widely available in the organic section of most US grocery stores, so highly recommended for that accessibility. edenfoods.com

United Kingdom and Europe

The Wasabi Company: The sole grower of wasabi in the UK, also distributed throughout Scandinavia and the EU. They sell a range of Japanese products online of varying quality – though this is scheduled to change dramatically with a revamp of their line, including adding Wadaman sesame and Yamaki Jozo shoyu, miso and *ume* products. The Wasabi Company directly imports vinegars and various vinegar-related sauces from Marusho, a venerable Kyoto vinegar maker. The brown rice vinegar is exceptional. thewasabicompany.co.uk

Nishikidori: An online and brick-and-mortar store in Paris, with distribution to retail and restaurants. Includes knives and kitchen equipment (look for the mini-katsuobushi shaver!). Nishikidori imports some of my favorite products: Iio Jozo vinegars, Mikawa mirin and Kushino Nouen yuzu kosho (page 270), and is under negotiation with Yamaki Jozo to bring in their shoyu-related products and misos. Nishikidori also carries high-quality sea greens such as konbu, *oboro konbu* (similar to *tororo konbu*) and nori. Some products are not recommended – read the content labels. nishikidori.com

Umami Paris: An online shop and distributor that also runs Matcha Café, a popular teashop in Paris. Umami is the source for Wadaman sesame (seeds and pastes, see page 212), Sennari vinegars (highly recommended is the 'pure organic' rice vinegar, brown rice vinegar and apple vinegar), a rare abalone liver soy sauce (*awabi no sei*) and high-quality green teas (sencha and matcha). Read the ingredients in other products, because they may contain several additives, thickeners or sugars that would not normally appear in artisanal versions. umamiparis.com

Clearspring: A reliable source for Japanese artisanal condiments, keeping in mind the caveat mentioned on page 272 regarding the use of Chinese organics. The family-owned and -run company has very close ties to Japan and does an outstanding job of sourcing Japanese materials. Clearspring products are available in Bio stores in the UK and EU. clearspring.co.uk

KITCHEN TOOLS

Essential

Hocho: Japanese knives. Without a razor-sharp, fine-bladed all-purpose kitchen knife (*bunka bocho*), your cuts will not be as fine as needed for slicing vegetables. A small *deba bocho* is also useful for cutting through fish and poultry bones, as is a long, thin sashimi knife (*sashimi bocho*).

Makisu: Small bamboo mat for rolling sushi, and also useful for draining things.

Mushiki: Bamboo or metal steamer.

Oroshigane/Oroshiki: Although a microplane can substitute in a pinch, these sharp-toothed metal or ceramic grinding plates are the best tools to properly grate root vegetables and rhizomes such as daikon, mountain yam, ginger and wasabi – and are not expensive.

Otoshibuta: Wooden or metal drop lids used to keep simmering ingredients submerged.

Shamoji: Bamboo, ceramic, wood or plastic rice paddle for fluffing and serving rice.

Suribachi: Ceramic bowl with grooves etched into the inside surface to facilitate grinding seeds, nuts and tofu with a large wooden pestle (*surikogi*). Small ones are virtually useless, so buy the largest one you can find.

Surikogi: Wooden pestle traditionally made from the branch of a *sansho* (prickly ash) tree with the bark intact – used to grind food in the *suribachi*.

Tawashi: Rather than peeling root vegetables such as daikon, carrot and turnips, this coconut-fiber brush is used to scrub and refresh the skin. Seek out the original 'turtle brand' made by the Kamenoko company. It is the best.

Very Useful

Donabe: Lidded, flameproof ceramic casserole used to cook rice as well as soupy stews (*nabemono*) at the table.

Handai: Wide, shallow cedar tub used for cooling rice.

Sarashi: Muslin (cheesecloth) for wrapping fish or vegetables for pickling.

Seimenki: Standing noodle-rolling machine. Very sturdy and an extremely useful addition to any kitchen, be it Japanese or western.

Shichirin: Tabletop charcoal brazier crafted from diatomaceous earth. Although more pricey than in Japan, they are available online abroad. Considered the best method to cook air-dried fish (*himono*, page 186), and also handy for communal grilled meat and vegetable (*yakiniku*) parties.

Uragoshi: Flat, fine-meshed sieve used for sifting flour, straining batters and smashing fish or bean pastes.

Washi: Japanese paper used for calligraphy practice, but also handy as a liner for tempura plates to blot oil. Fold artfully on a diagonal.

Chopsticks

Hashi: Made of lacquered or unlacquered wood, bone or plastic, with pointed ends. (Korean chopsticks are often metal since they frequently cook communally over fire.) Japanese chopsticks are 18–24 cm (7–9½ in) long. Chinese chopsticks are generally longer and have blunt tips – useful for serving others across a wide table.

Konabashi: Thick wooden cooking chopsticks used for dipping pieces of fish and vegetables into batter when making tempura.

Moribashi: Thin metal chopsticks with fine pointed tips and wooden handles. Used for serving food in the kitchen or cooking tempura.

Saibashi: Wooden cooking chopsticks, about 32 cm (13 in) long.

Tetsubashi: Iron chopsticks for cooking over fire.

CUTTING STYLES

Butsugiri: 3 cm (1¼ in) crosswise-cut pieces; *negi*, chicken (cut through the bone).

Hangetsu-kiri: Thin or thick half moons; cucumber, carrot (thin), daikon, eggplant (aubergine), tomato (slightly thick).

Hitokuchi Dai ni Kiru: 3 cm (1¼ in) bite-sized pieces.

Hosogiri: Medium julienne, 3 mm × 5 cm (⅛ in × 2 in); cucumber, potato, daikon, carrot, burdock, *negi*, *piman* (green pepper).

Hyoshigi-kiri: 1 × 5 cm (½ × 2 in) batonnets; carrot, daikon.

Itchogiri: Halved lengthwise, cut crosswise into 5 mm (¼ in) half moons, and again in half for rounded triangular pieces resembling ginkgo leaves; daikon, carrot.

Kokuchi-giri: Small bite-sized pieces.

Kushigata-giri: 'Comb'-shaped cuts resembling wedges; tomato, onion, cabbage.

Mijingiri: Fine dice; ginger, onion, *negi*, carrot.

Rangiri: 'Random' triangular-like chunks made by alternating diagonal cuts; cucumber, eggplant (aubergine), potato, *piman* (green pepper), lotus root, daikon.

Sasagaki: Fine feather cuts made by holding the root and shaving like a pencil; carrot, burdock.

Sengiri: Fine julienne; cabbage (2 mm × 5 cm/⅛ in × 2 in); carrot, daikon, ginger (2 mm × 3 cm/⅛ in × 1¼ in).

Sogigiri: A 12 mm (½ in) thick diagonal cut; chicken, squid, shiitake, napa (Chinese) cabbage stems.

Tanzaku-giri: Very fine ribbon strips, 2 cm (¾ in) wide by 4 cm (1½ in) long; daikon, carrot.

Usugiri: Finely sliced crosswise. Long thin vegetables such as burdock and *negi* are sliced at a diagonal. Other vegetables are halved lengthwise and sliced crosswise.

Wagiri: Cut crosswise into thick or thin round slices, depending on the vegetable and the recipe.

Zakugiri: Greens cut crosswise into 4 cm (1½ in) pieces.

VEGETABLES

ROOT VEGETABLES

Bamboo Shoot (*Takenoko*): Dug up in the early spring, often when snow is still on the ground. *Takenoko* is like corn and should be eaten as soon after harvest as possible. When fresh, bamboo shoot can be cooked as is, after peeling. When not as fresh, they require soaking in water with rice bran overnight to remove bitterness. When fresh shoots are not available, substitute vacuum-packed shoots. *Nemagari takenoko* is a thin variety of bamboo shoot, which juts out from the earth in a curve (hence the name 'curved shoot'). To harvest, break off the soft top-third portion or so, where the shoot wants to naturally break – exactly in the same manner as breaking off the hard part of asparagus.

Burdock (*Gobo*): A long, thin, beige, fibrous root; it turns light brown when simmered or stir-fried. Scrub with a vegetable brush, but do not peel. If not using right away after cutting, soak in a bowl of water with a splash of rice vinegar to prevent discoloration.

Daikon: Typically a fat, white cylindrical radish, daikon may be plumply round or thin and elongated. Though relatively rare, there are different colors: purple, red, orange, variegated, also *koshin daikon* (**watermelon radish**). Avoid dry, out-of-season daikon – substitute small turnips or western radishes. Scrub, but do not peel.

Lily Bulb (*Yuri Ne*): Used to add texture and a delicate flavor to savory egg custards (*chawan mushi*) or soups, lily bulbs are only sold fresh in Japan and can be found from late winter to spring. Resembling flat garlic cloves, the pieces are called scales in English. Pare off discolored portions before separating the scales from the bulb.

Lotus Root (*Renkon*): The fat tuber of a lotus flower plant, with Swiss cheese–like cavities visible in cross-section pieces. The creamy white flesh has a lovely crunch, so adds texture to soups and holds up well in stir-fries. Peel, and if not using right away, soak in cold water with a dash of vinegar. Avoid roots that are discolored.

Mountain Yam (*Yama Imo*): A tan-skinned, hairy tuber with bright white flesh, which is usually grated to a glorious viscous mass and eaten raw, but can also be cooked or pickled. Mountain yam might be difficult to find outside of Japan, though is sometimes sold as Chinese yam. Starchy yams or sweet potatoes are not suitable substitutes since the slimy consistency of the mountain yam is essential to dishes where it is used.

Sweet Potato (*Satsuma Imo*): Japanese sweet potatoes are dense-fleshed and almost fluff up when roasted. Varieties from other countries should be cooked until soft and succulent. Although most commonly yellow-fleshed with red skin, there are also purple and white sweet potatoes.

Taro (*Sato Imo*): These small to medium, round or slightly oblong roots have a sticky but appealingly creamy grey-white flesh. Peel off the brown fibrous skin before simmering, or roast whole and pop out of the skin, dip in salt and eat as a snack.

Turnip (*Kabu*): Golf ball–sized turnips work best for Japanese cuisine. Scrub but do not peel, leaving a small portion of the green stem ends intact – perhaps not traditional, but much prettier than when lopped off and the turnip left bald.

MOUNTAIN VEGETABLES

Butterbur (*Fuki*): Resembling celery in appearance but not in taste, *fuki* can grow to great heights in some areas of Japan, though usually is sold in lengths of about 90 cm (3 ft). Remove strings from mature stems of *fuki* before using. This is definitely a vegetable worth cultivating outside of Japan, though it does seem to enjoy hot and humid mountainous areas.

Butterbur Buds (*Fuki no To*): Given *fuki no to*'s naturally bitter yet appealing profile, it makes the most delicious tempura ever, but is also irresistible as a condiment when sautéed with miso and mirin. *Fuki no to* appear in the spring, when the plant is just poking through the earth, and have wide open buds about the size of ping-pong balls.

Fiddlehead Ferns: Fiddleheads are most often blanched, then dressed. *Kogomi* are furry and tight-headed ferns with thick stems, whereas *warabi* are long and thin fiddleheads with finely curled tops.

Tara no Me/Koshi Abura: Another lovely bitter spring mountain vegetable that makes outstanding tempura. It has finger-thick stems from which small, slightly furry leaves and tiny stems shoot out.

Udo: Thanks to greenhouse cultivation, this soft, complex-flavored mountain vegetable (with a gentle licoricy note) is available outside of the spring season, though true mountain *udo* is spectacular. Peel before using. Substitute celery if not available.

OTHER VEGETABLES

Cucumber (*Kyuri*): Small thin cucumbers with few seeds and mild skin, which is not peeled. Substitute other small Asian cucumbers or English cucumbers in a pinch. If the cucumbers are large, best to seed them; if the skin is bitter or tough, peel it off.

Eggplant/Aubergine (*Nasu*): Japanese eggplants are usually slender and almost egg-shaped, and the skin is often eaten. *Mizu nasu* is a small eggplant used for salt-pickling because their flesh is a bit spongy and juicy, so is good eaten raw or lightly salted.

***Manganji Togarashi* (Capsicum):** A sweet green pepper that is a cross between a Californian bell pepper and a Japanese shishito pepper. Manganji peppers were an experiment originating at a temple in Kyoto in the late 1920s or early '30s, and recently, these peppers are achieving popularity among chefs in Japan as well as abroad.

***Piman* (Capsicum):** Thin-skinned, small green peppers similar to poblanos.

Shishito Pepper (Capsicum): A small, sweet (though occasionally hot!) green pepper that is technically a chili. Used whole, shishito are grilled, battered and quick fried.

***Togarashi* (Chile Japones):** A small chili eaten fresh or dried; substitute cayenne or chile de árbol.

LEAFY GREENS

Bok Choy (*Chingensai*): Use tender young heads and cut lengthwise into wedges before simmering or stir-frying.

Chrysanthemum Greens (*Shungiku*): Appealingly bitter culinary chrysanthemum, available in the spring. Good blanched quickly and dressed, or in sukiyaki, one-pot dishes (*nabe*) and soups.

Flowering Brassica (*Nanohana*): Brassicas such as turnip, komatsuna or mustard, which resemble rapini (broccoli rabe) when flowering. Rapini can be used as a substitute.

Komatsuna: A versatile green available almost year-round. Japanese komatsuna is a bit more tender than the komatsuna I have seen abroad, perhaps because it is often grown in greenhouses in Japan to avoid rain and dirt splash-back. In the mustard family, komatsuna is similar to bok choy but has softer leaves and finer stems.

Malabar Spinach (*Tsuru Murasaki*): A succulent vine found mostly in Asia, with mild, heart-shaped purple or green leaves reminiscent of spinach.

Mustard (*Karashina*): Spicy, prickly greens that do well pickled or in one-pot dishes (*nabemono*).

Shakushina: Similar leaves to bok choy with long narrow stems. Native to the Chichibu area of Saitama prefecture, northwest of Tokyo.

MUSHROOMS

Enoki: Used more for texture than taste, these small, white-capped cultivated mushrooms appear in savory custards, soups and dressed dishes.

***Eryngii* (King Oyster Mushrooms):** Cultivated mushrooms with flat tan caps and thick white stems.

***Maitake* (Hen of the Woods):** A favorite for tempura, but also good sautéed in butter and sake. *Maitake* grow in frilly, dusky tan clumps in the forest or cultivation houses.

***Matsutake*:** Mostly imported from China or Korea, Japanese *matsutake* are hard to find and quite expensive. Grilling lightly before using brings out their heavenly aroma, which has been called 'the essence of autumn'.

***Nameko* (Butterscotch Mushrooms):** Small clumped mushrooms with golden brown caps, which have a naturally slimy coating and are particularly delicious in miso soup.

***Sakura Shimeji* (Pinkmottle Woodwax Mushrooms):** A popular wild mushroom for gathering, since they grow in large patches, thus making efficient use of one's time. The stems are short, and the medium-sized caps show a reddish wine color in the center, which dissipates into a lighter color on the perimeter. Good for stir-frying and soupy dishes.

***Shibatake* (Scotch Bonnet Mushrooms):** Light brown caps with wide gills, and pithy stems that should be removed. Mild tasting, *shibatake* grow in meadows or coastal dunes in the summer and autumn. Naturally sweet from the presence of trehalose, they are good in soups and stews.

Shiitake: Fresh and dried shiitake have different culinary uses, so unless specified as dried, use fresh. The undersides should be snowy white without discoloration, and the tops should be dry, preferably with deep fissures, not moist or saturated. Shiitake are cultivated on logs in forests.

Shimeji: Cultivated shimeji are easy to source and can be used in soups, stir-fries, gratins and just about anything else. The naturally propagating variety, *hon shimeji*, has a more pronounced flavor and grows in the forests.

KONNYAKU PRODUCTS

***Konnyaku*:** A firm, gelatinous grey or white block made from the devil's tongue corm. *Konnyaku* is a zero-calorie, high-fiber food that is sliced then added to stir-fries, soups and simmered things.

***Shirataki*:** Noodles made from *konnyaku*, used in sukiyaki, soups and simmered dishes. Avoid the tofu 'shirataki' recently seen in health food stores, as it is not the same.

SOY PRODUCTS

Soy Milk: There are many soy milks on the market, but not many good ones. In Japan, Yamaki Jozo's soy milk has a nutty soybean taste that is eminently quaffable as well as rich enough to produce creamy, delicious soft tofu. In the US, Hodo Foods and Meiji Tofu make excellent soy milks. Otherwise, try Clearspring (UK) or local tofu makers.

Fresh Tofu: Quite difficult to find outside of Japan, though there are a number of tofu makers around the world who are trying their best, so this should become more and more available. Fresh tofu is often eaten plain with grated ginger, chopped scallions (spring onions) and shoyu, with an optional sprinkling of katsuobushi.

Cotton-style Tofu (*Momendofu*): Soft and custard-like, but with some structure, cotton tofu is made by stirring *nigari* (a coagulant that occurs naturally during the artisanal salt-making process) into hot soy milk, which, in turn, is poured into muslin (cheesecloth)-lined molds, and wrapped and weighted until set. Substitute the best quality, freshest, not firm type of tofu available. For this book I have specified 'Japanese-style soft-block tofu' as the closest. If making smashed tofu dishes (*shira-ae*), Japanese cotton tofu is weighted then mashed in a grinding bowl (*suribachi*). However, since true Japanese cotton tofu is not readily available outside of Japan, this step can probably be skipped, and you might not get the tofu to cream up unless you mash it in a food processor.

Soy Products continued

Silken-style Tofu (*Kinudofu*): Smooth textured and lightly gelatinous, this delicate tofu is produced by stirring nigari into heated soy milk before pouring into a large mold. Once set, the tofu is cut into small blocks.

Fried Tofu: Fried tofu products are ubiquitous in Japanese cuisine, but not readily available outside of Japan. (Look in the freezer case for *usuage*, but you might only find the version made by House, one of the largest food companies in Japan, so the quality will not be very high.) ***Usuage/Abura-age***: Thinly sliced, weighted tofu that is deep-fried twice to form a pouch useful for stuffing and simmering, also used in stir-fries. ***Atsuage***: Deep-fried, weighted blocks of tofu, often included in simmered treatments. ***Ganmodoki***: Deep-fried croquettes made from smashed tofu mixed with grated mountain yam to bind, and flavored with finely chopped carrot, konbu, shimeji mushroom and dried shrimp (for homemade *ganmodoki*, see page 207).

Yakidofu: Pressed tofu that is grilled (or singed with a blowtorch). Used in sukiyaki or other one-pot dishes, though cotton tofu substitutes admirably.

Yuba: Skin skimmed off the surface of soy milk as it is heated in the tofu-making process. Fresh *yuba* is like burrata cheese in texture, but has a lighter profile with soy undertones. Making *yuba* is a special, limited process, so the product is not inexpensive.

***Okara* (Soybean Pulp)**: The by-product of making soy milk. Available dried, frozen or sometimes fresh in Japanese markets. Traditionally stir-fried with julienned root vegetables for a thrifty farm or temple dish.

Natto: Fermented soybeans with a pronounced funky, slimy characteristic. Often spooned over rice for breakfast. Even in Japan, artisanal natto is hard to find, but there are some local natto makers in various pockets around the world, so it is definitely on the upward swing. Otherwise, natto available outside of Japan is made by large Japanese food companies and has been previously frozen.

FLOURS, STARCHES AND DRIED THINGS

FLOURS

All-purpose Flour (*Kyorikiko*): Flour used for western sweets and breads.

Buckwheat Flour (*Sobako*): A highly perishable fine flour made from the pyramidal inner kernel of the buckwheat seed. Coarsely milled buckwheat flour cannot be used for making soba noodles.

Cake Flour (*Hakurikiko*): Low-gluten flour used for udon, tempura and Japanese sweets such as steamed buns (*manju*).

Glutinous Rice Flour (*Mochiko*): Flour made from washed and dried glutinous rice, often called 'sweet rice flour' outside of Japan. Used for mochi sweets and *shiratama dango*. Also known as *shiratama ko*.

Potato Flour (*Imo no Kona*): Flour made in Iwate prefecture from air-dried potatoes (page 56).

Rice Flour (*Joshinko*): Rice flour made from washed and dried short-grain rice. Used for *dango* sweets and occasionally for dusting foods before deep-frying. Also known as *komeko*.

STARCHES

Agar: A natural gelatin extracted from red algae. Sold in flakes and used to solidify desserts.

Kudzu Powder (*Kuzuko*): Extracted from the root of the kudzu vine, *kuzuko* is a brilliant white powder that tends to clump up, so needs to be smashed well before using. Mostly used as a thickener or coagulating agent for savory or sweet squares. Avoid the brown kudzu found in health food stores, as it is not suitable for Japanese culinary applications.

Potato Starch (*Katakuriko*): The most common starch used in the Japanese kitchen. Potato starch is lighter than cornstarch and if used sparingly, can thicken simmering juices ever so slightly to make a silky sauce.

Uchiko: Technically a starch, *uchiko* is a by-product of milling Japanese buckwheat flour (*sobako*), and is only used for dusting soba dough in the noodle-rolling process.

DRIED THINGS

Gourd Ribbons (*Kanpyo*): Produced by cutting the flesh of the *yugao* gourd into long ribbons and sun-drying. Used for tying foods that will be simmered in a bundle or stack, or as an ingredient in thick country sushi rolls.

Wheat Gluten (*Fu*): Obtained by kneading wheat dough in water to separate out the gluten, *fu* is mostly sold in small colored shapes for adding to soups, or in large bread-like coils for simmered dishes, but also is found raw in Japan. Said to have been brought to Okinawa prefecture by Zen priests from China early in the Muromachi period (1336–1573), *fu* is a mainstay ingredient in temple food (*shojin ryori*).

INDEX

D

E

F

THANKS

An off-hand comment made by Adam James (@roughrice) while visiting me in Japan led me to approach Jane Willson at Hardie Grant Publishing in Melbourne, Australia, with the idea for this book.

By virtue of blurb comments for Sharon Flynn's *Ferment for Good* (Hardie Grant), a connection was forged with the publishing house, for which I am eternally grateful. I also deeply appreciate that the team at Hardie Grant immediately understood my vision for this book and gave me the contract to write it. Professional, kind and supportive every step of the way, I have nothing but awe and gratitude for everyone at Hardie Grant.

At the end of the day though, I rely on Kim Schuefftan for always being my sounding board, editor of my words, and friend. Without him I would be lost.

I have become a champion for all the artisans and chefs who appear in this book because they touched my heart. And for that, I thank them profoundly. Although no story was written about Yamaki Jozo – makers of artisanal shoyu, miso, tofu and pickles in my town – I swear my undying devotion to the Kitani family because of the incredible work they do to maintain Japanese-sourced raw materials that are as much as possible organic, with all products still made in the traditional way.

And as always, I thank my family for their patience and understanding, and the mothers in my small immersion preschool for supporting my dual dedication to Japanese foodways as well as their children.

Published in 2019 by Hardie Grant Books,
an imprint of Hardie Grant Publishing

Hardie Grant Books (Melbourne)
Building 1, 658 Church Street
Richmond, Victoria 3121

Hardie Grant Books (London)
5th & 6th Floors
52–54 Southwark Street
London SE1 1UN

hardiegrantbooks.com

A catalogue record for this book is available from the National Library of Australia

Food Artisans of Japan
ISBN 978 1 74379 465 4

10 9 8 7 6 5 4 3 2 1

Publishing Director: Jane Willson
Project Editor: Anna Collett
Editor: Rachel Pitts
Editorial Assistants: Mallory Evans, Stephanie McClelland
Design Manager: Jessica Lowe
Designer: Michelle Mackintosh
Photographers: Kenta Izumi, Kenji Miura, Nancy Singleton Hachisu, Yoko Nakamura, Thomas Schiller, Anna Schwaber
Production Manager: Todd Rechner
Production Coordinator: Mietta Yans

Colour reproduction by Splitting Image Colour Studio
Printed in China by Leo Paper Products LTD.

This book uses 15 ml (½ fl oz) tablespoons and metric cup measurements, i.e. 250 ml (8½ fl oz) for 1 cup; in the US a cup is 8 fl oz, just smaller, and American cooks should be generous in their cup measurements; in the UK a cup is 10 fl oz and British cooks should be scant with their cup measurements.